A Million Little Pieces
of Close to Home

Other *Close to Home* Books
by John McPherson

Close to Home
One Step Closer to Home
Dangerously Close to Home
Home: The Final Frontier
The Honeymoon Is Over
The Silence of the Lamberts
Striking Close to Home
The Close to Home Survival Guide
Close to Home Uncut
The Scourge of the Vinyl Car Seats
Close to Home Exposed
Ferociously Close to Home
When Bad Things Happen to Stupid People

Treasury Collections
Close to Home Revisited
Close to Home Unplugged

Also from John McPherson
High School Isn't Pretty
Close to Home: A Book of Postcards
The Barber of Bingo
The Get Well Book
Give Mommy the Superglue and Other Tips on Surviving Parenthood
Get Well, Doctor's Orders! A Close to Home Get Well Box

A Million Little Pieces
of Close to Home

A *Close to Home* Collection by John McPherson

Andrews McMeel
PUBLISHING®

Close to Home is distributed internationally by Andrews McMeel Syndication.

Andrews McMeel Publishing
a division of Andrews McMeel Universal
1130 Walnut Street, Kansas City, Missouri 64106

www.andrewsmcmeel.com
www.closetohome.com

ISBN: 978-0-7407-6198-0

Library of Congress Control Number: 2006925371

For Griffin

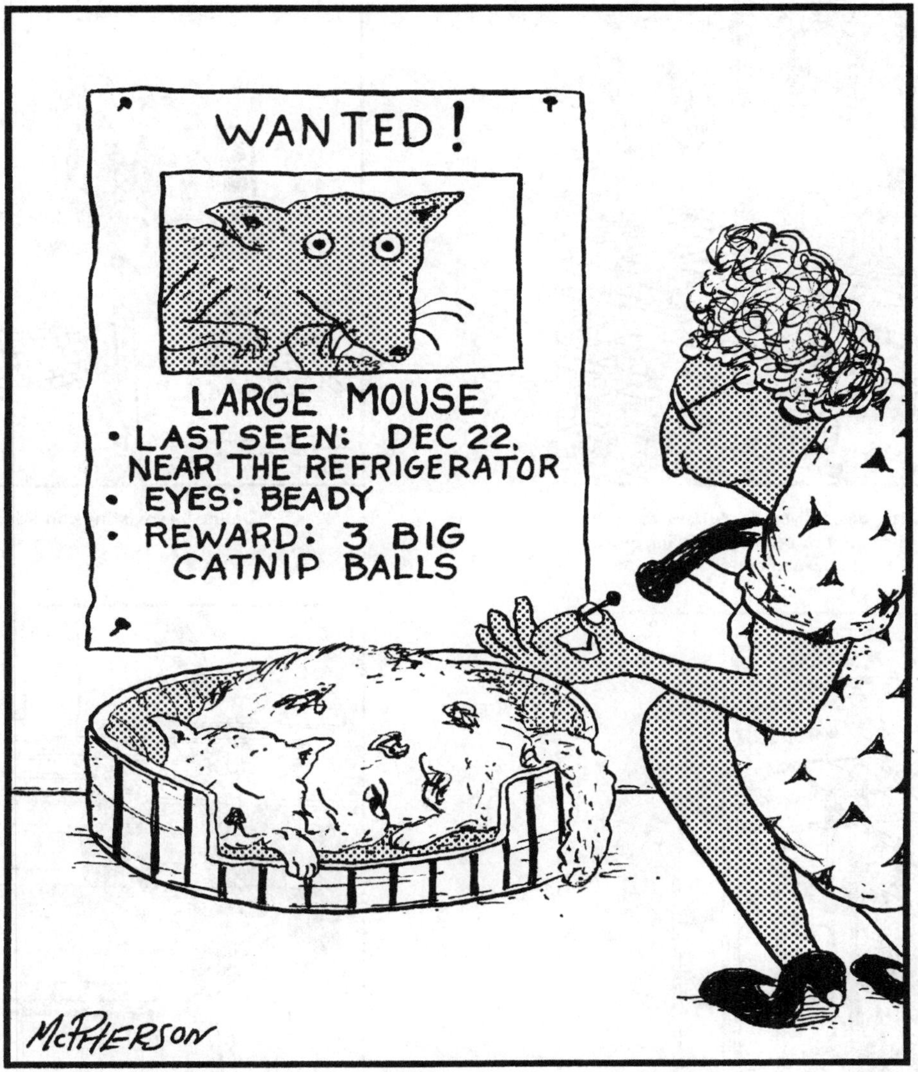
WANTED!
LARGE MOUSE
• LAST SEEN: DEC 22, NEAR THE REFRIGERATOR
• EYES: BEADY
• REWARD: 3 BIG CATNIP BALLS
McPHERSON

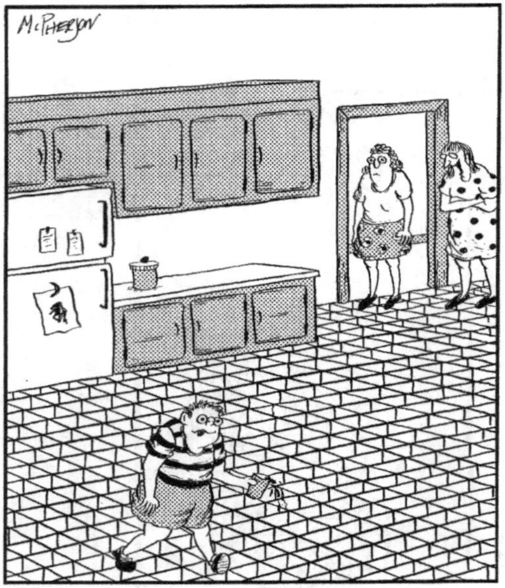
McPHERSON

"Spills, crumbs, dirt . . . you don't have to worry about any of them. I'm tellin' ya, Sheila, grated kitchen floors have changed my life."

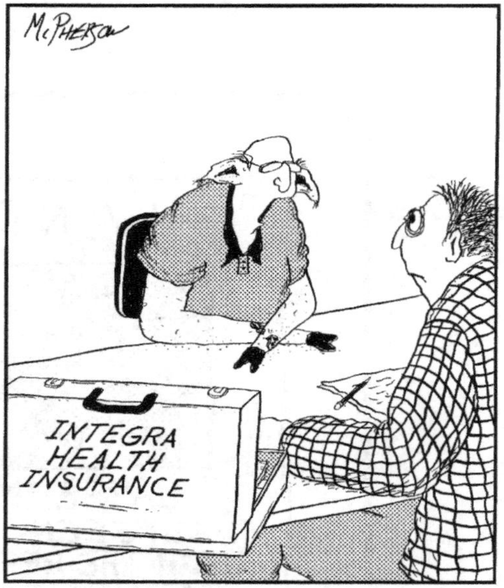
McPHERSON
INTEGRA
HEALTH
INSURANCE

"Define 'preexisting condition.'"

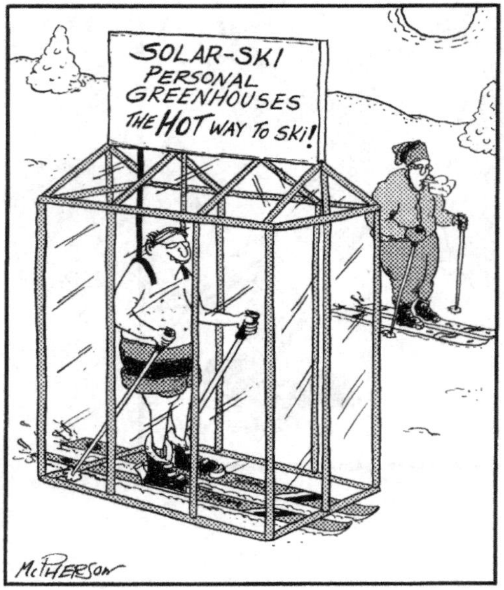
SOLAR-SKI
PERSONAL
GREENHOUSES
THE HOT WAY TO SKI!
McPHERSON

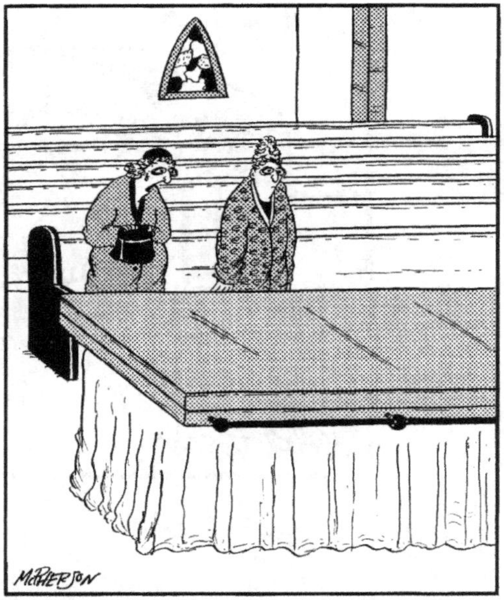
McPHERSON

"I yelled to him three times! 'Frank, look out for the steamroller!'"

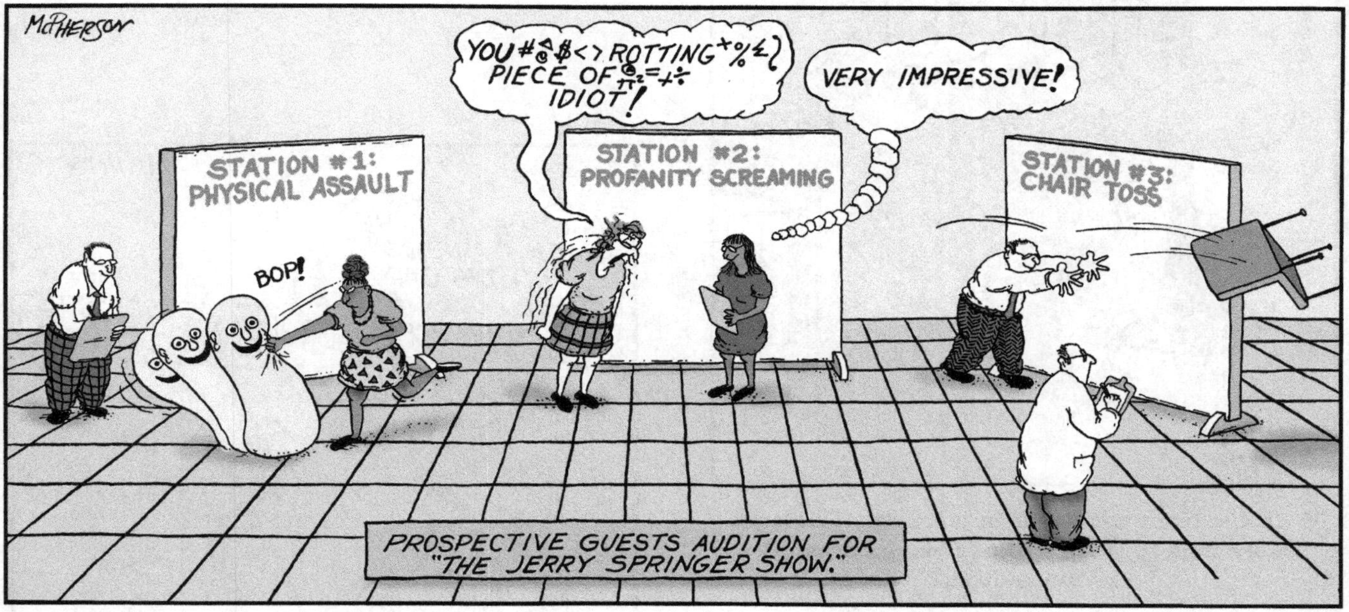
McPHERSON
YOU #$<> ROTTING %£ PIECE OF =+÷ IDIOT!
VERY IMPRESSIVE!
STATION #1: PHYSICAL ASSAULT
BOP!
STATION #2: PROFANITY SCREAMING
STATION #3: CHAIR TOSS

PROSPECTIVE GUESTS AUDITION FOR "THE JERRY SPRINGER SHOW."

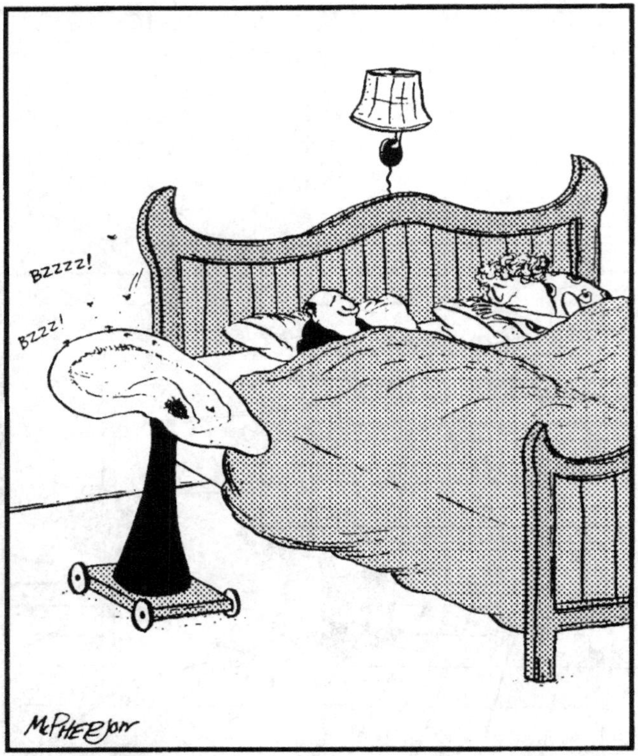
BZZZZ!
BZZZ!
McPHERSON

With the giant decoy ear in place, the Gurtsons were able to sleep without being harassed by mosquitoes.

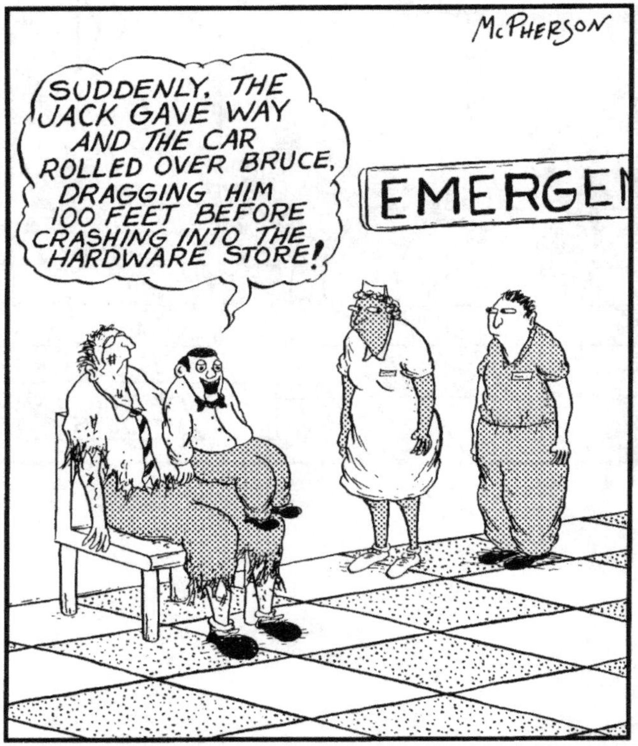
McPHERSON
SUDDENLY, THE JACK GAVE WAY AND THE CAR ROLLED OVER BRUCE, DRAGGING HIM 100 FEET BEFORE CRASHING INTO THE HARDWARE STORE!
EMERGE

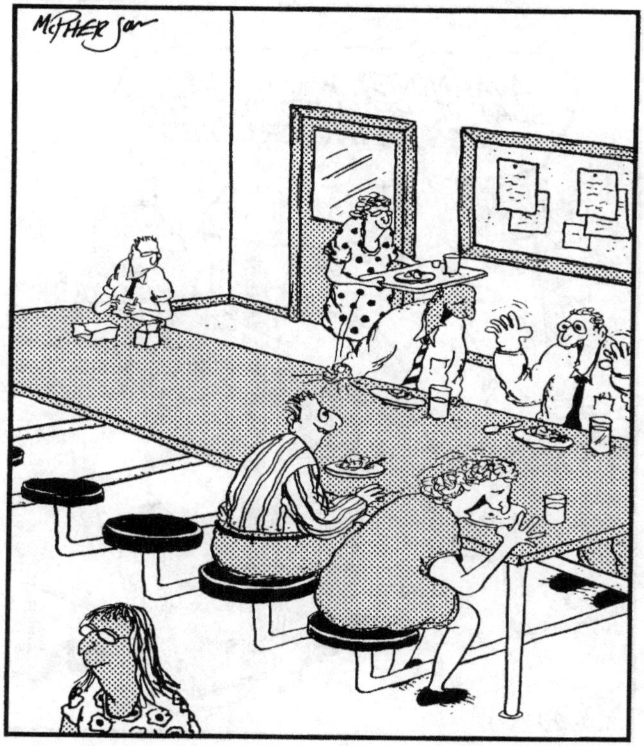

McPHERSON

Having announced that he would never surf the Net for anything other than strictly company business, Dwayne is immediately ostracized by his coworkers.

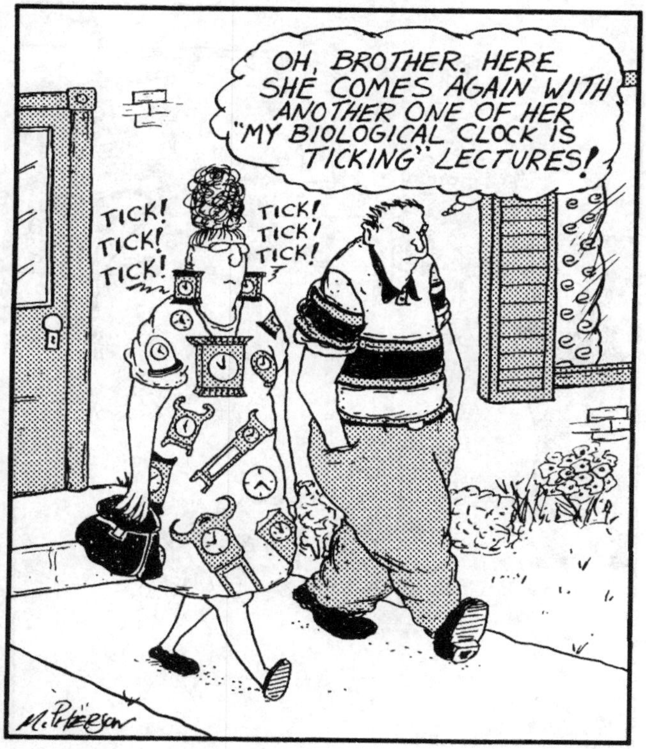

OH, BROTHER. HERE SHE COMES AGAIN WITH ANOTHER ONE OF HER "MY BIOLOGICAL CLOCK IS TICKING" LECTURES!
TICK! TICK! TICK!
TICK! TICK! TICK!
McPHERSON

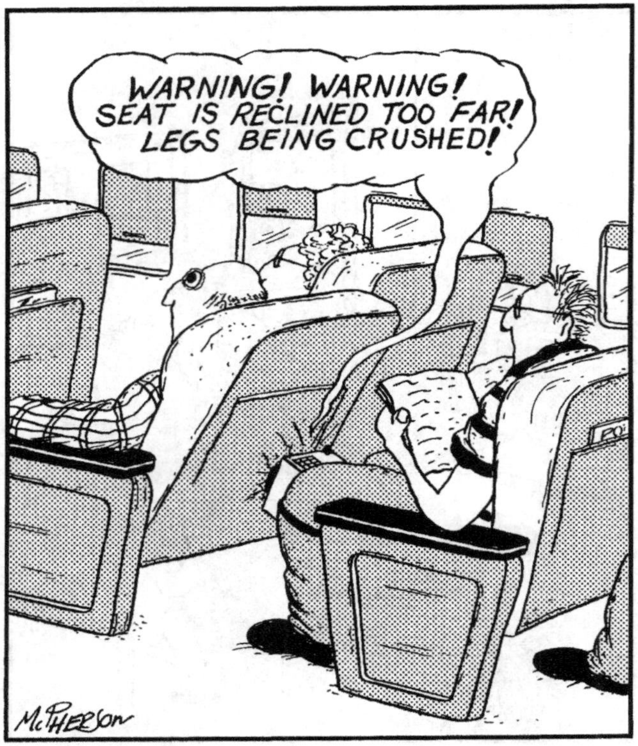

WARNING! WARNING!
SEAT IS RECLINED TOO FAR!
LEGS BEING CRUSHED!
McPHERSON

Vince never flew without his Airline Travel Knee Alarm™.

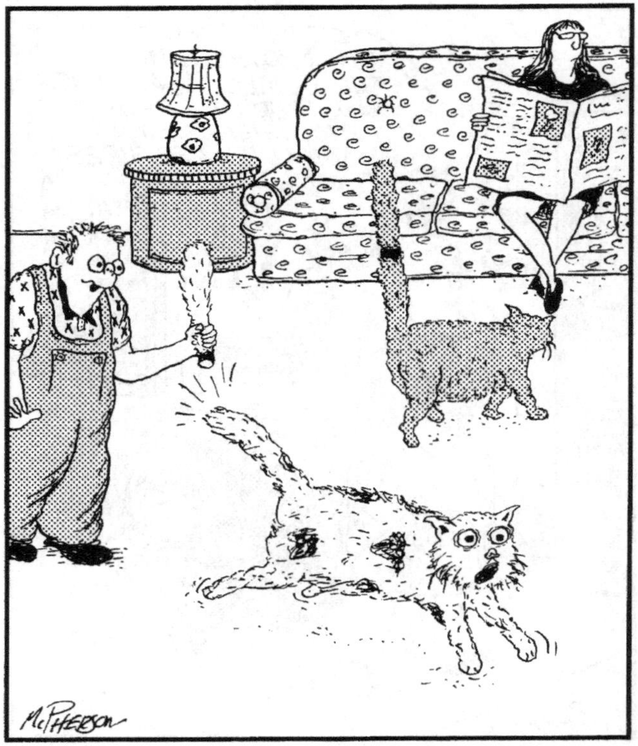

McPHERSON

To spare their cats from the wrath of their toddler, the Wagners outfitted both felines with artificial tear-away tail extensions.

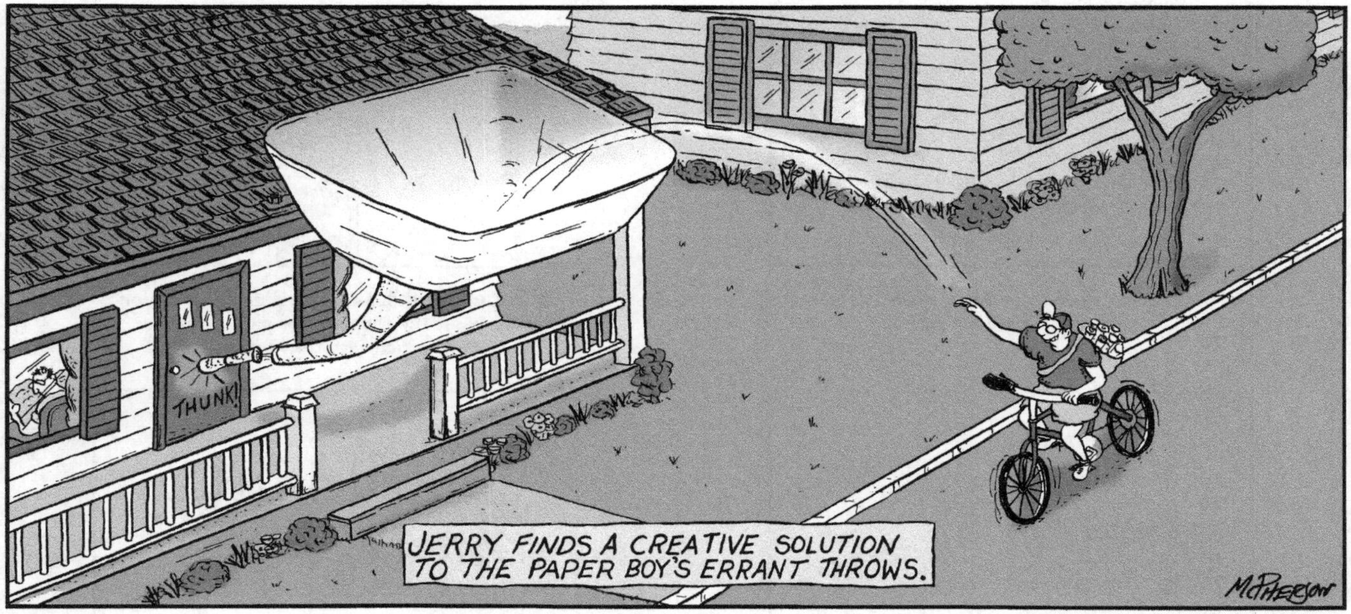
THUNK!
JERRY FINDS A CREATIVE SOLUTION TO THE PAPER BOY'S ERRANT THROWS.
McPHERSON

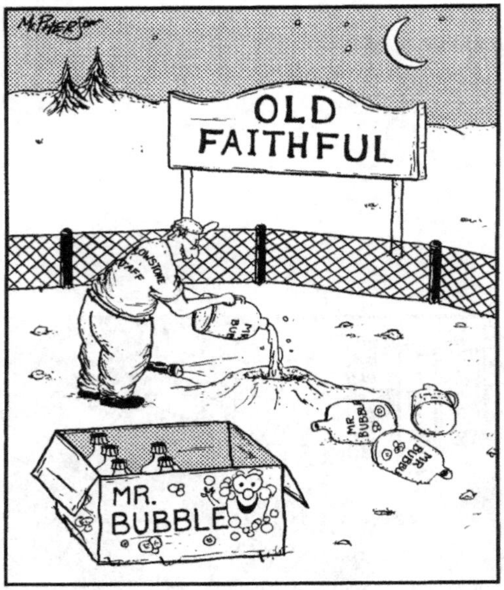
OLD FAITHFUL
MR. BUBBLE

Yellowstone park employee Reggie Nordell pulls the practical joke of a lifetime.

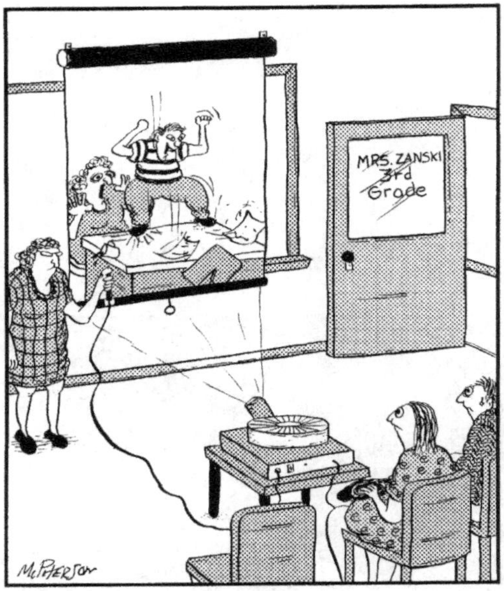
MRS. ZANSKI 3rd Grade

Mrs. Zanski's fifteen-minute slide presentation quickly set the tone for her parent-teacher conference with the Murdocks.

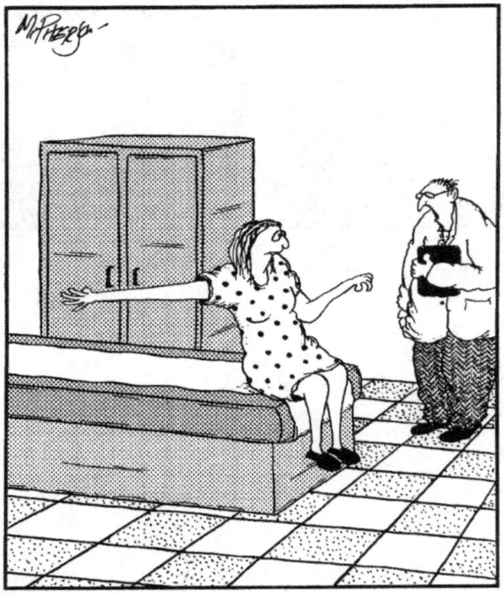

"You've got Minivanitis, Mrs. Keppler, commonly known as Reaching Back to Retrieve Your Screaming Toddler's Juice Cup While Driving Syndrome."

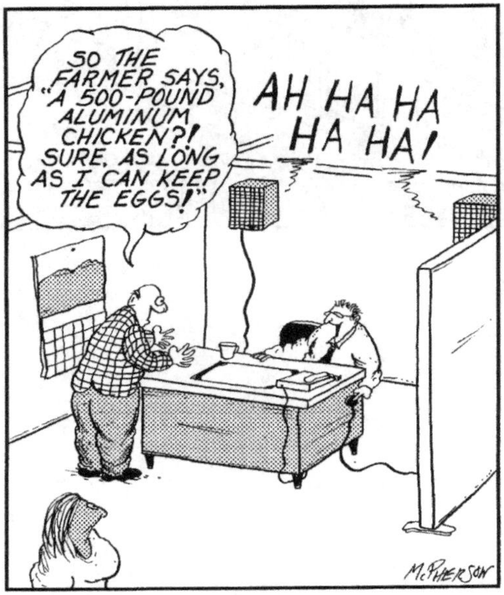
SO THE FARMER SAYS, "A 500-POUND ALUMINUM CHICKEN?! SURE, AS LONG AS I CAN KEEP THE EGGS!"
AH HA HA HA HA!

Having installed a laugh track that he could activate anytime his boss told a joke, Mel quickly ascended the corporate ladder.

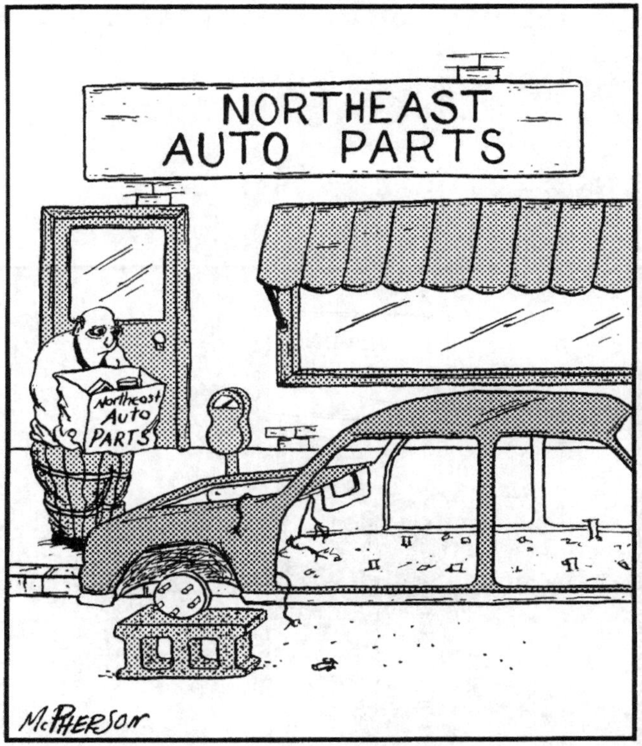
NORTHEAST
AUTO PARTS
Northeast
Auto
PARTS
McPHERSON

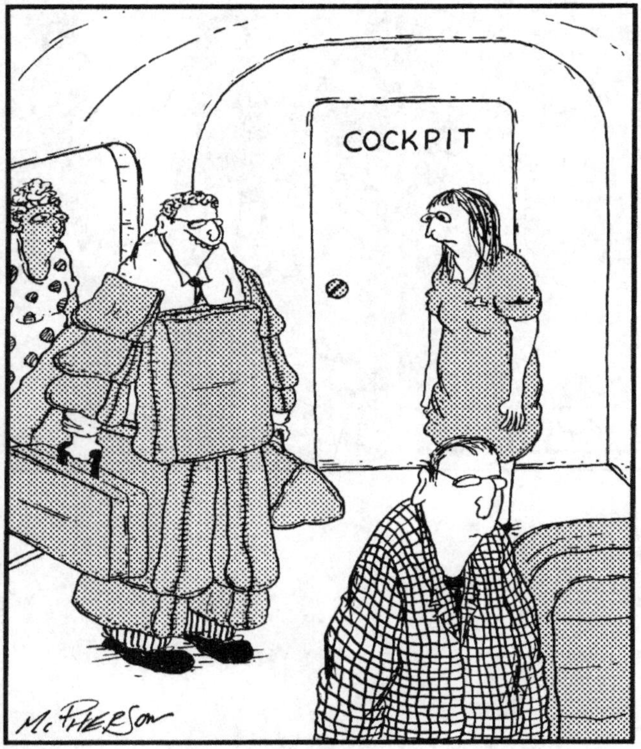
COCKPIT
McPHERSON

Thanks to his new Body Luggage™, Art was able to evade the airline's two-carry-on-bags rule.

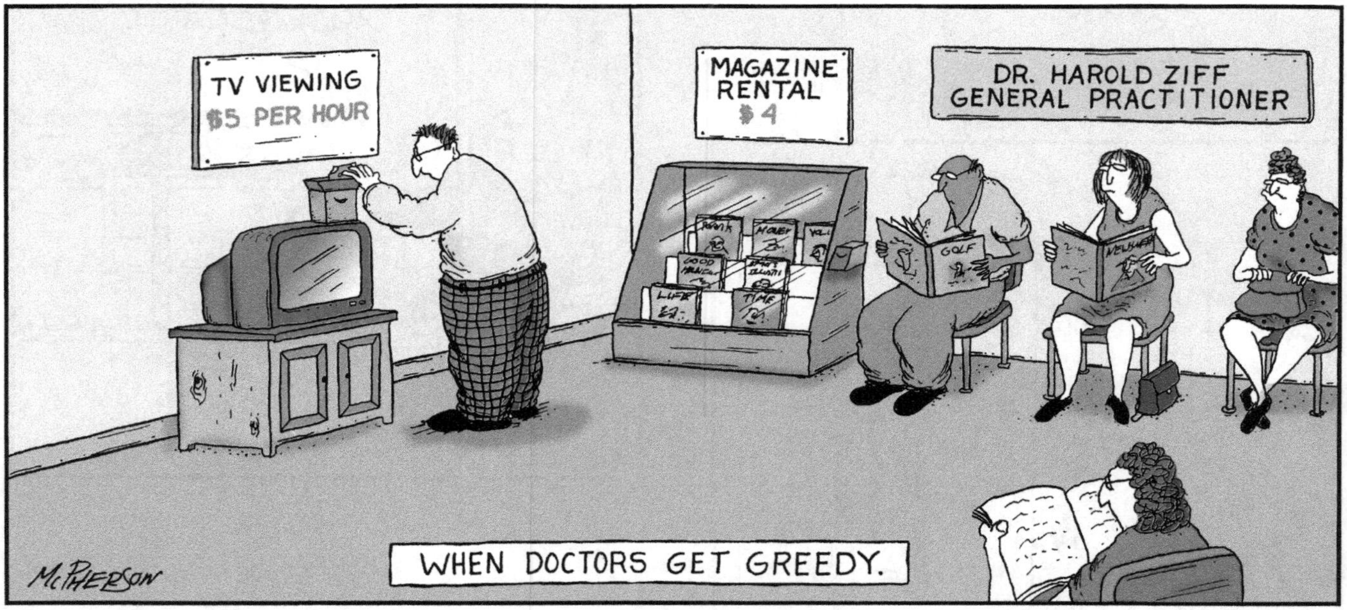
TV VIEWING
$5 PER HOUR
MAGAZINE RENTAL
$4
DR. HAROLD ZIFF
GENERAL PRACTITIONER
GOLF
LIFE
TIME
McPHERSON

WHEN DOCTORS GET GREEDY.

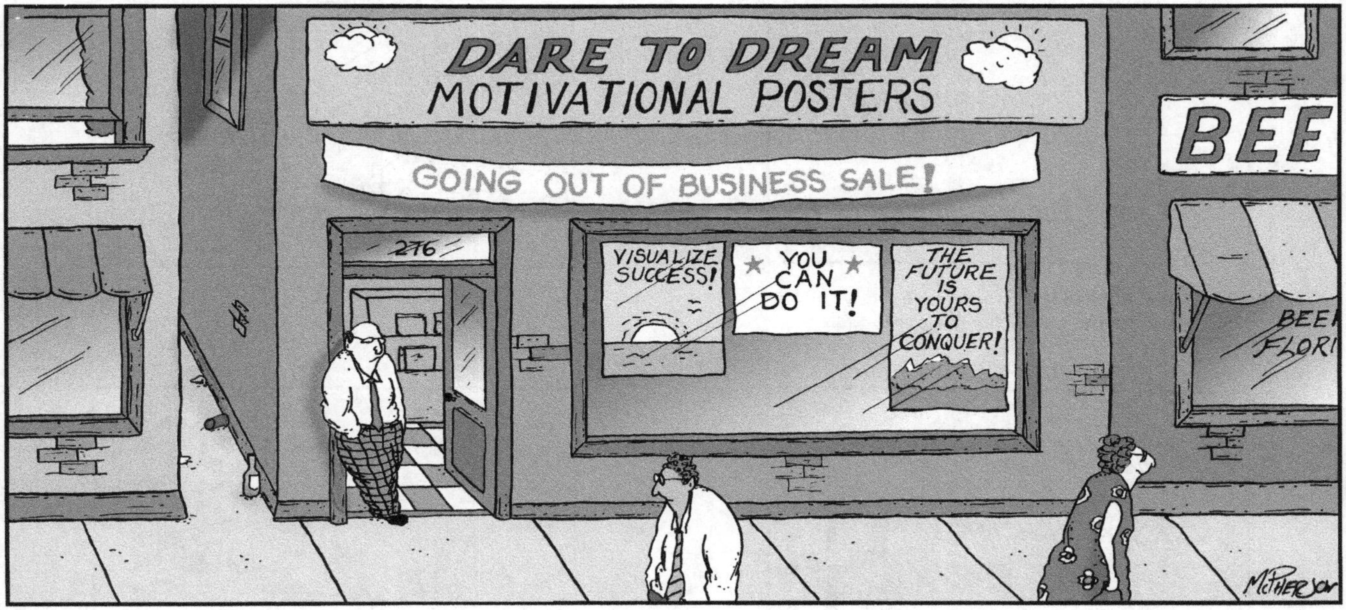
DARE TO DREAM
MOTIVATIONAL POSTERS
GOING OUT OF BUSINESS SALE!
276
VISUALIZE SUCCESS!
YOU CAN DO IT!
THE FUTURE IS YOURS TO CONQUER!
BEE
McPherson

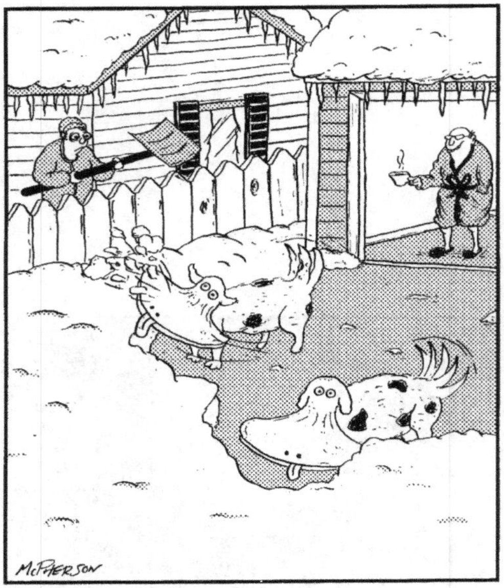

Bert's new Alaskan show-shoveling hounds quickly became the talk of the neighborhood.

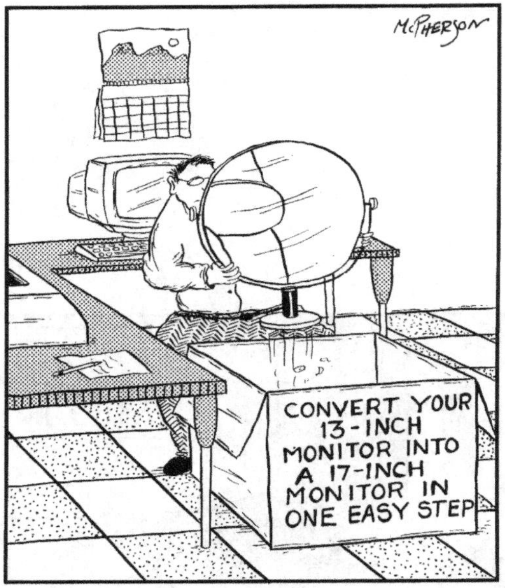

CONVERT YOUR 13-INCH MONITOR INTO A 17-INCH MONITOR IN ONE EASY STEP

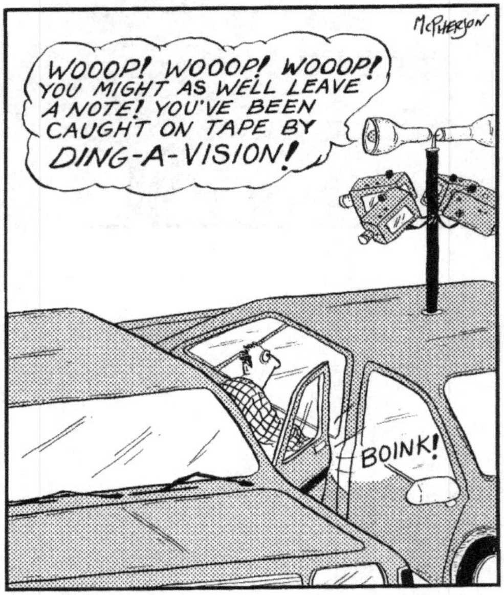

WOOOP! WOOOP! WOOOP! YOU MIGHT AS WELL LEAVE A NOTE! YOU'VE BEEN CAUGHT ON TAPE BY DING-A-VISION!
BOINK!

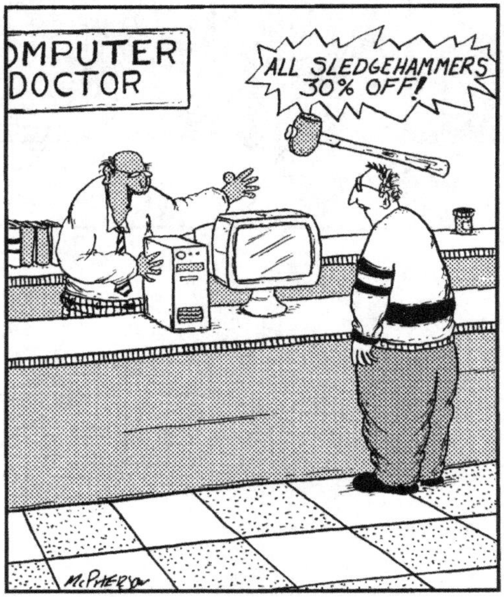

MPUTER DOCTOR
ALL SLEDGEHAMMERS 30% OFF!

"Unfortunately we don't do repairs on computers made prior to 1995. We do, however, have a sale on sledgehammers."

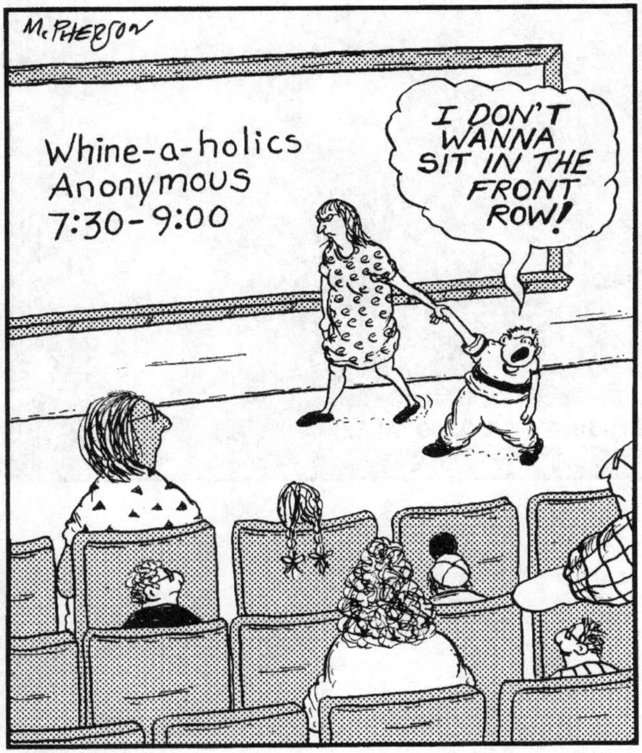
McPHERSON
Whine-a-holics
Anonymous
7:30-9:00
I DON'T WANNA SIT IN THE FRONT ROW!

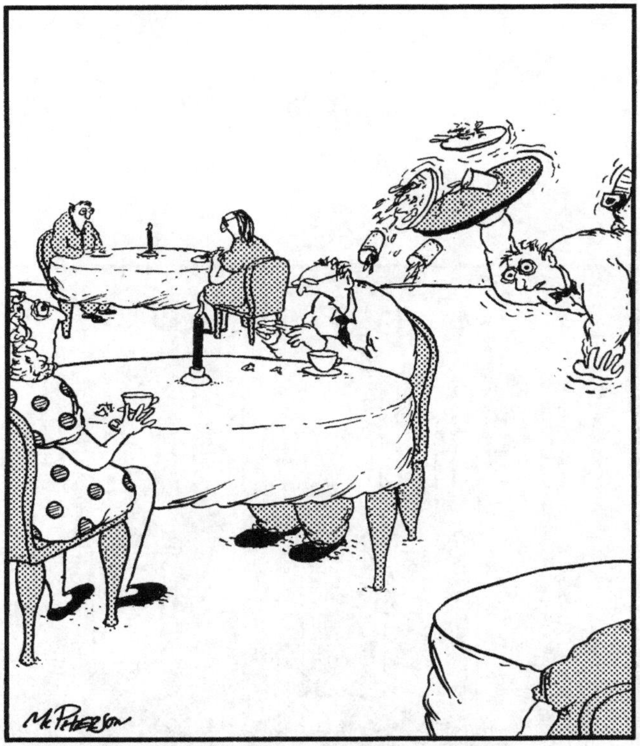
McPHERSON

"That's weird. All this fortune cookie says is 'Look out!'"

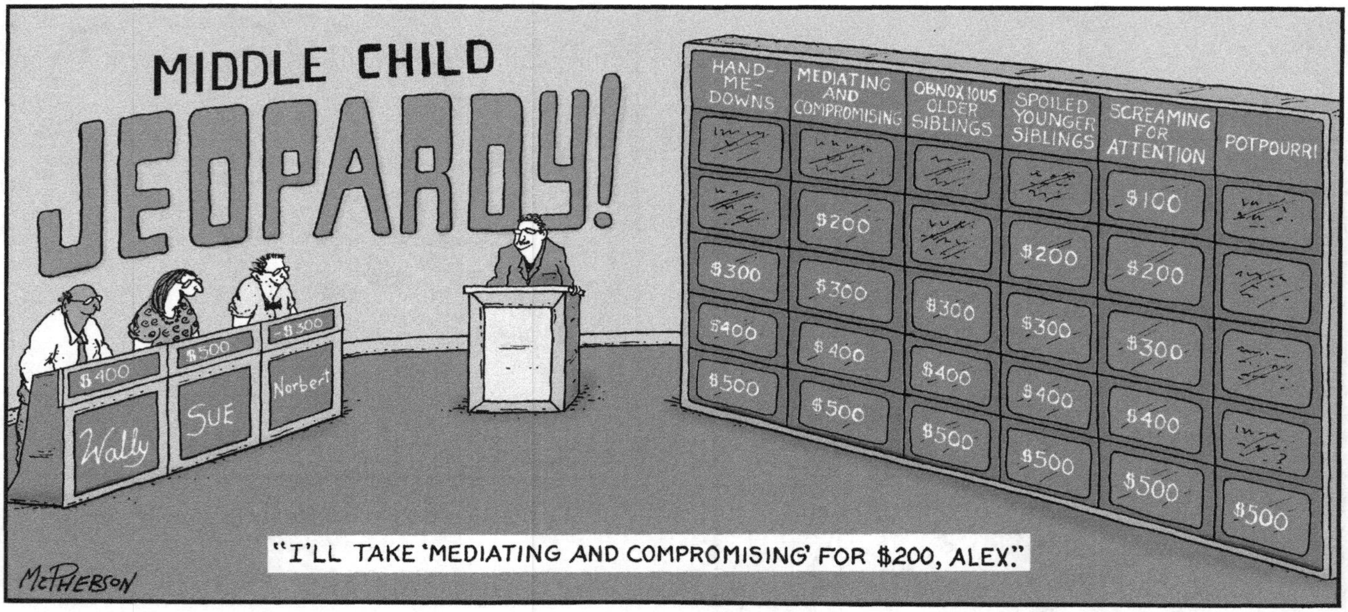
MIDDLE CHILD
JEOPARDY!
HAND-ME-DOWNS
MEDIATING AND COMPROMISING
OBNOXIOUS OLDER SIBLINGS
SPOILED YOUNGER SIBLINGS
SCREAMING FOR ATTENTION
POTPOURRI
$100
$200
$200
$200
$300
$300
$300
$300
$300
$400
$400
$400
$400
$400
$500
$500
$500
$500
$500
$500
$400
$500
-$300
Wally
SUE
Norbert
McPHERSON

"I'LL TAKE 'MEDIATING AND COMPROMISING' FOR $200, ALEX."

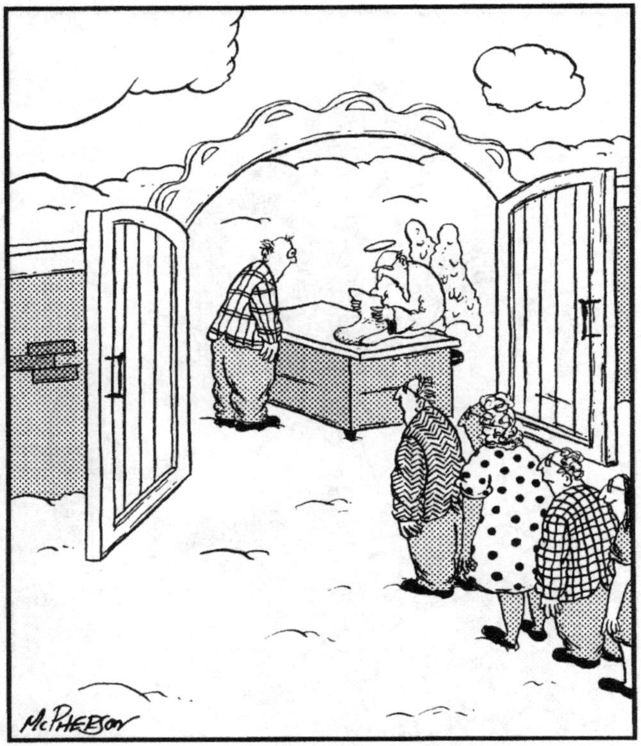
McPHERSON

"OK, let's see . . . Myron Wuffle, president of one of America's largest HMOs. It says you're allowed in, but you can stay for only twenty-four hours."

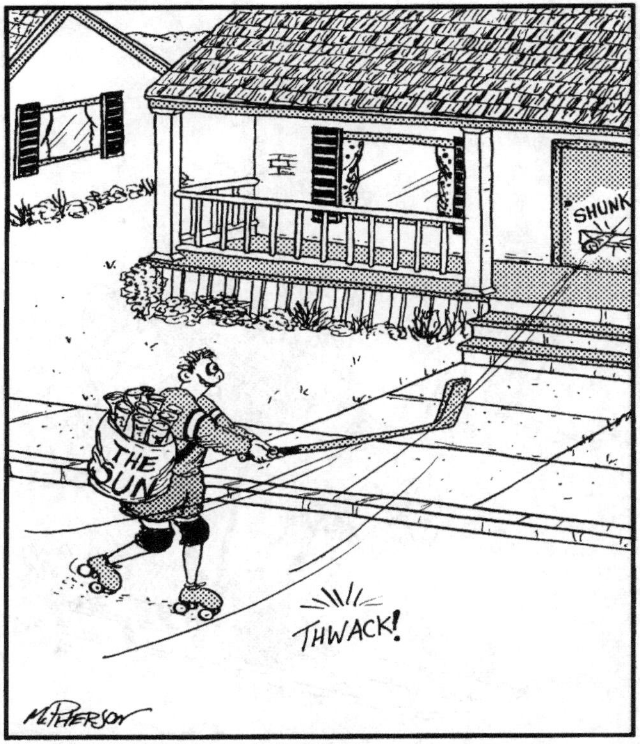
SHUNK
THE SUN
THWACK!
McPHERSON

Wayne Gretzky, age ten.

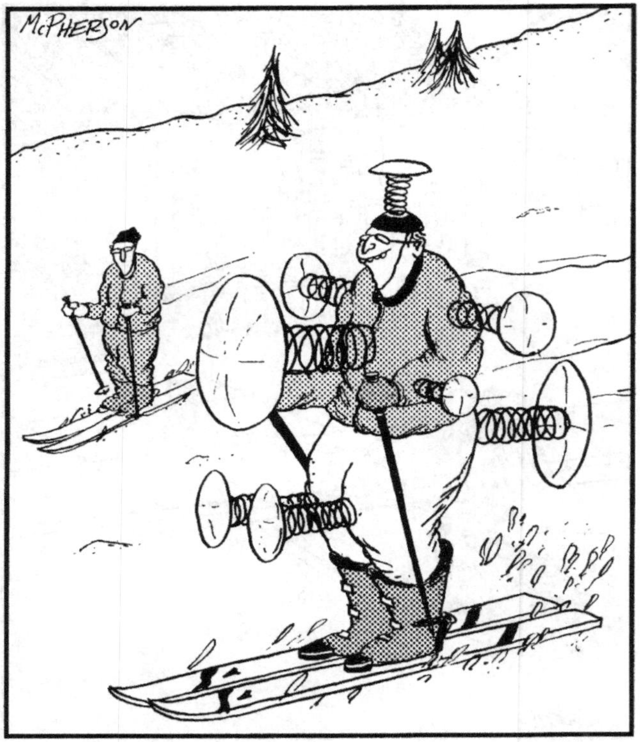
McPHERSON

Greg's new wipeout-resistant ski outfit allowed him to cruise black diamond trails with confidence.

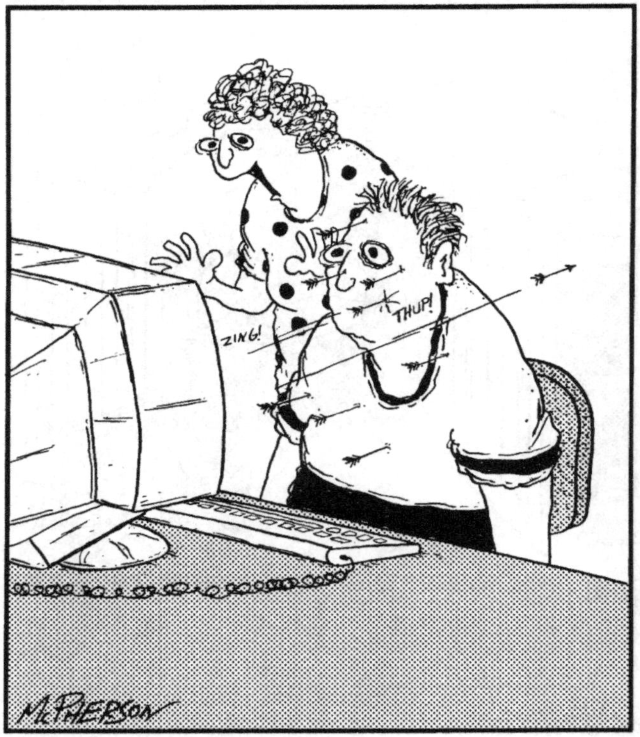
ZING!
THUP!
McPHERSON

"I just read about this in the paper! It's called the Robin Hood Virus!"

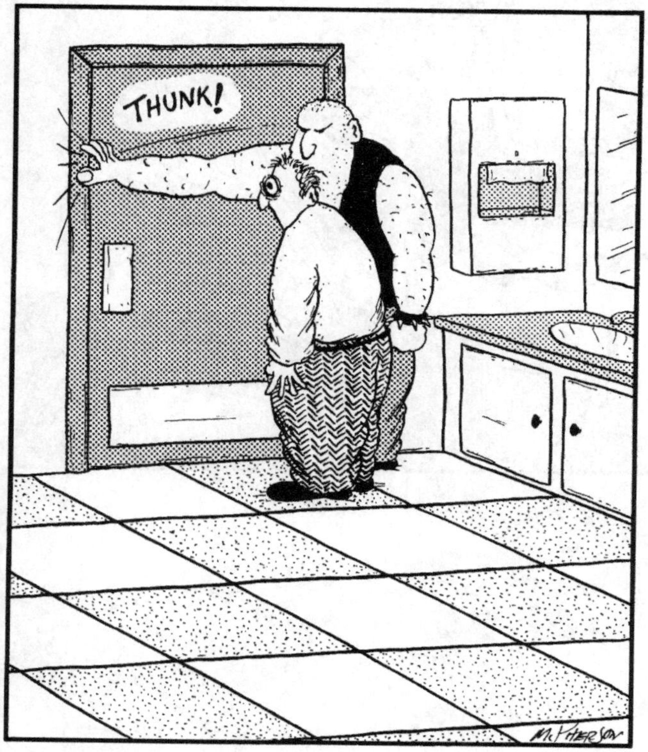
THUNK!

To help reduce illnesses among employees, many companies have placed hand-washing bouncers in all restrooms.

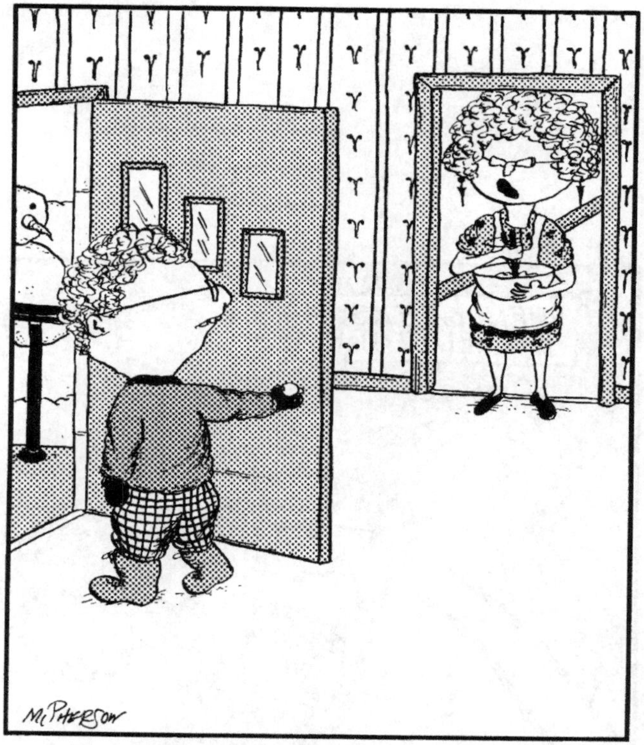

"You're not going anywhere without a hat, young man! I read an article just yesterday that said we lose 90 percent of our body heat through our heads."

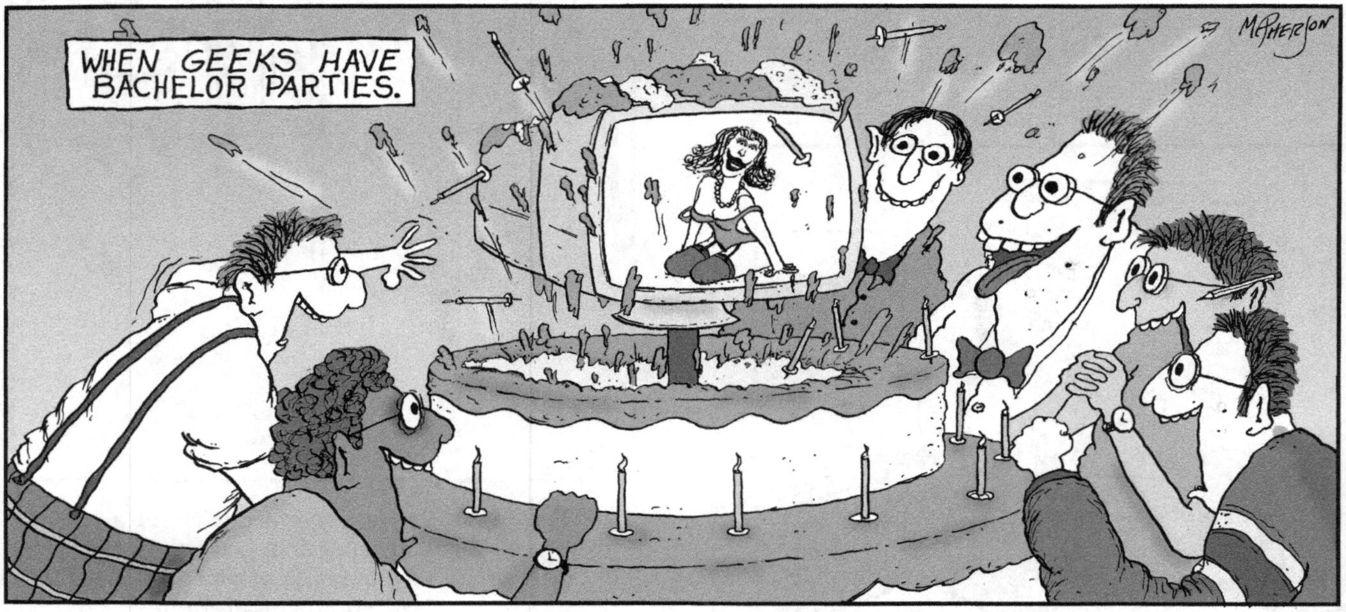
WHEN GEEKS HAVE BACHELOR PARTIES.
McPHERSON

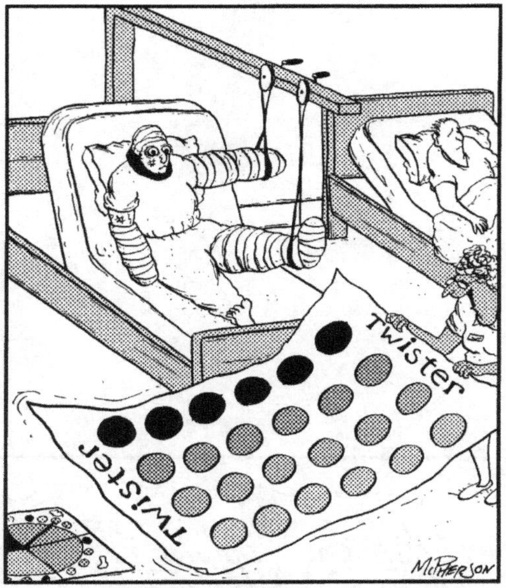
Twister
Twister
McPHERSON

"OK, Mr. Gridley! Time to start your rehab!"

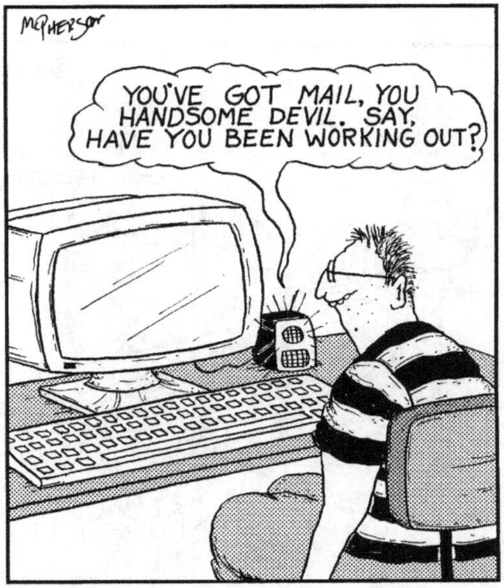
McPHERSON
YOU'VE GOT MAIL, YOU HANDSOME DEVIL. SAY, HAVE YOU BEEN WORKING OUT?

AOL's new personalized e-mail greeting was an instant hit with its customers.

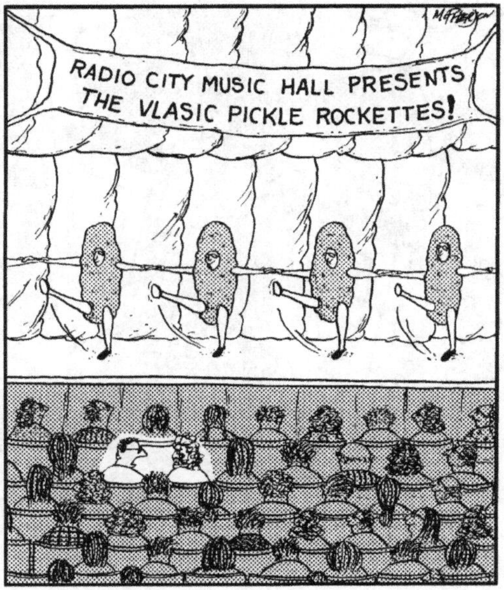
McPHERSON
RADIO CITY MUSIC HALL PRESENTS THE VLASIC PICKLE ROCKETTES!

"Personally I think this whole corporate sponsorship thing is getting way out of hand."

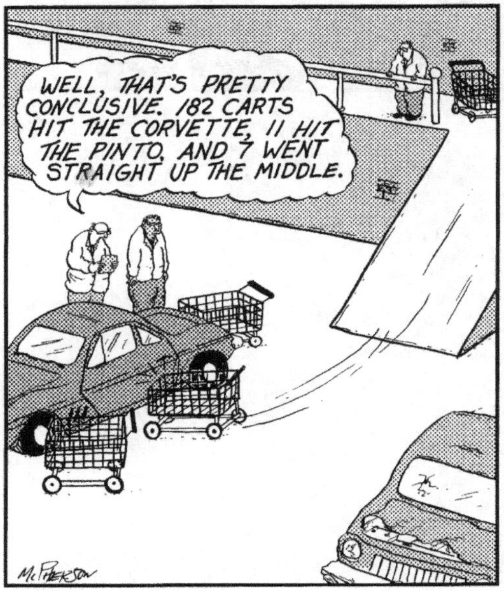
WELL, THAT'S PRETTY CONCLUSIVE. 182 CARTS HIT THE CORVETTE, 11 HIT THE PINTO, AND 7 WENT STRAIGHT UP THE MIDDLE.
McPHERSON

Researchers at MIT prove that rolling shopping carts will almost invariably hit the most expensive car in their vicinity.

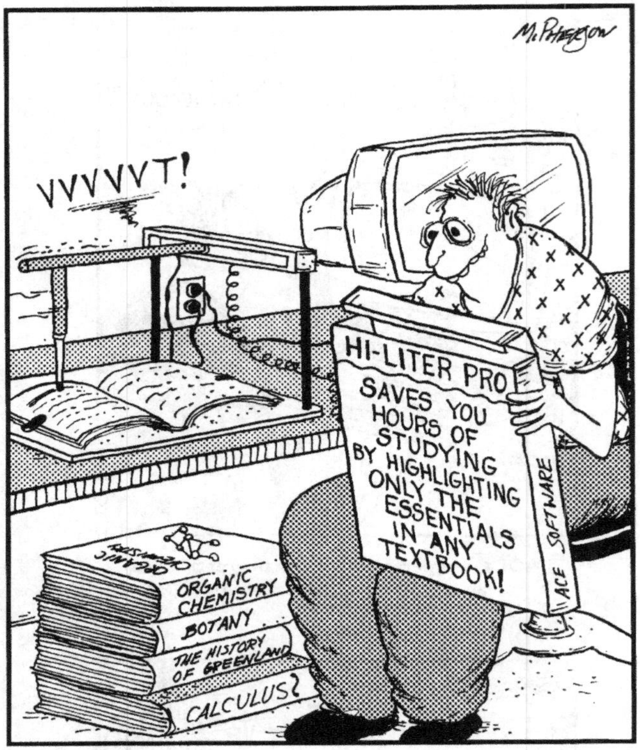
M. PETERSON
VVVVVT!
HI-LITER PRO
SAVES YOU HOURS OF STUDYING BY HIGHLIGHTING ONLY THE ESSENTIALS IN ANY TEXTBOOK!
ACE SOFTWARE
ORGANIC CHEMISTRY
BOTANY
THE HISTORY OF GREENLAND
CALCULUS

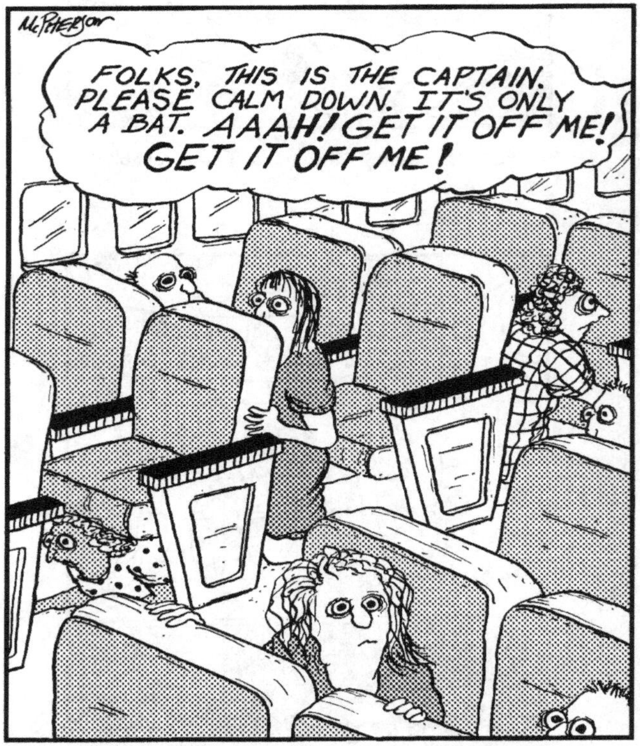
M. PETERSON
FOLKS, THIS IS THE CAPTAIN. PLEASE CALM DOWN. IT'S ONLY A BAT. AAAH! GET IT OFF ME! GET IT OFF ME!

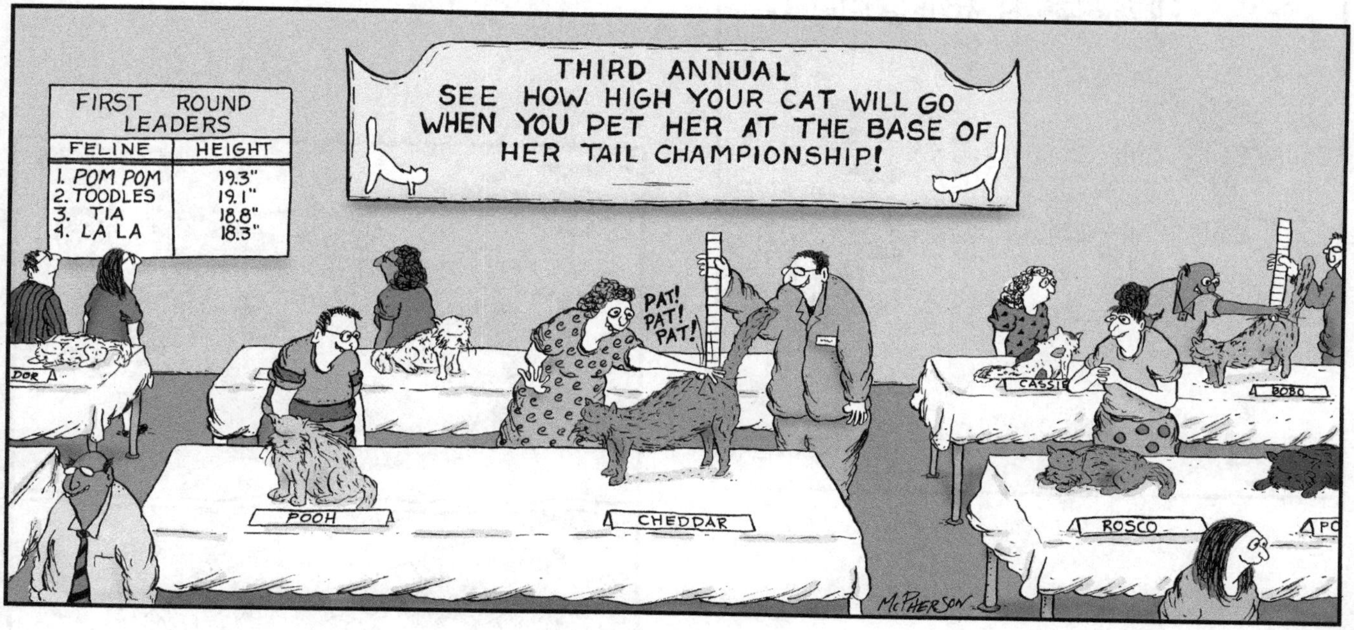

FIRST ROUND LEADERS
FELINE HEIGHT
1. POM POM 19.3"
2. TOODLES 19.1"
3. TIA 18.8"
4. LA LA 18.3"
THIRD ANNUAL
SEE HOW HIGH YOUR CAT WILL GO
WHEN YOU PET HER AT THE BASE OF
HER TAIL CHAMPIONSHIP!
PAT! PAT! PAT!
POOH
CHEDDAR
CASSIE
BOBO
ROSCO
McPHERSON

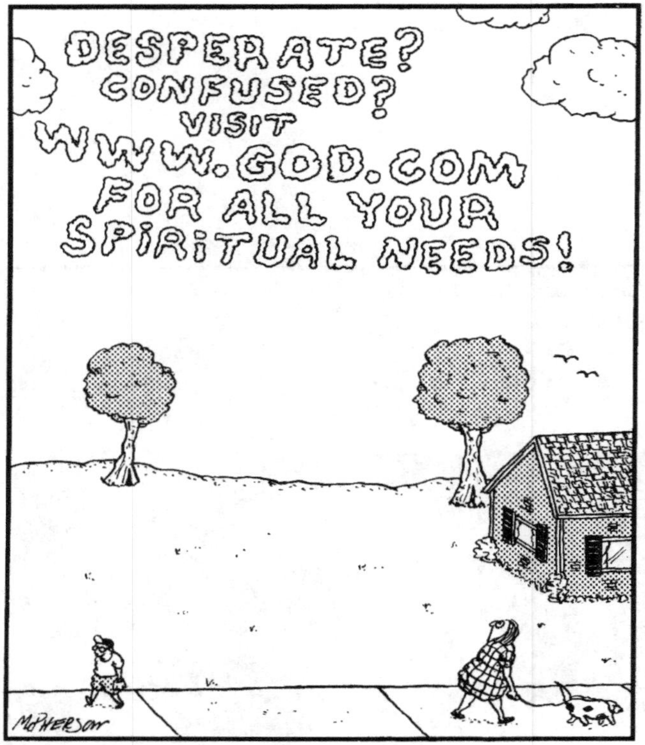
DESPERATE?
CONFUSED?
VISIT
WWW.GOD.COM
FOR ALL YOUR
SPIRITUAL NEEDS!
McPHERSON

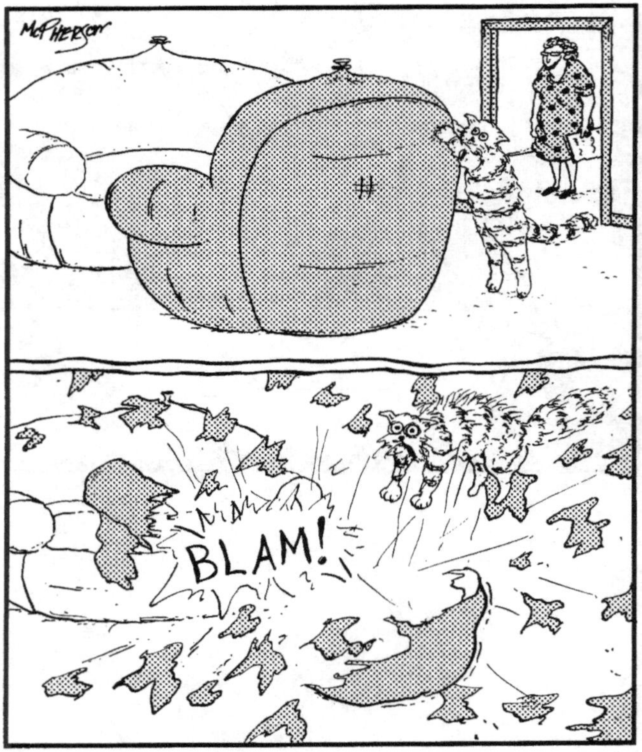
McPHERSON
BLAM!

Claire's decoy balloon furniture quickly broke Muffin of her claw-sharpening habit.

McPHERSON
DELI

Though expensive, hiring a professional actor dressed as death to stalk his every move finally broke Ted of his smoking addiction.

McPHERSON
SPROING!
NUTS

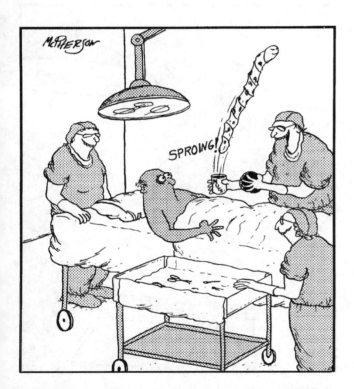

"Your pacemaker will need to be replaced in five years. Mind if we play a little prank on your future surgeons by implanting this harmless spring-snake gag in your chest?"

McPHERSON
DOWN COMFORTER WITH BUILT-IN "LABRADOR RETRIEVER"
★ HEATS UP TO A DOG'S BODY TEMPERATURE AND OCCASIONALLY SCRATCHES ITS EAR!

"See? It looks like a real dog, feels like a real dog, but without the hassles of owning a real dog!"

McPHERSON

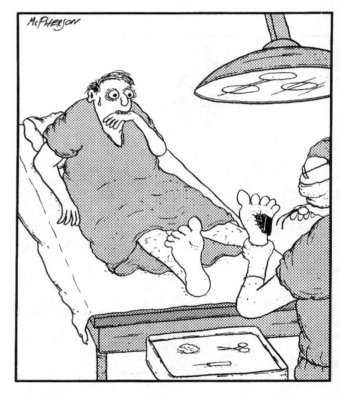

Despite warnings to parents not to walk through their kids' playrooms barefoot, Lego-ectomies continue to be the most common operation in ERs.

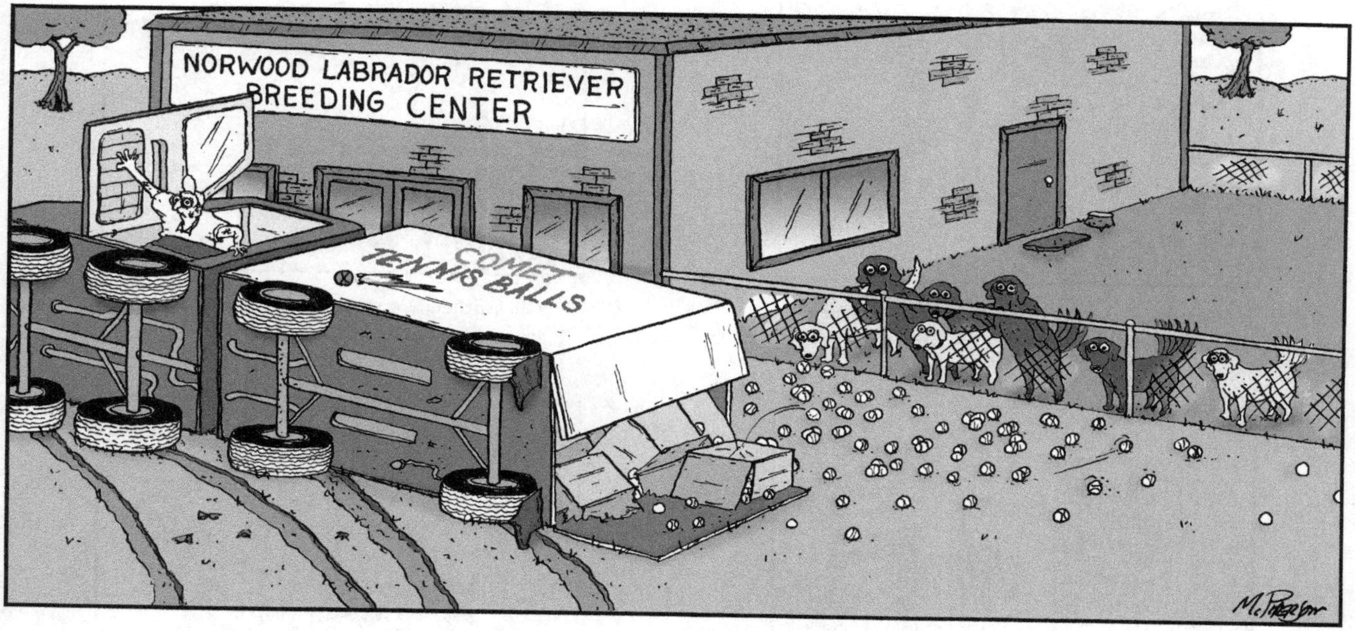
NORWOOD LABRADOR RETRIEVER
BREEDING CENTER
COMET
TENNIS BALLS
McPherson

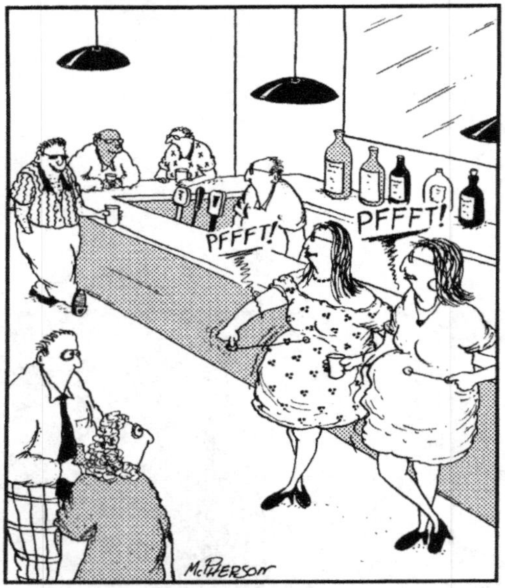
PFFFT!
PFFFT!

Having spotted the lounge lizard approaching, Peggy and Joanne quickly activated their pregnancy-simulation systems.

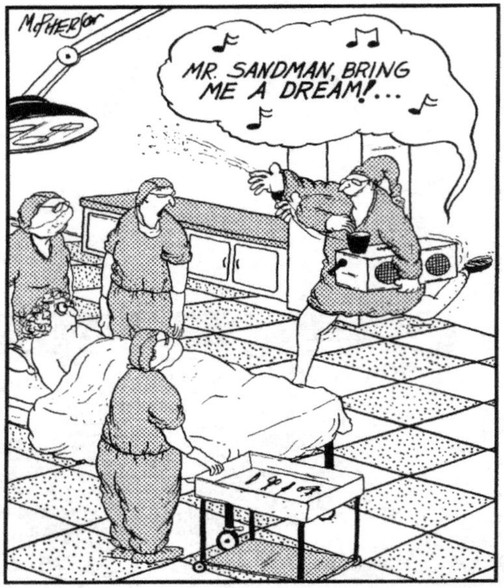
MR. SANDMAN, BRING ME A DREAM!...

"Oh, brother. Not this anesthesiologist again!"

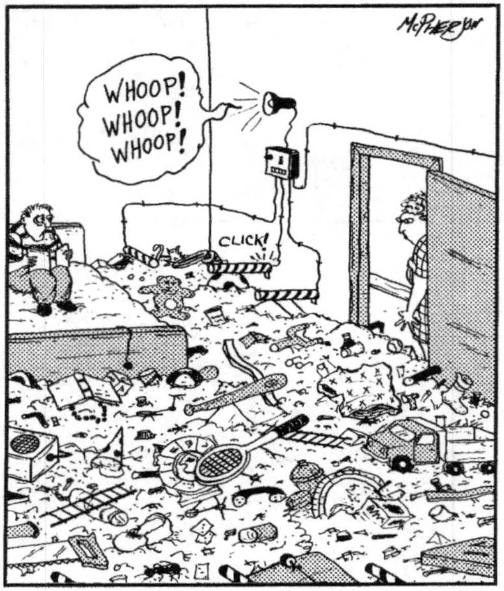
WHOOP! WHOOP! WHOOP!
CLICK!

As soon as the Excessive Trashiness Alarm™ sounded in his room, Matt knew he was in big trouble.

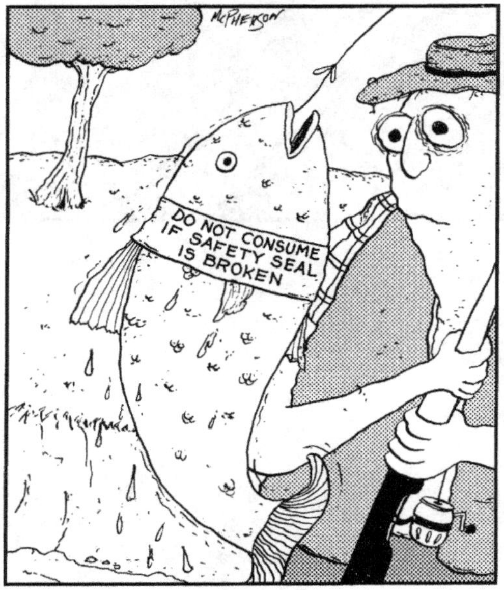
DO NOT CONSUME IF SAFETY SEAL IS BROKEN

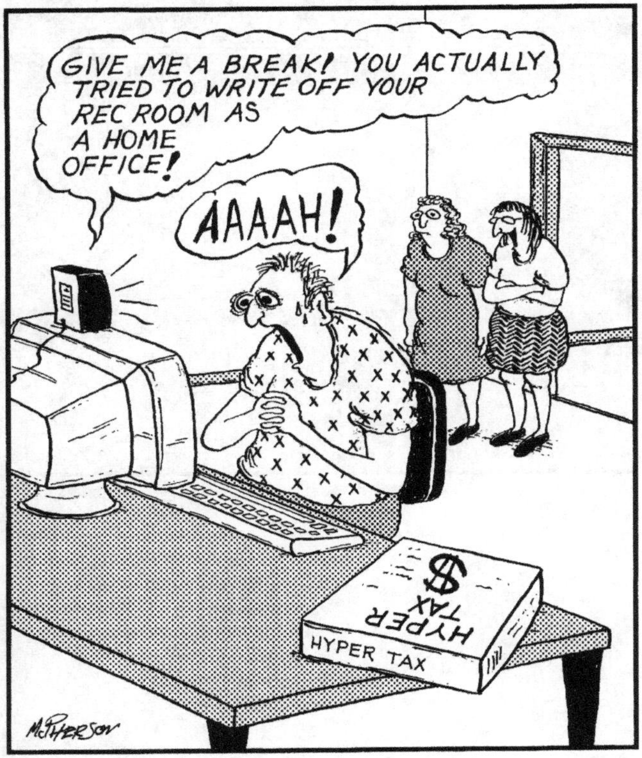
GIVE ME A BREAK! YOU ACTUALLY TRIED TO WRITE OFF YOUR REC ROOM AS A HOME OFFICE!
AAAAH!
HYPER TAX
HYPER TAX
McPHERSON

"Tim's new tax software includes a virtual-reality IRS audit."

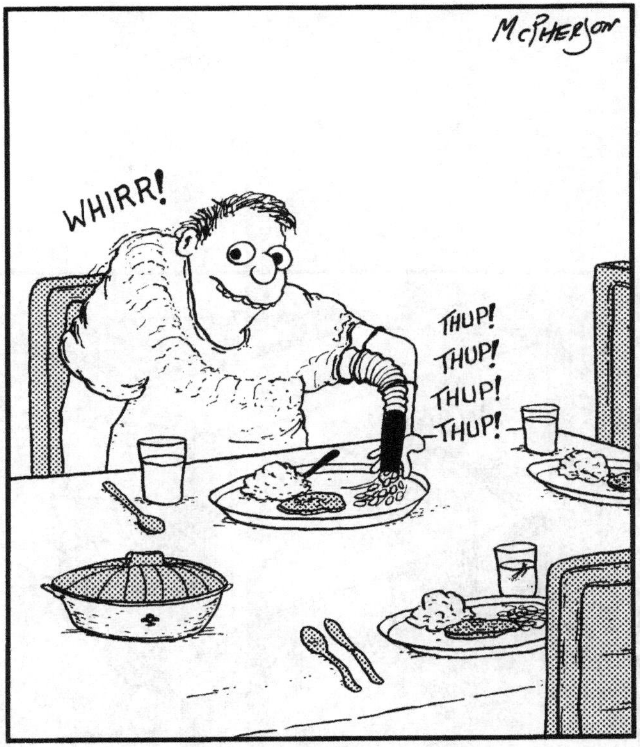
McPHERSON
WHIRR!
THUP!
THUP!
THUP!
THUP!

With his parents momentarily out of the room, Willie quickly used his Veggie-Vac™ on his lima beans.

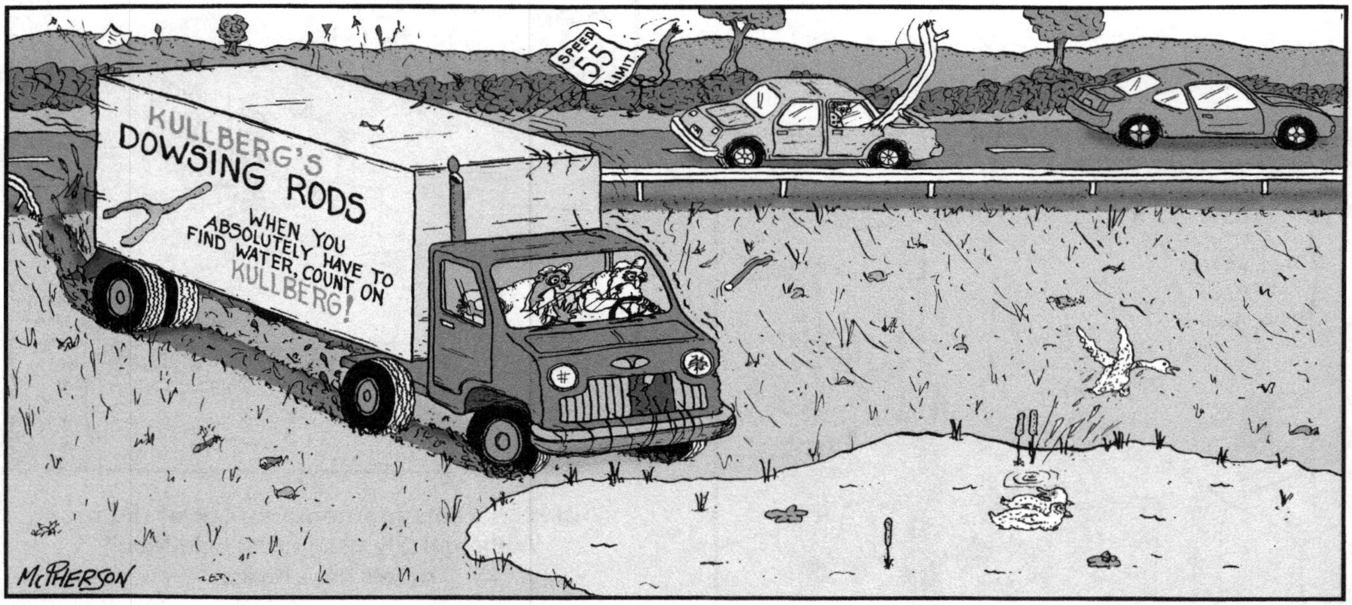
KULLBERG'S
DOWSING RODS
WHEN YOU ABSOLUTELY HAVE TO FIND WATER, COUNT ON KULLBERG!
SPEED 55 LIMIT
McPHERSON

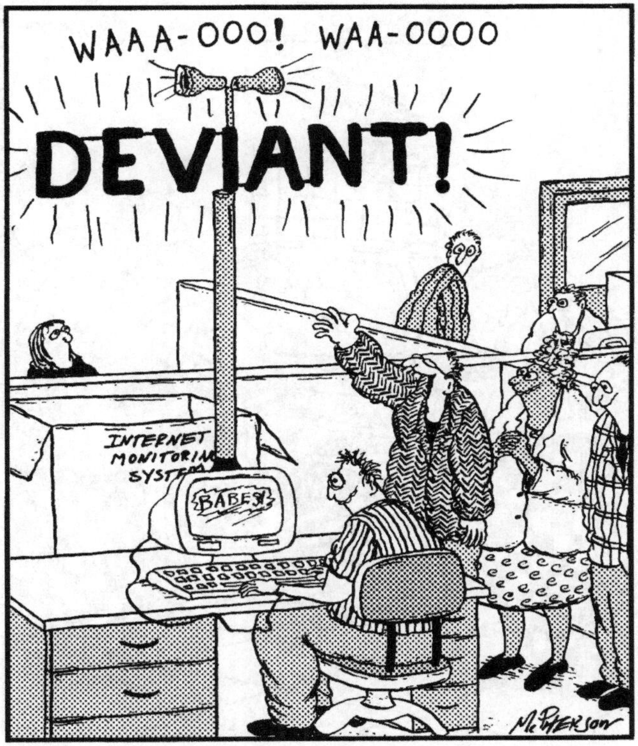
WAAA-OOO! WAA-OOOO
DEVIANT!
INTERNET MONITORING SYSTEM
BABES!

"... and when the user's blood pressure goes over one hundred, the computer shuts down, the siren sounds, and the neon sign begins to flash!"

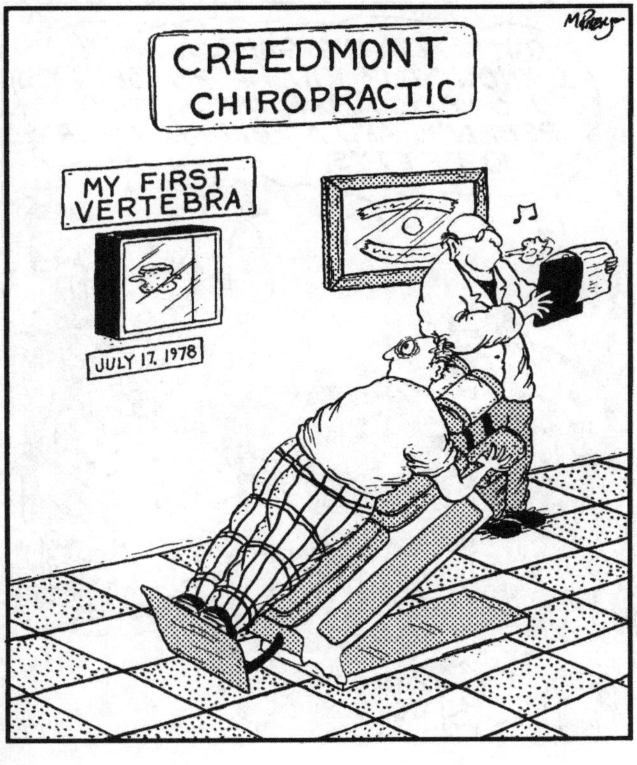
CREEDMONT CHIROPRACTIC
MY FIRST VERTEBRA
JULY 17, 1978

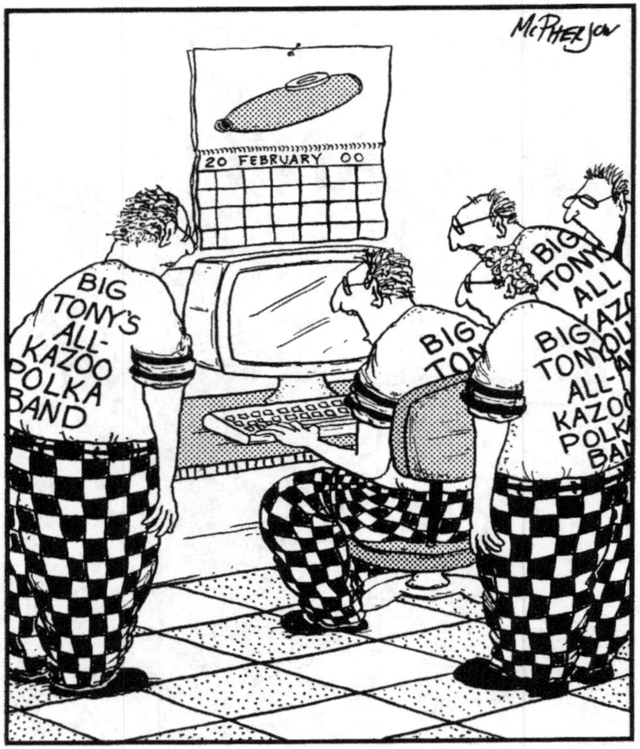
McPherson
20 FEBRUARY 00
BIG TONY'S ALL-KAZOO POLKA BAND

"What the . . . ?! Oh, for cryin' out loud! BigTonysAllKazooPolkaBand.com is already taken as a domain name!"

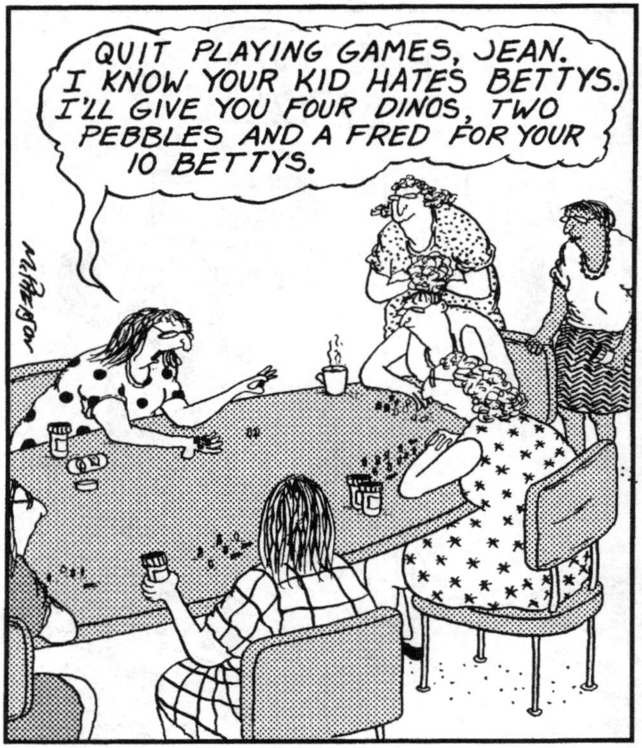
QUIT PLAYING GAMES, JEAN. I KNOW YOUR KID HATES BETTYS. I'LL GIVE YOU FOUR DINOS, TWO PEBBLES AND A FRED FOR YOUR 10 BETTYS.
McPherson

At the Mayfield Mothers Group's weekly Flintstones Vitamins trading session.

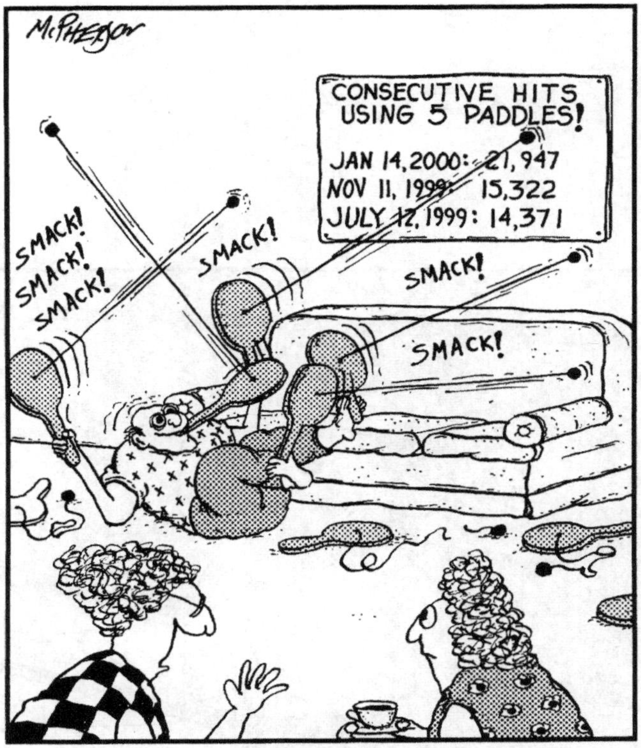
McPHERSON
CONSECUTIVE HITS
USING 5 PADDLES!
JAN 14, 2000: 21,947
NOV 11, 1999: 15,322
JULY 12, 1999: 14,371
SMACK!
SMACK!
SMACK!
SMACK!
SMACK!
SMACK!

"For the first year after he retired, Bob just seemed lost, as though he had no passion in life. And then, one day . . ."

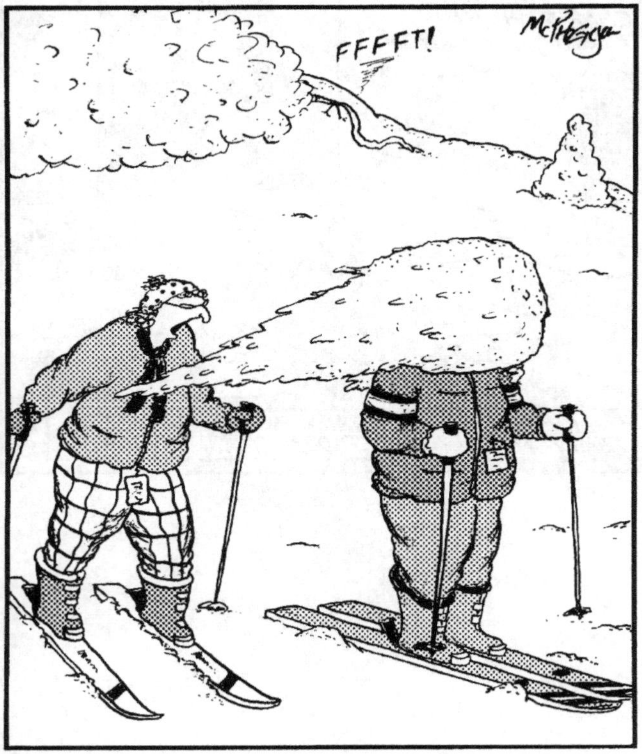
FFFFT!
McPHERSON

"I warned you not to ski so close to that snow gun!"

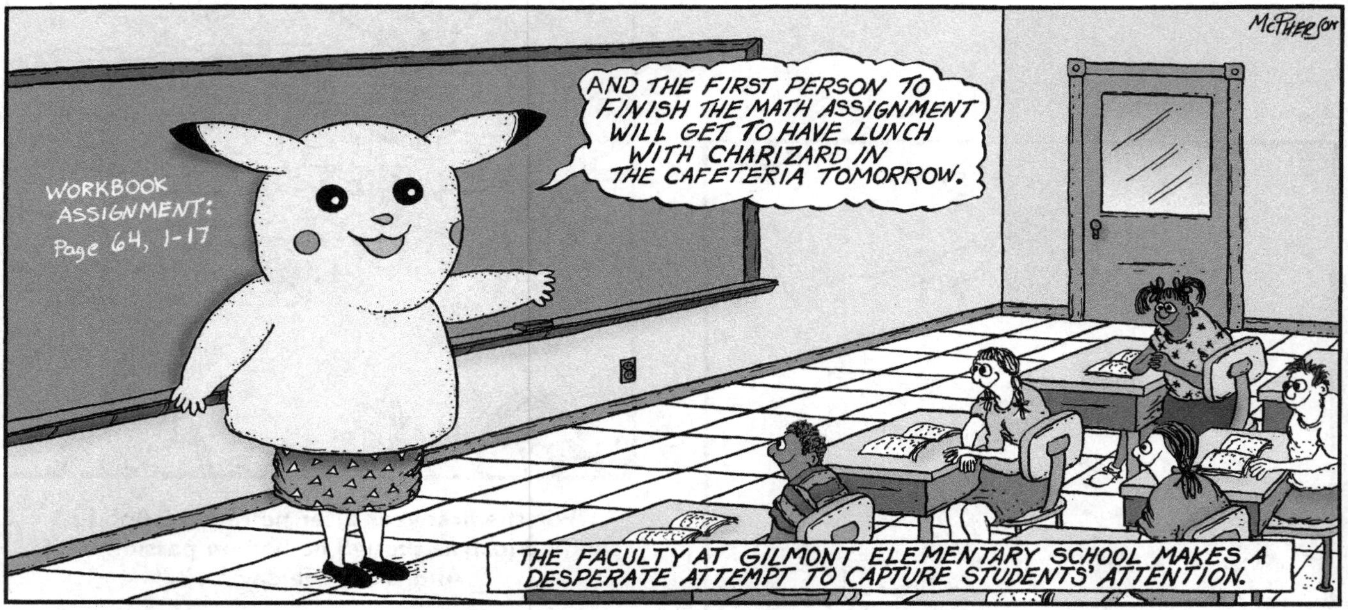
McPHERSON
WORKBOOK ASSIGNMENT: Page 64, 1-17
AND THE FIRST PERSON TO FINISH THE MATH ASSIGNMENT WILL GET TO HAVE LUNCH WITH CHARIZARD IN THE CAFETERIA TOMORROW.
THE FACULTY AT GILMONT ELEMENTARY SCHOOL MAKES A DESPERATE ATTEMPT TO CAPTURE STUDENTS' ATTENTION.

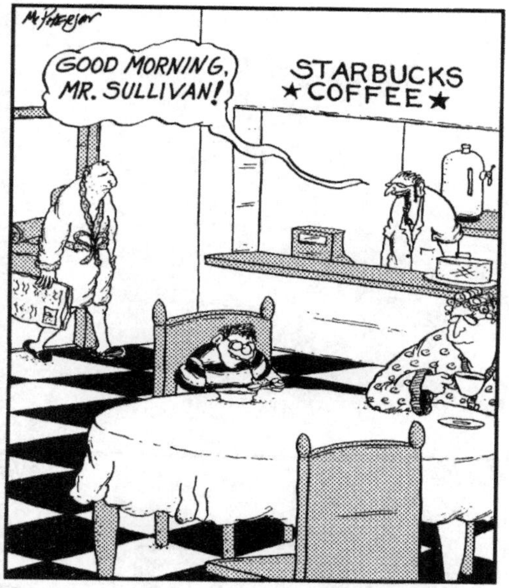
McPherson
GOOD MORNING, MR. SULLIVAN!
STARBUCKS ★ COFFEE ★
Looking to expand its territory even further, Starbucks opens the first of many private-residence coffee shops.

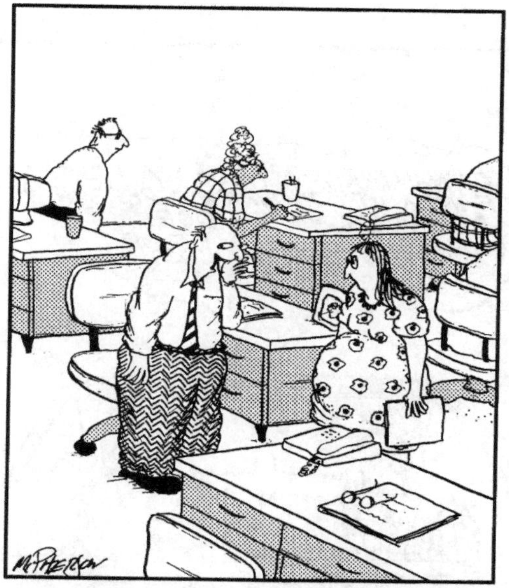
McPherson
"Psst! Carol! I'll split the office pool with you if you'll induce labor on the 17th, 10 a.m."

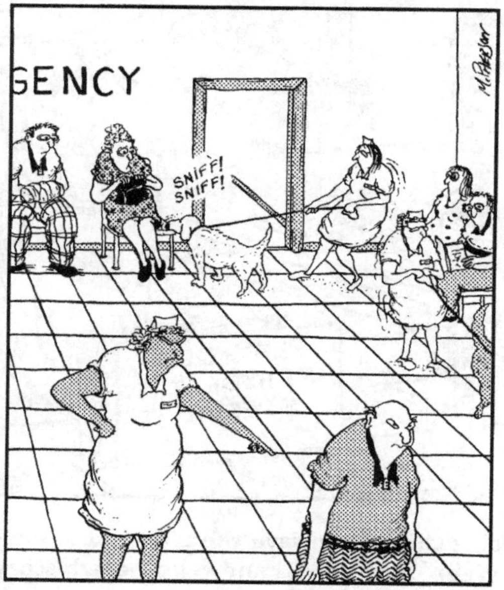
GENCY
McPherson
SNIFF! SNIFF!
Hoping to filter out frivolous visits to the ER, nurses at Ackwood Memorial Hospital brought out hypochondriac-sniffing dogs.

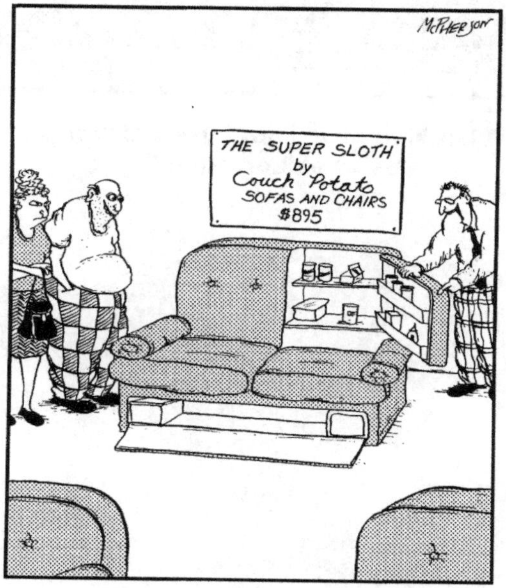
McPherson
THE SUPER SLOTH by Couch Potato SOFAS AND CHAIRS $895
"Here's our top seller! On the right side you've got a 3.3-cubic-foot refrigerator, and down below is the freezer, complete with ice maker and mug froster."

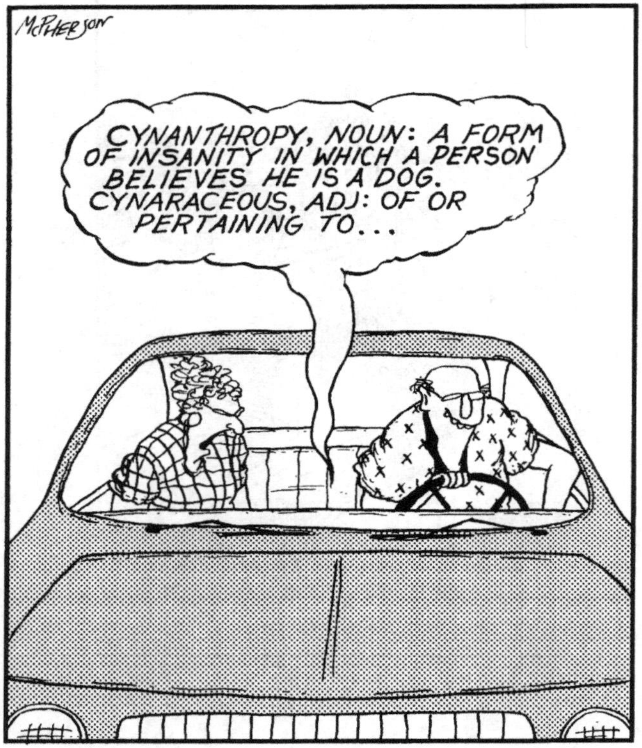
McPHERSON
CYNANTHROPY, NOUN: A FORM OF INSANITY IN WHICH A PERSON BELIEVES HE IS A DOG. CYNARACEOUS, ADJ: OF OR PERTAINING TO...

"What kind of an idiot buys a dictionary as a book on tape?!"

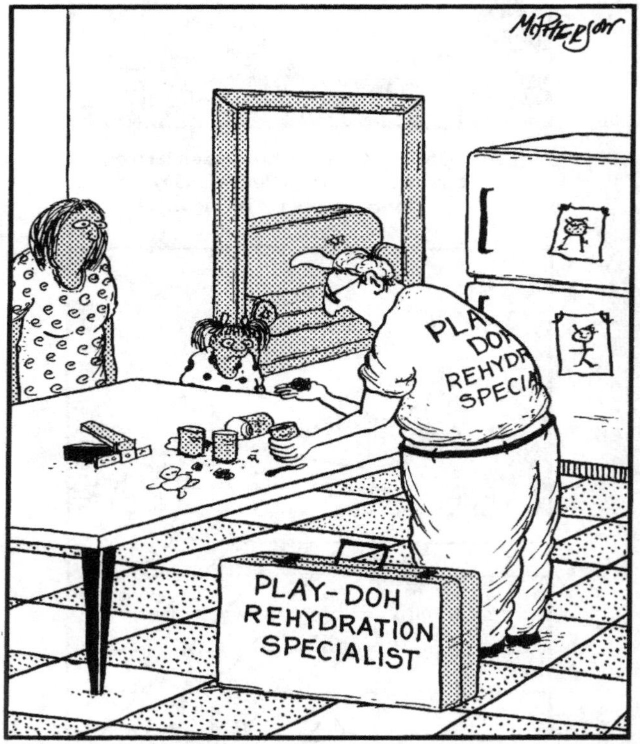
McPHERSON
PLAY-DOH REHYDRATION SPECIALIST

"Well, I think I can save the blue and some of the green, but the red and yellow are history."

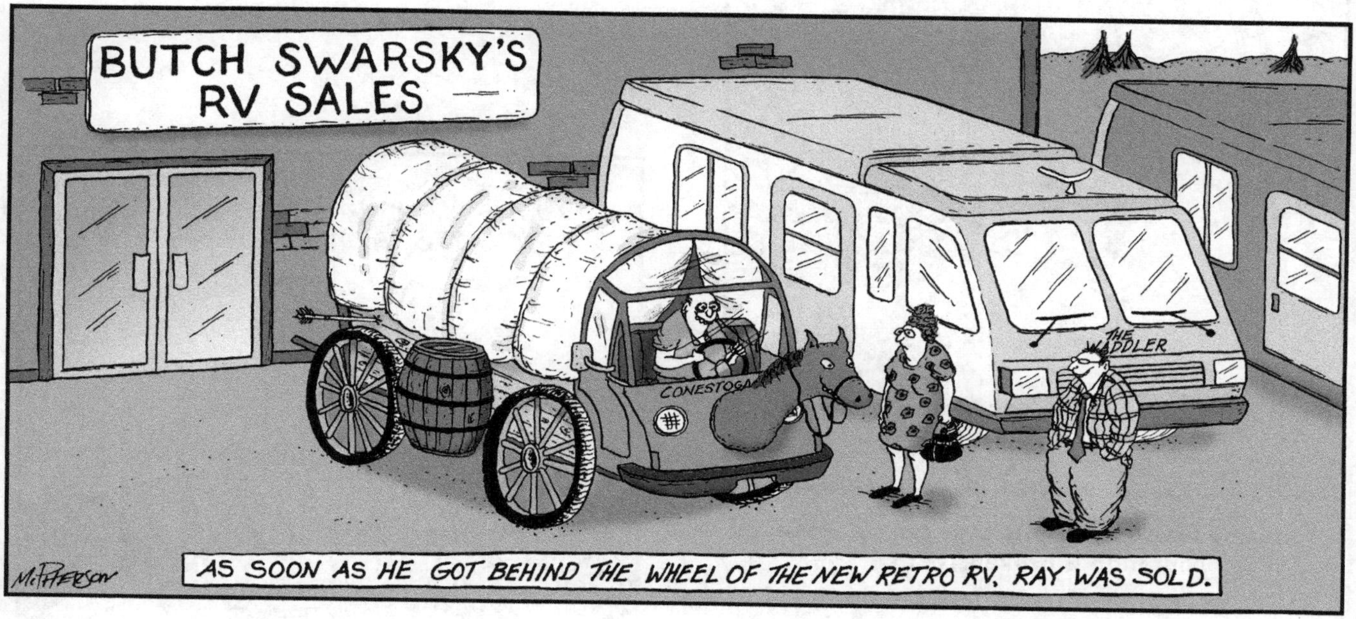
BUTCH SWARSKY'S
RV SALES
CONESTOGA

AS SOON AS HE GOT BEHIND THE WHEEL OF THE NEW RETRO RV, RAY WAS SOLD.

PAT!
PAT!
PAT!
McPHERSON

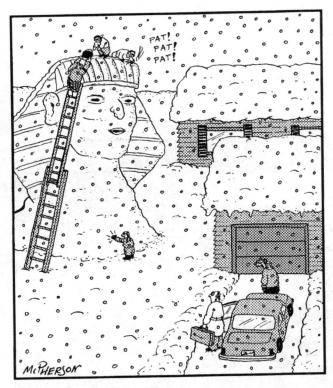

"Amazing how industrious they can be when the Nintendo is broken, isn't it?"

WHEW! <GAG>... YEAH, THAT'S HIM ALL RIGHT!

A powerful new weapon in the war on crime: scratch-and-sniff mug shots.

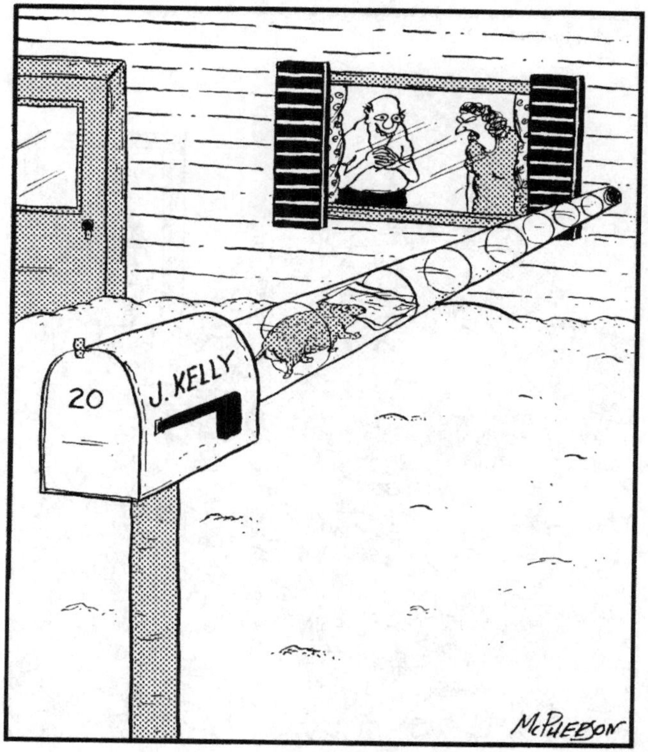

20
J. KELLY
McPHERSON

"For cryin' out loud, would it kill you to put on a coat and hat and get the mail yourself now and then?!"

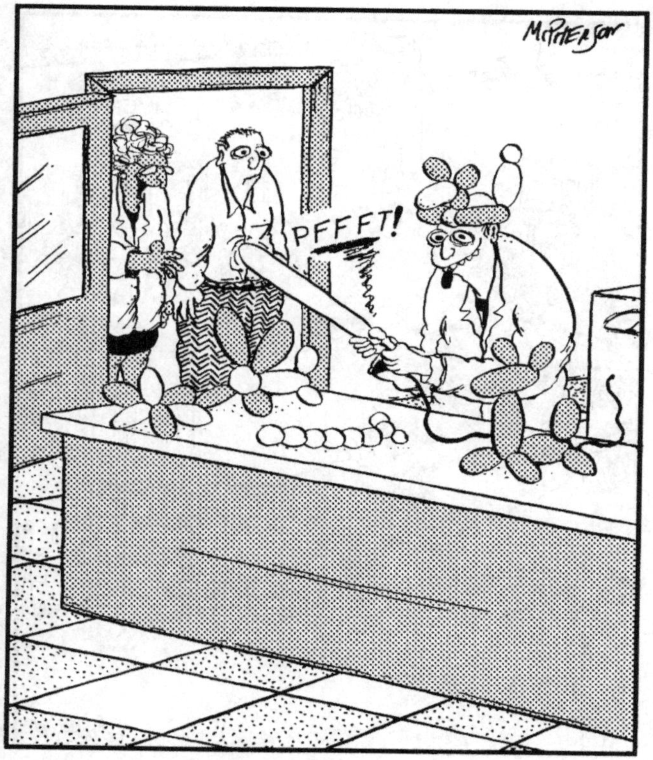

McPHERSON
PFFFT!

"And this is Dr. Sanborn. He's the one who will actually be performing your balloon angioplasty procedure."

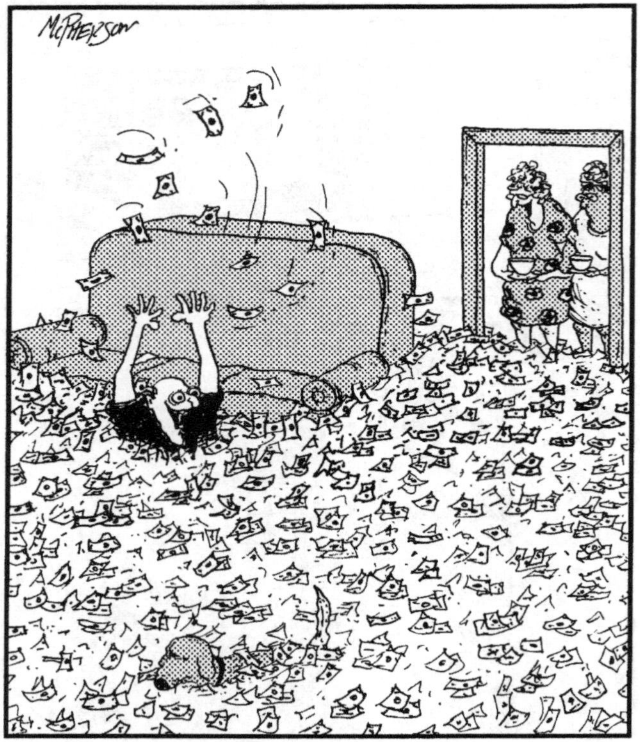
McPHERSON

"Arnie asked to receive his lump-sum retirement entirely in ones."

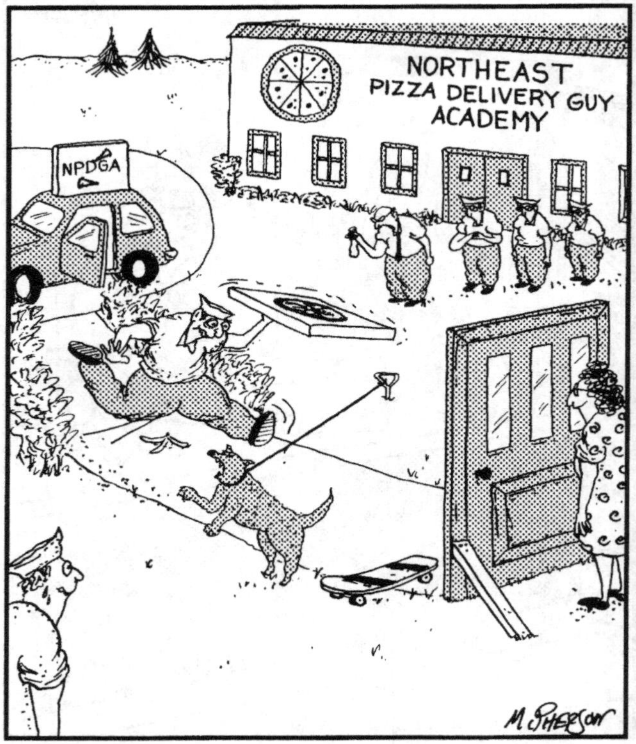
NORTHEAST
PIZZA DELIVERY GUY
ACADEMY
NPDGA
M. PHERSON

"Move! Move! Move! You're seven-tenths of a second behind your last time! Jump over the dog! That's it. The pizza! You're tipping the pizza!"

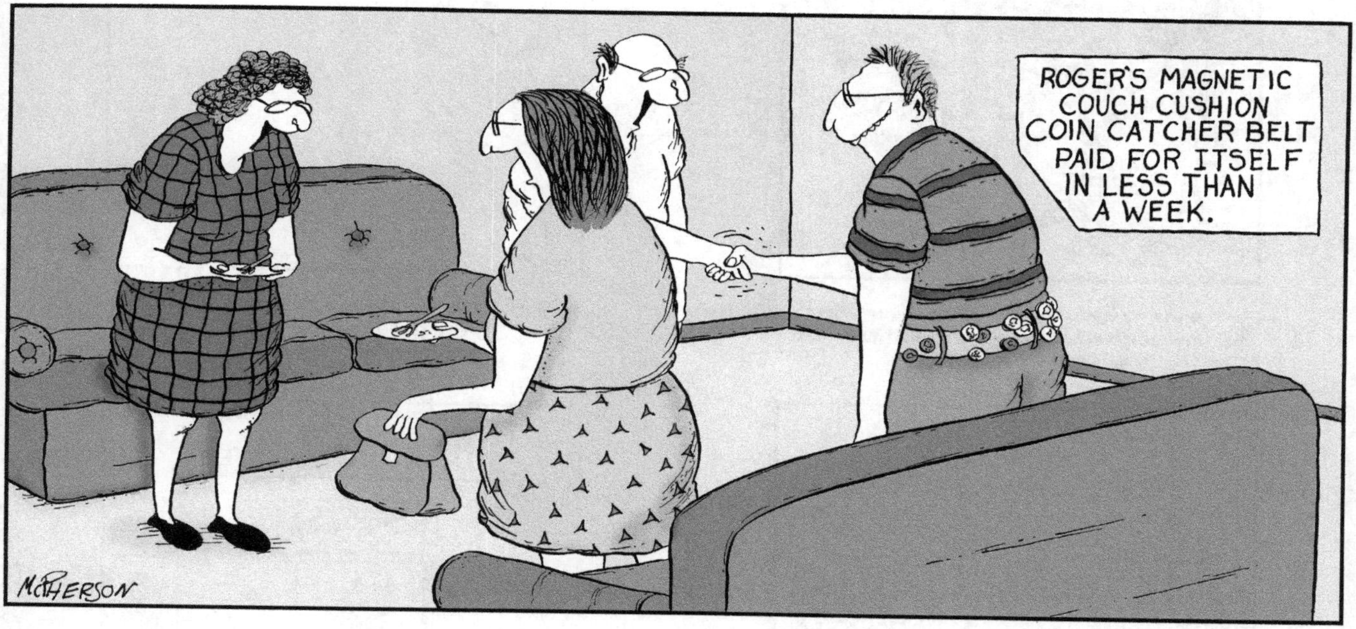
ROGER'S MAGNETIC COUCH CUSHION COIN CATCHER BELT PAID FOR ITSELF IN LESS THAN A WEEK.
McPHERSON

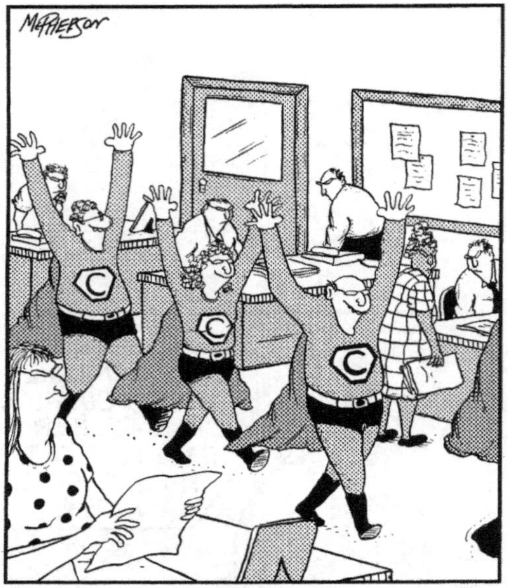
McPHERSON

From the moment the new consultants arrived, full-time employees at Watkins Industries sensed an air of condescension.

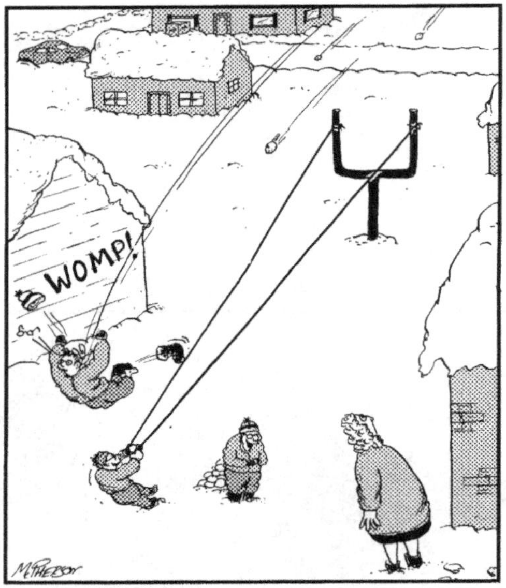
WOMP!
McPHERSON

"Check it out, Mom! We're having a snowball fight with three kids in Syracuse!"

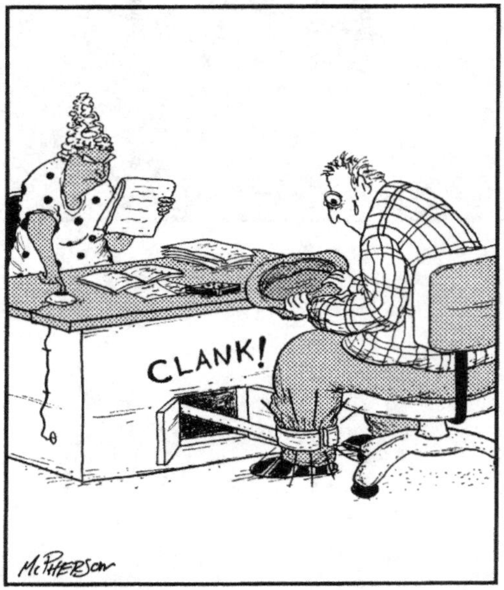
CLANK!
McPHERSON

Tim's meeting with the IRS takes a sudden turn for the worse.

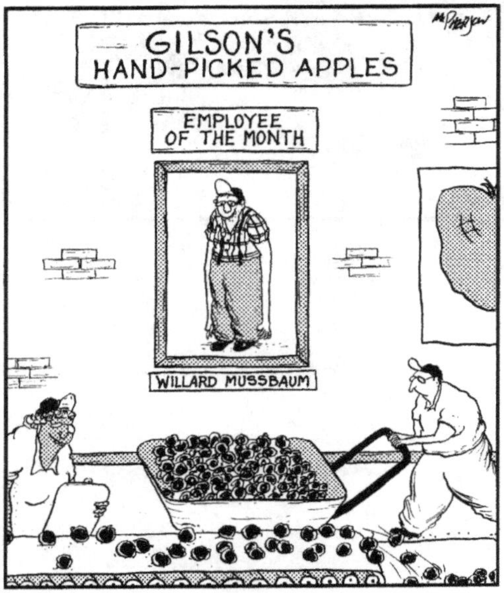
GILSON'S
HAND-PICKED APPLES
EMPLOYEE OF THE MONTH
WILLARD MUSSBAUM

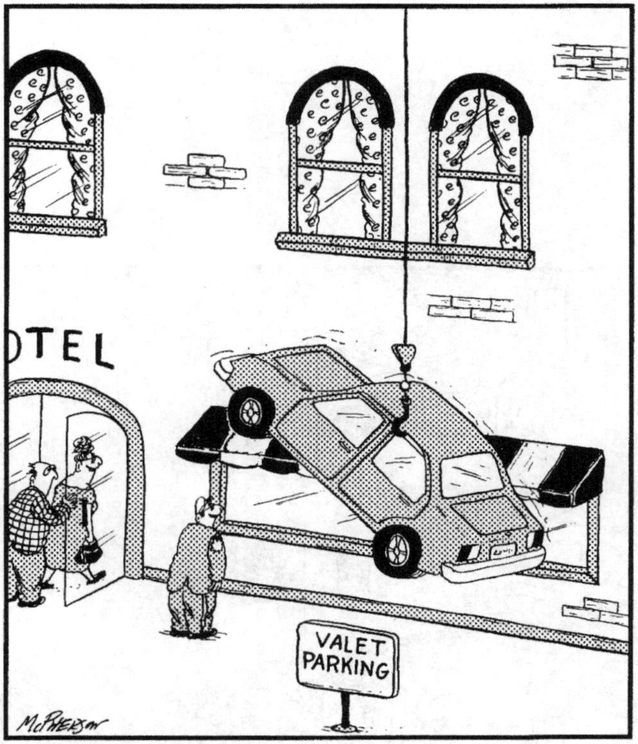
OTEL
VALET PARKING
McPHERSON

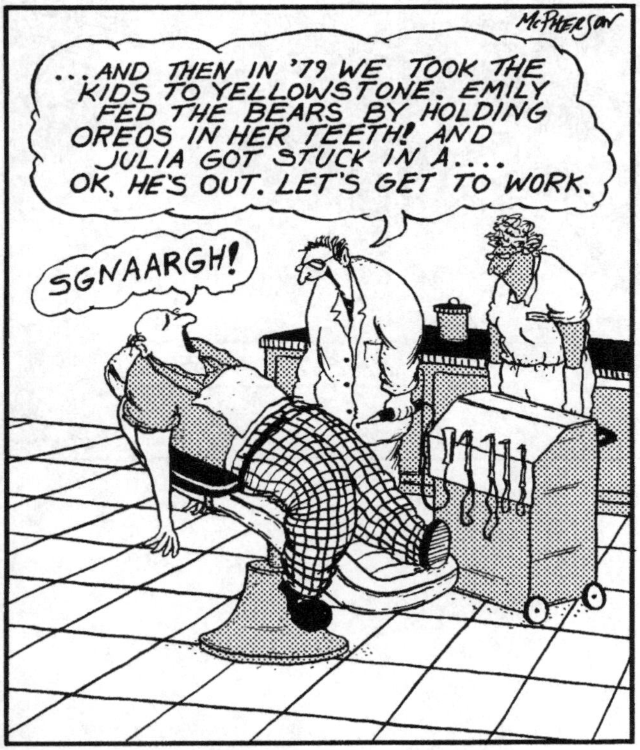
McPHERSON
...AND THEN IN '79 WE TOOK THE KIDS TO YELLOWSTONE. EMILY FED THE BEARS BY HOLDING OREOS IN HER TEETH! AND JULIA GOT STUCK IN A.... OK, HE'S OUT. LET'S GET TO WORK.
SGNAARGH!

By recounting family vacations, Dr. Ingersoll was able to perform extractions without the use of anesthetics.

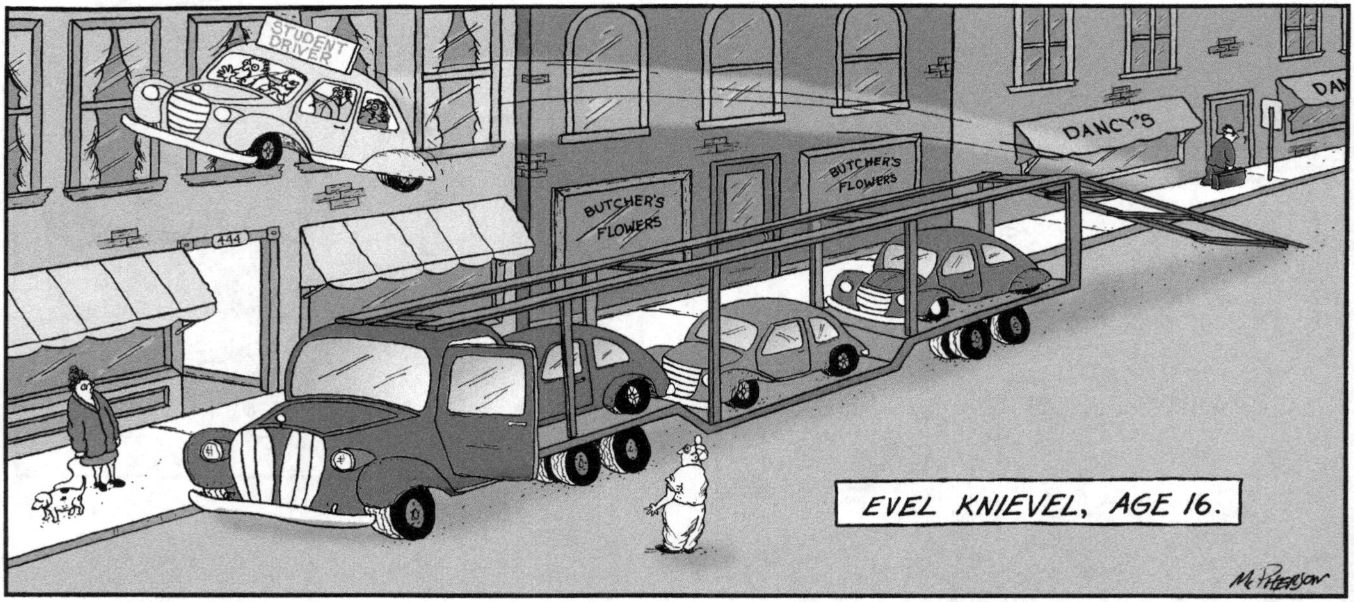
STUDENT DRIVER
444
BUTCHER'S
FLOWERS
BUTCHER'S
FLOWERS
DANCY'S
McPherson
EVEL KNIEVEL, AGE 16.

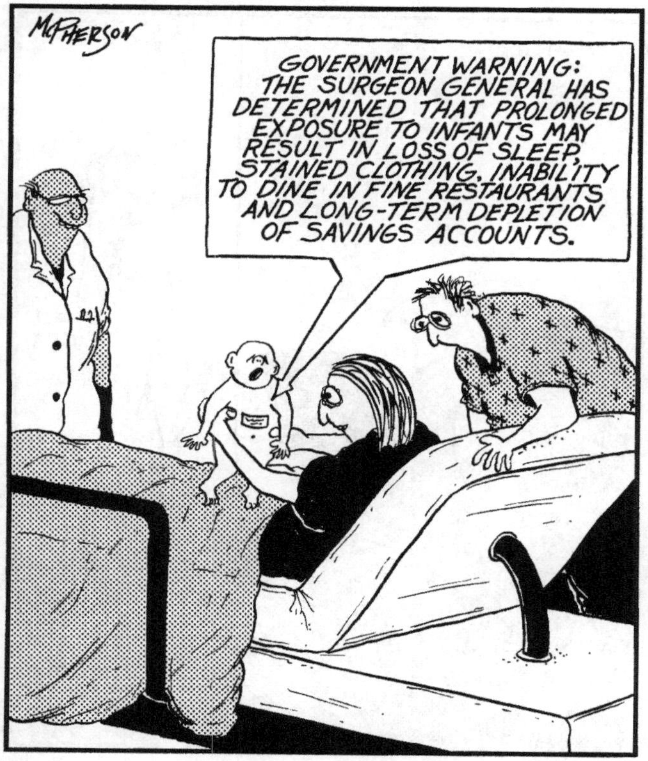
McPHERSON
GOVERNMENT WARNING: THE SURGEON GENERAL HAS DETERMINED THAT PROLONGED EXPOSURE TO INFANTS MAY RESULT IN LOSS OF SLEEP, STAINED CLOTHING, INABILITY TO DINE IN FINE RESTAURANTS AND LONG-TERM DEPLETION OF SAVINGS ACCOUNTS.

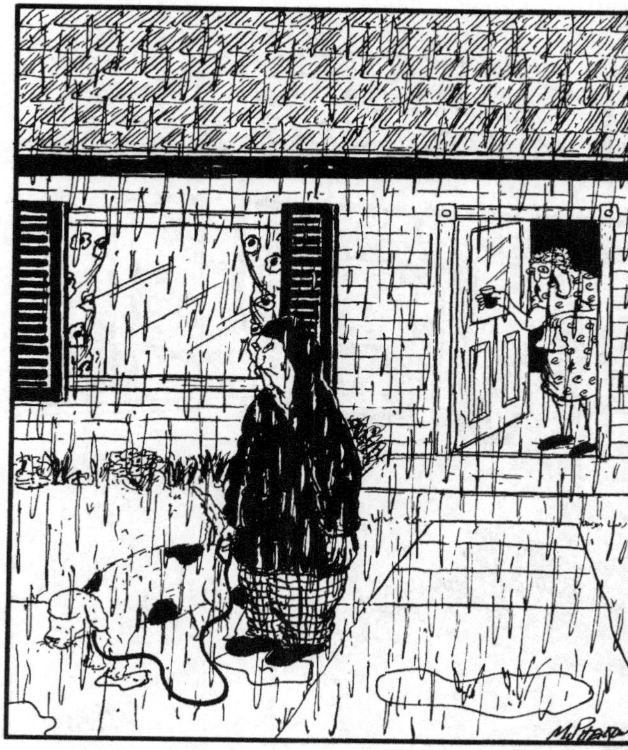

"Bill! Don't forget! The vet wants samples!"

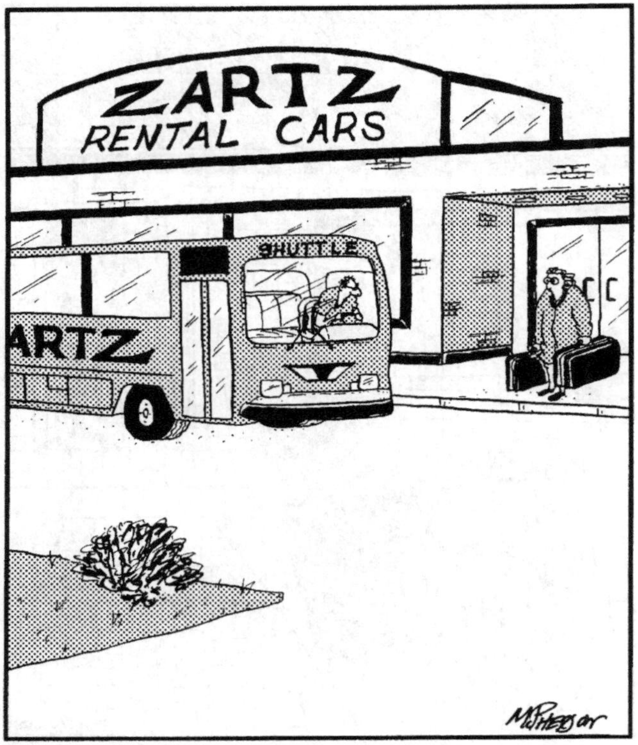
ZARTZ
RENTAL CARS
SHUTTLE
ARTZ

"Hop in, Gail! This is all they had left."

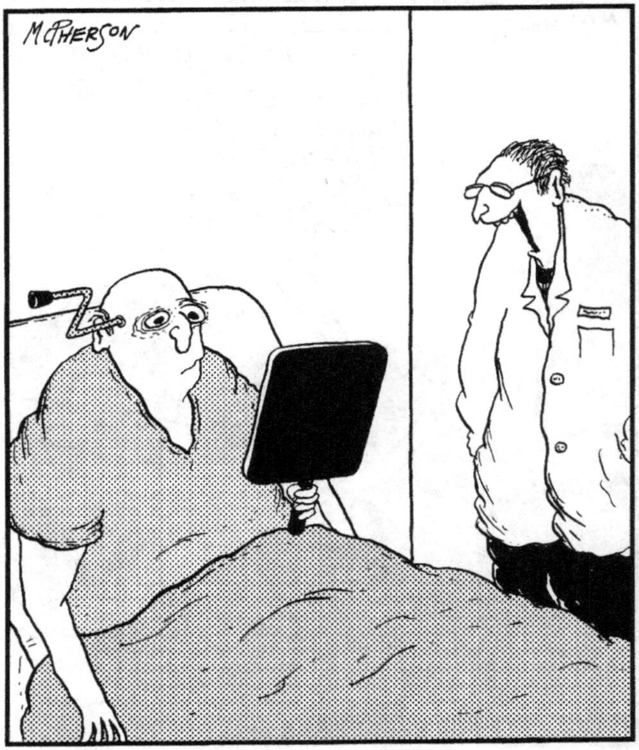

"When you notice yourself becoming forgetful, just give it twenty hard cranks and your memory should be sharp for a good two or three days."

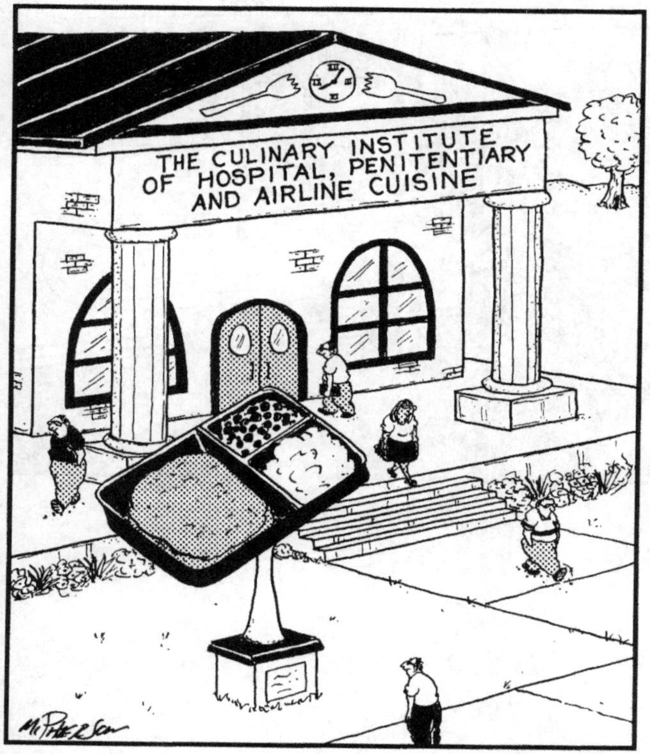
MCPHERSON
THE CULINARY INSTITUTE
OF HOSPITAL, PENITENTIARY
AND AIRLINE CUISINE

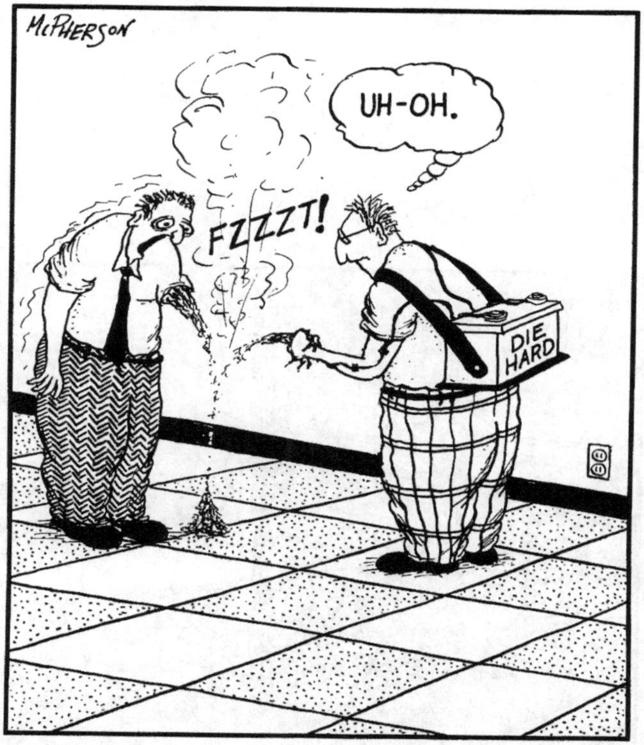
MCPHERSON
UH-OH.
FZZZT!
DIE HARD

Lenny's souped-up joy-buzzer gag goes awry.

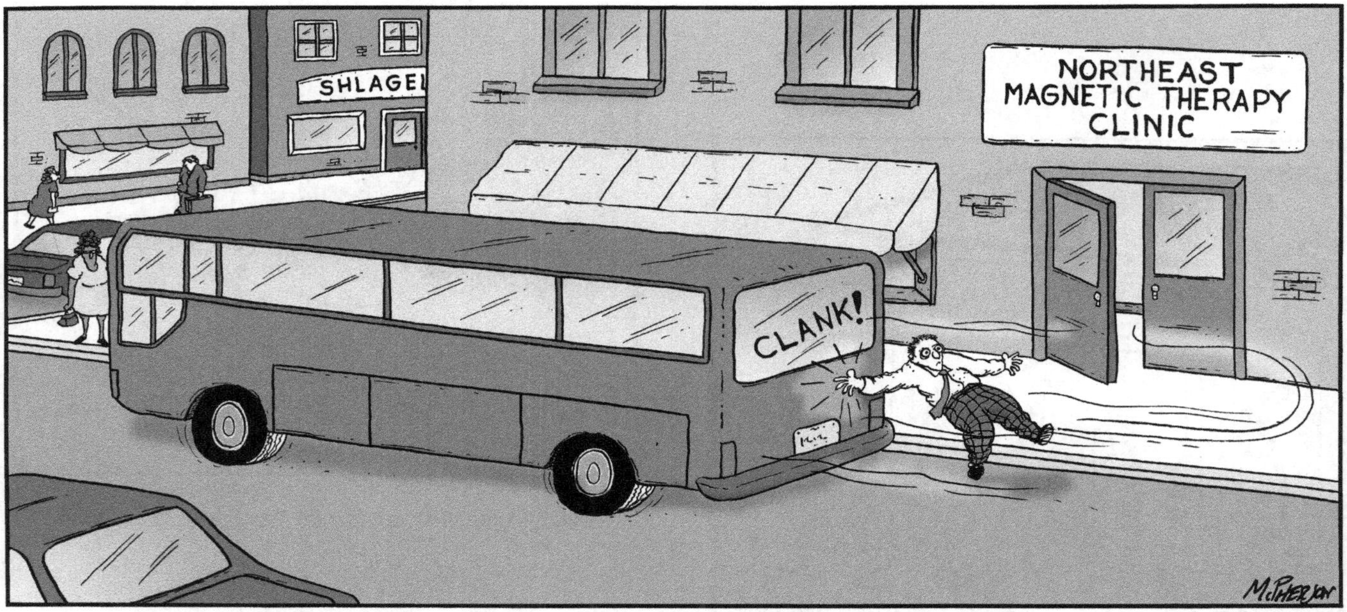
SHLAGEL
NORTHEAST
MAGNETIC THERAPY
CLINIC
CLANK!
McPHERSON

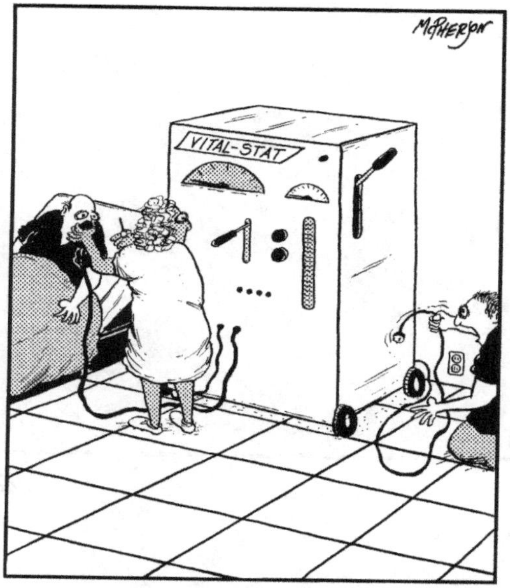
McPHERSON
VITAL-STAT

"Ms. Wahlstrom, run over to Wal-Mart and get a three-pronged adapter, stat!"

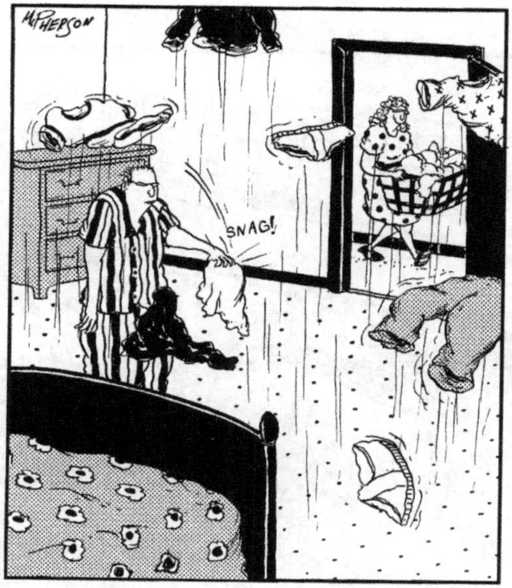
McPHERSON
SNAG!

Using the same technology as an air hockey table, the Stebers' new bedroom floor prevented Ed from leaving his dirty laundry lying around.

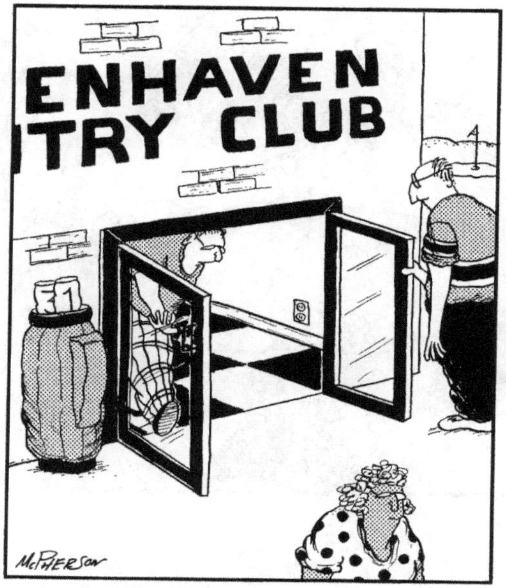
ENHAVEN
TRY CLUB
McPHERSON

To remind golfers to keep their heads down when they swing, doorways at Greenhaven Country Club are only four feet high.

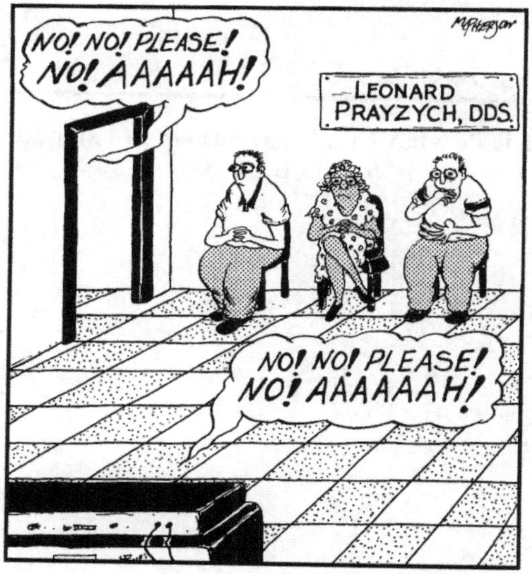
McPHERSON
NO! NO! PLEASE! NO! AAAAAH!
LEONARD PRAYZYCH, DDS
NO! NO! PLEASE! NO! AAAAAAH!

To drown out the screams coming from his inner offices, Dr. Prayzych kept videos of *Nightmare on Elm Street* and *Halloween* playing nonstop in the waiting room.

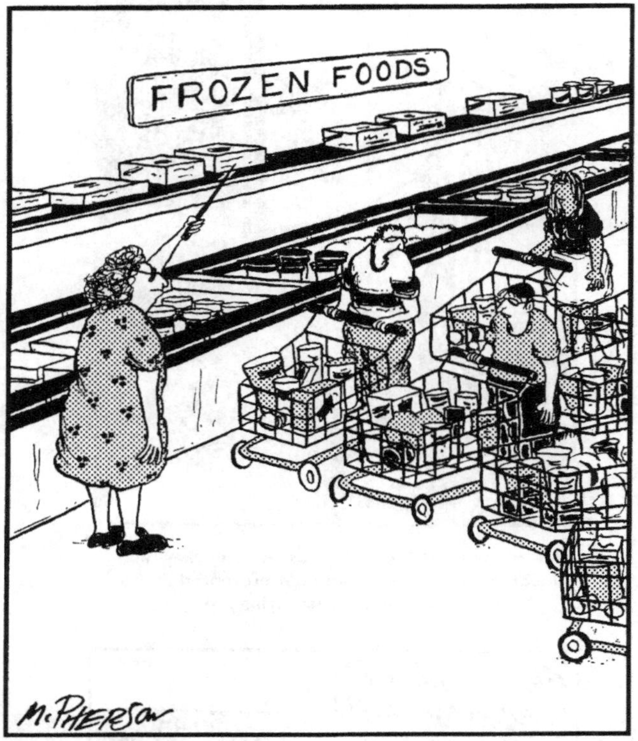
FROZEN FOODS
McPHERSON

"This isn't what I had in mind when I signed up for shop class."

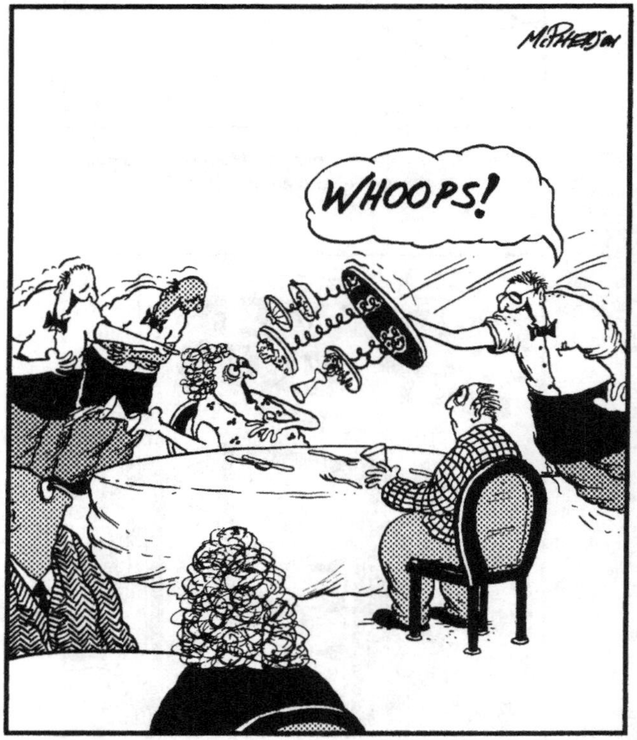
McPHERSON
WHOOPS!

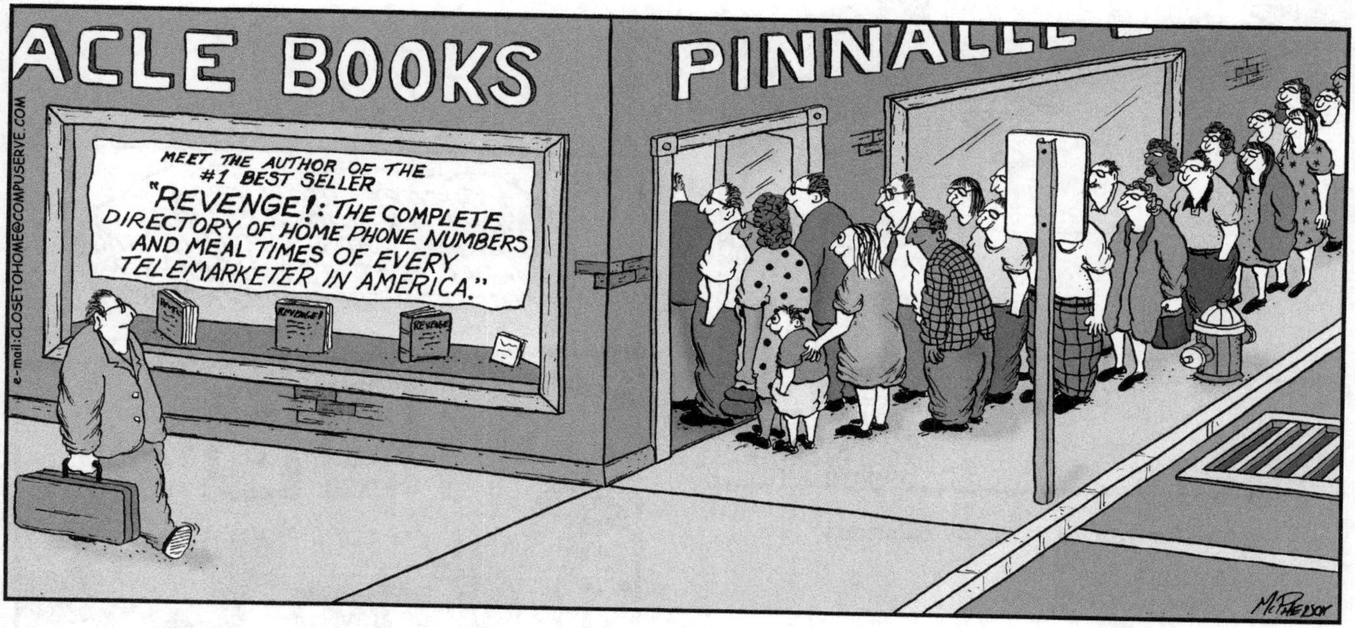
ACLE BOOKS
PINNACLE
MEET THE AUTHOR OF THE
#1 BEST SELLER
"REVENGE!: THE COMPLETE DIRECTORY OF HOME PHONE NUMBERS AND MEAL TIMES OF EVERY TELEMARKETER IN AMERICA."
e-mail:CLOSETOHOME@COMPUSERVE.COM
McPHERSON

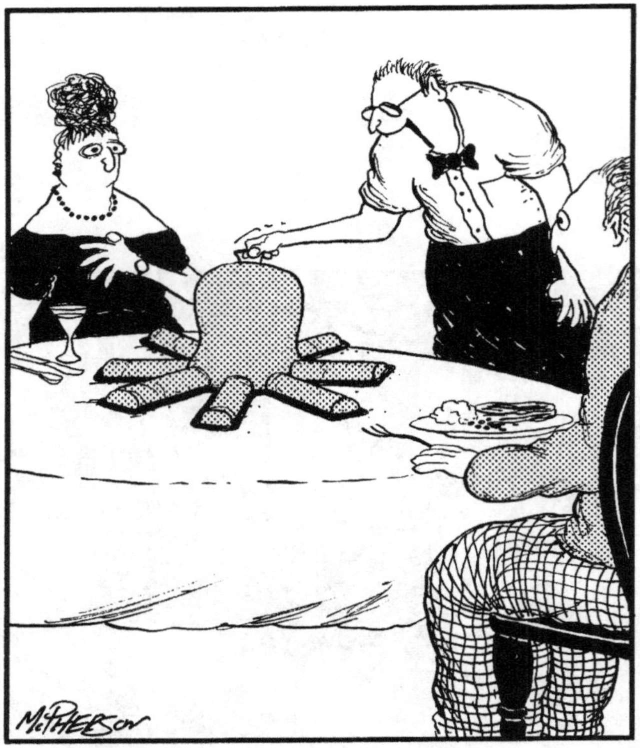

"And for you, ma'am, the calamari."

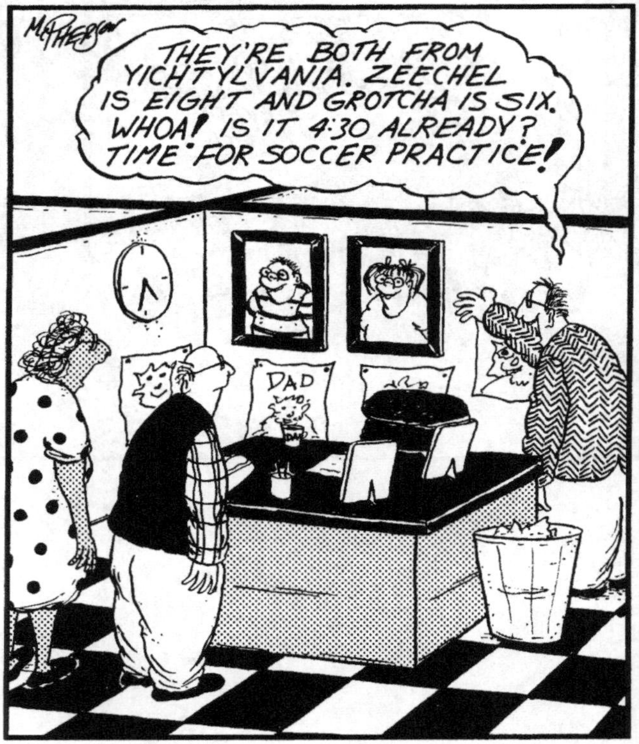
THEY'RE BOTH FROM YICHTYLVANIA. ZEECHEL IS EIGHT AND GROTCHA IS SIX. WHOA! IS IT 4:30 ALREADY? TIME FOR SOCCER PRACTICE!
DAD

Tired of constantly being singled out to work overtime because he's childless, Ted fakes adopting two kids.

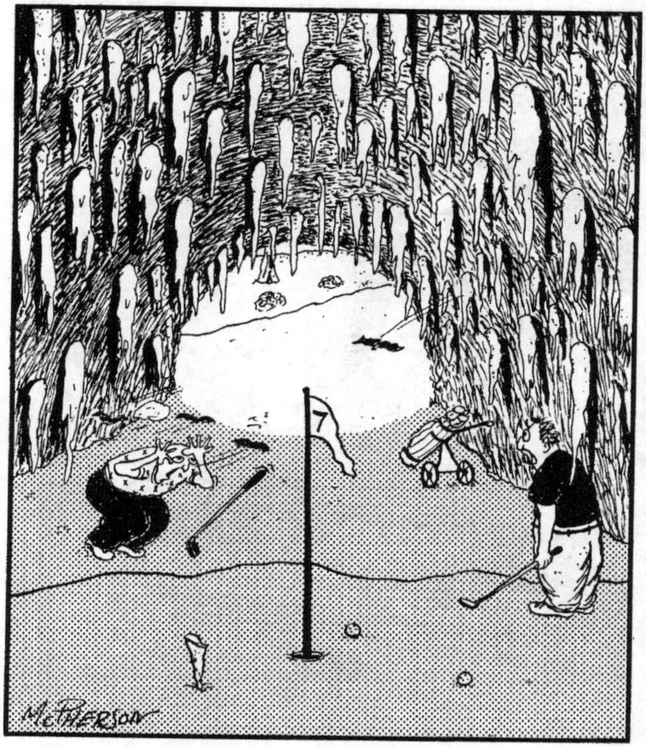
7
McPHERSON

"Now that is what I call a tough approach shot!"

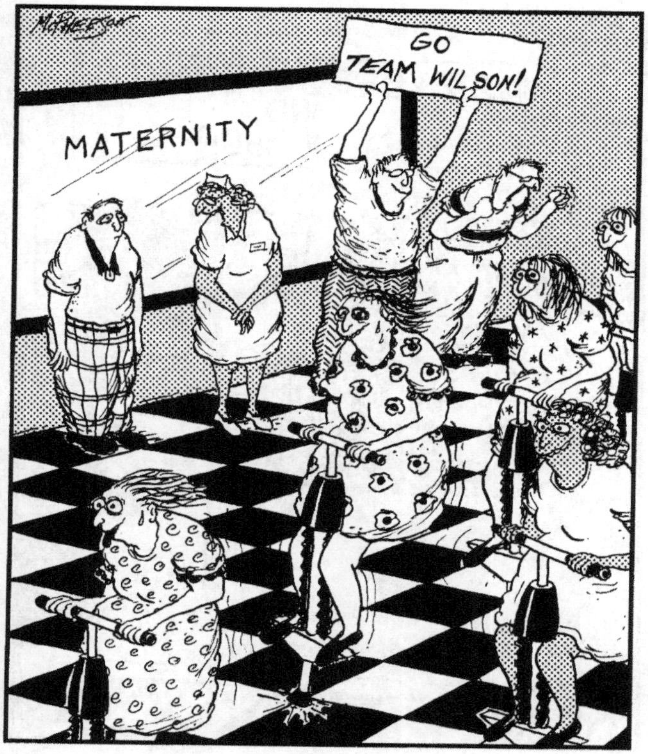
McPHERSON
GO TEAM WILSON!
MATERNITY

"We call it the Pogo-Prego 500. The moms love it, and it's reduced the average labor time by four hours."

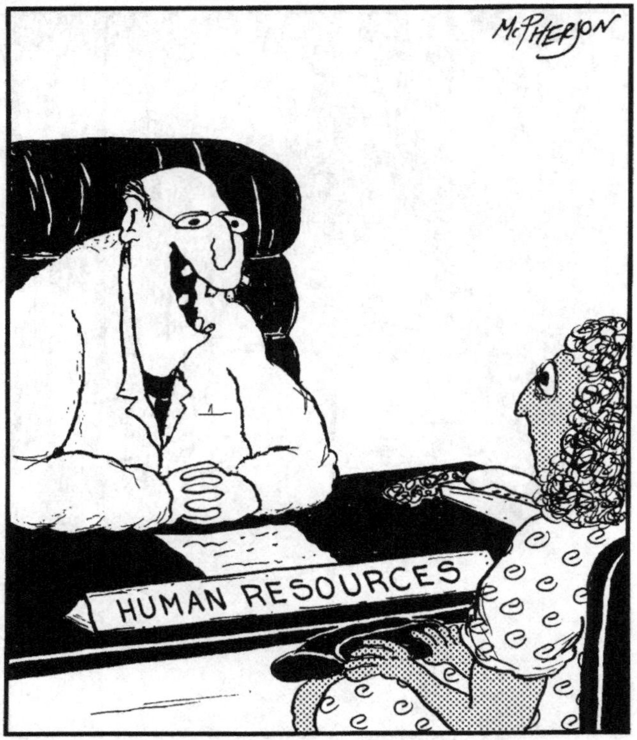
McPHERSON
HUMAN RESOURCES

"Our dental plan? Oh yeah we've got a great one. It's with . . . uh . . . well, I forget the name, but it's some really good dental outfit. Top-notch."

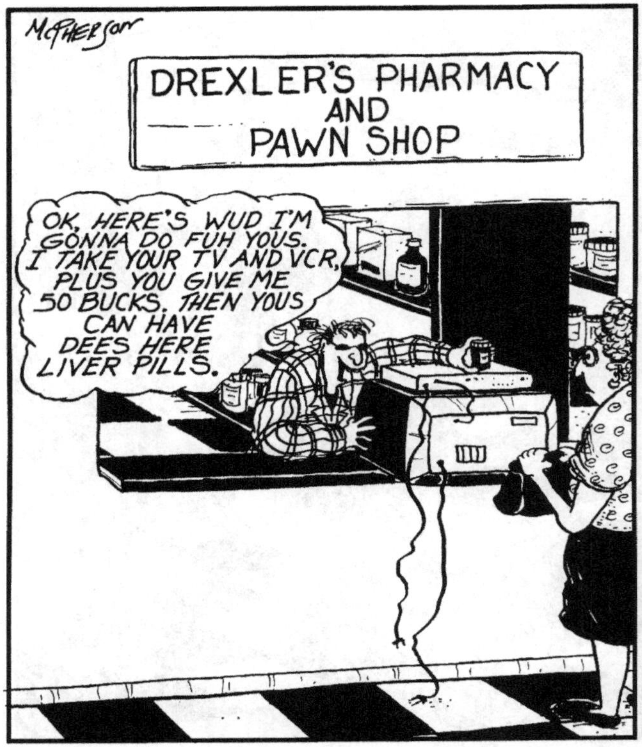
McPHERSON
DREXLER'S PHARMACY AND PAWN SHOP
OK, HERE'S WUD I'M GONNA DO FUH YOUS. I TAKE YOUR TV AND VCR, PLUS YOU GIVE ME 50 BUCKS. THEN YOUS CAN HAVE DEES HERE LIVER PILLS.

The skyrocketing prices of prescription drugs have affected the way many pharmacies do business.

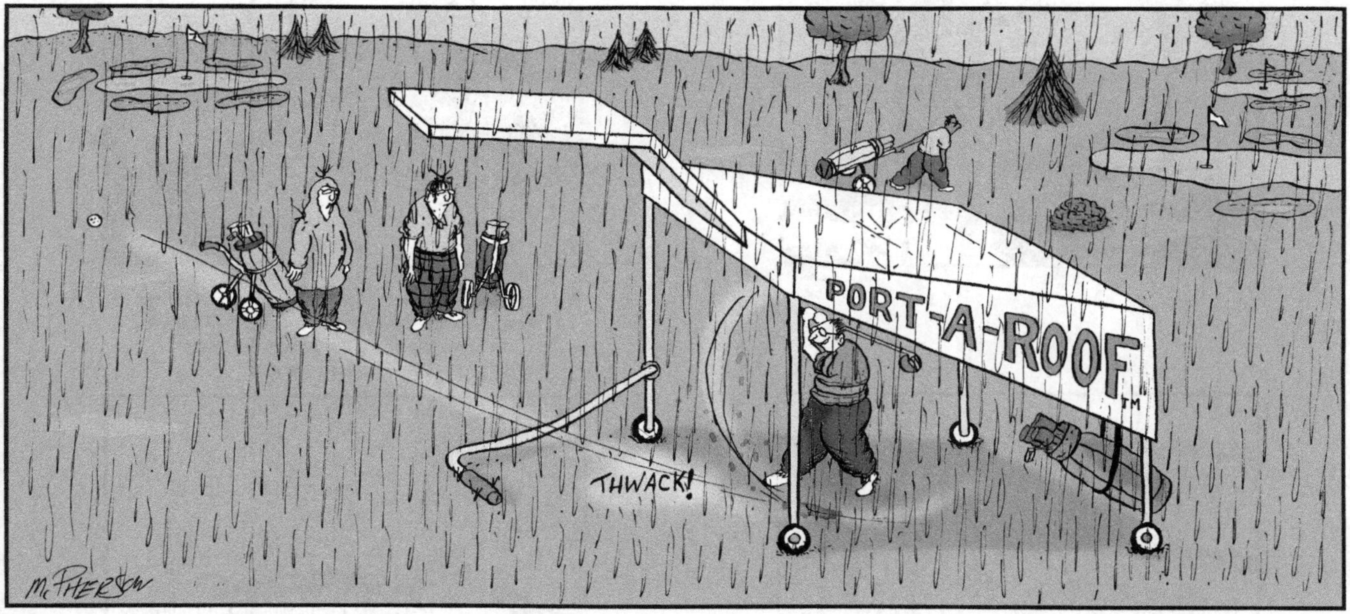
PORT-A-ROOF
TM
THWACK!
McPHERSON

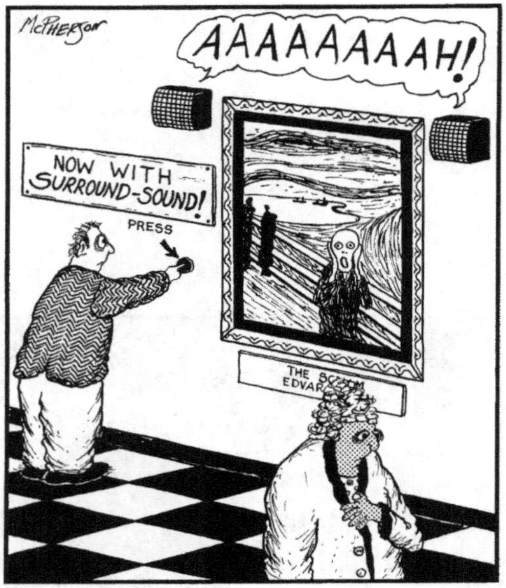
McPHERSON
AAAAAAAAH!
NOW WITH SURROUND-SOUND!
PRESS

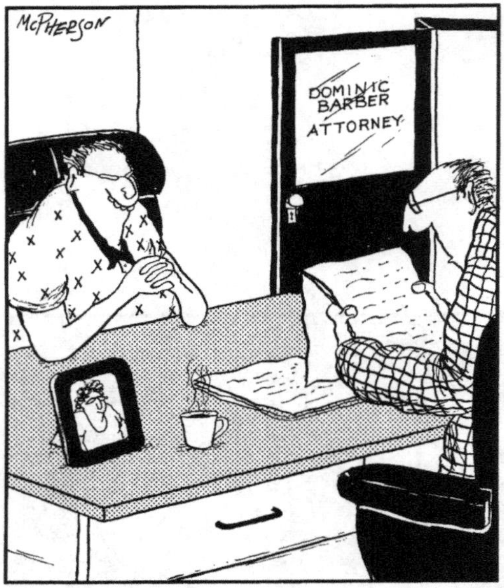
McPHERSON
DOMINIC BARBER
ATTORNEY

"... three Pete Rose rookie cards, a '54 Mantle ... I'd say you can sue your mom for $37,000 for throwing out your baseball cards when you were a kid."

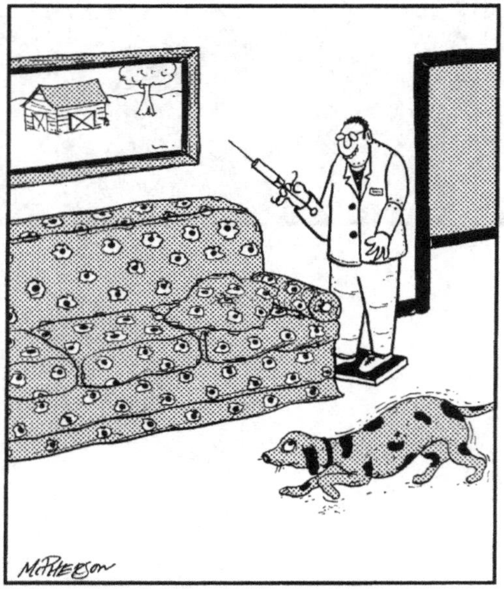
McPHERSON

Tired of cleaning dog hair off the furniture, the Lubermans placed several scarecrow veterinarians at strategic locations.

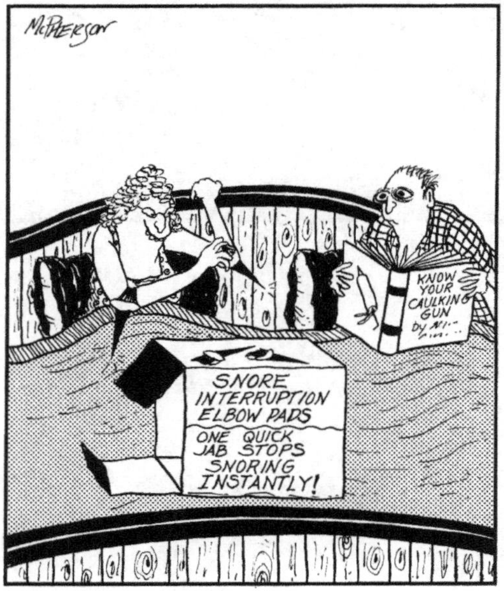
McPHERSON
KNOW YOUR CAULKING GUN
SNORE INTERRUPTION ELBOW PADS
ONE QUICK JAB STOPS SNORING INSTANTLY!

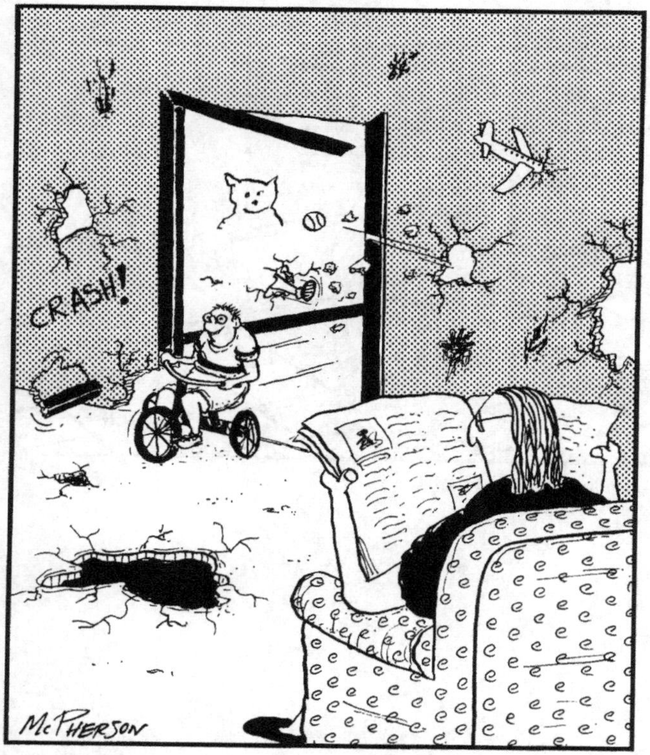
CRASH!
McPHERSON

Until the toddler years are well behind them, many parents opt for the new disposable houses.

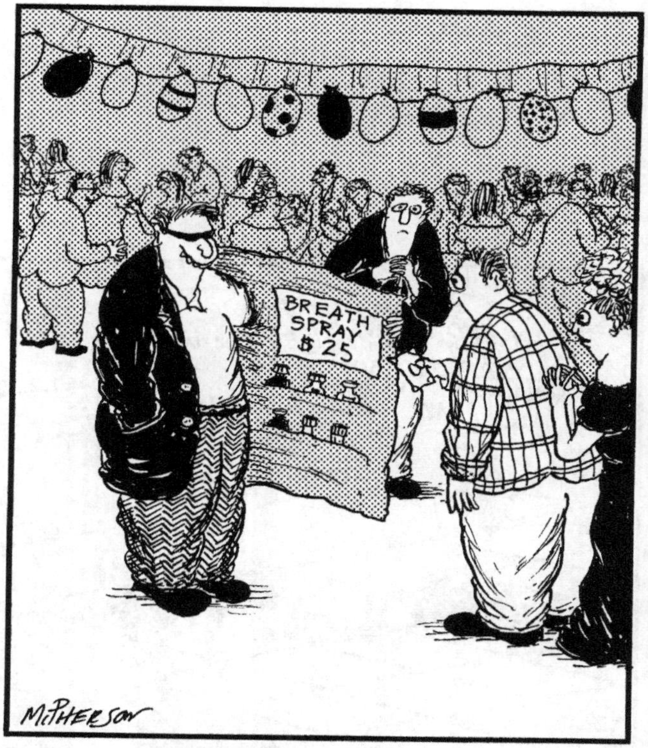
BREATH SPRAY $25
McPHERSON

Not long after the prom began, the scalpers opened up shop.

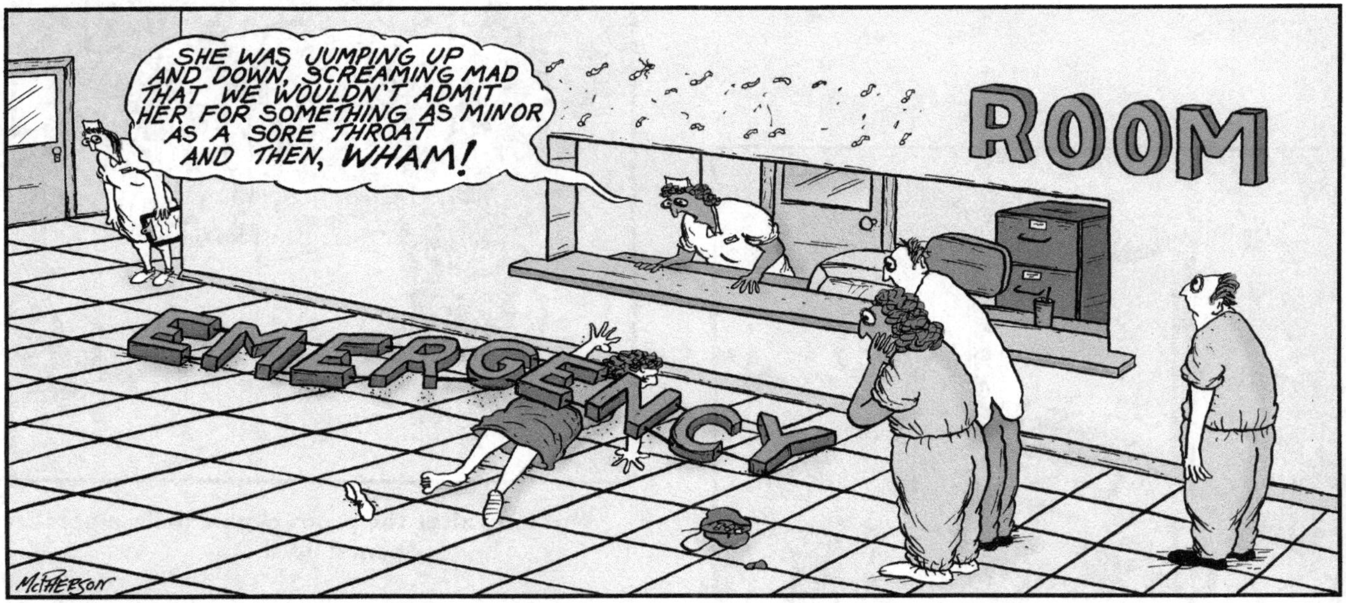
SHE WAS JUMPING UP AND DOWN, SCREAMING MAD THAT WE WOULDN'T ADMIT HER FOR SOMETHING AS MINOR AS A SORE THROAT AND THEN, WHAM!
ROOM
EMERGENCY
MCPHERSON

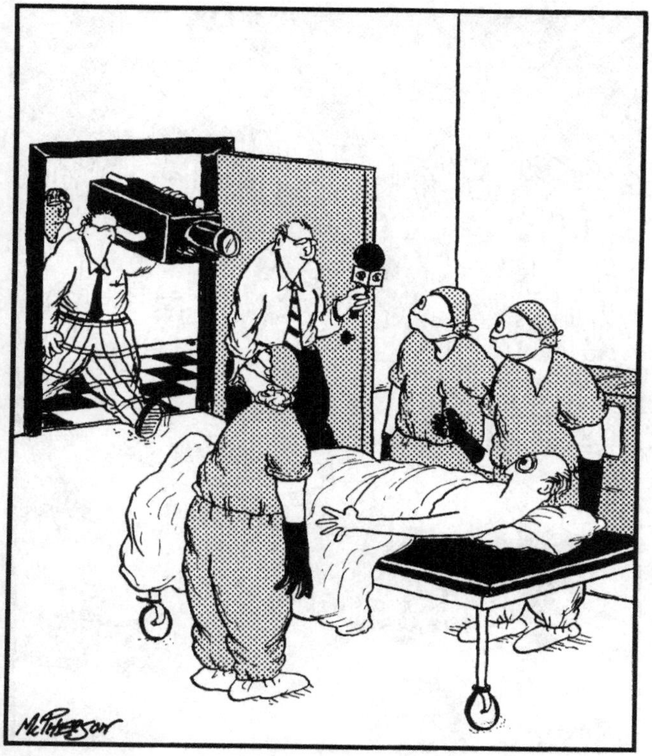

Walt was feeling calm and collected before his surgery until the crew from *60 Minutes* burst through the door.

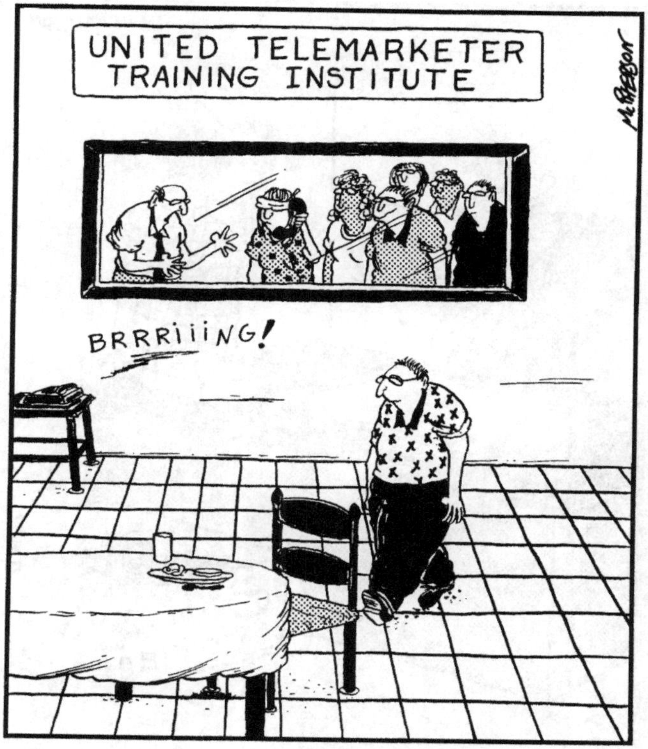
UNITED TELEMARKETER TRAINING INSTITUTE
BRRRiiiNG!

"No, no, you're rushing. Visualize the scene in your mind. Don't dial until you feel your target seated and eating dinner."

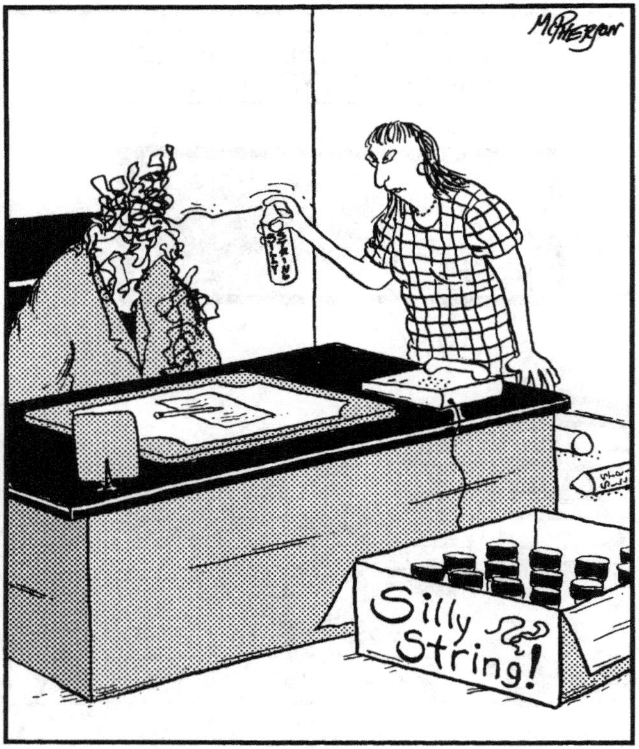
McPHERSON
Silly String!

"I take it you read your performance review."

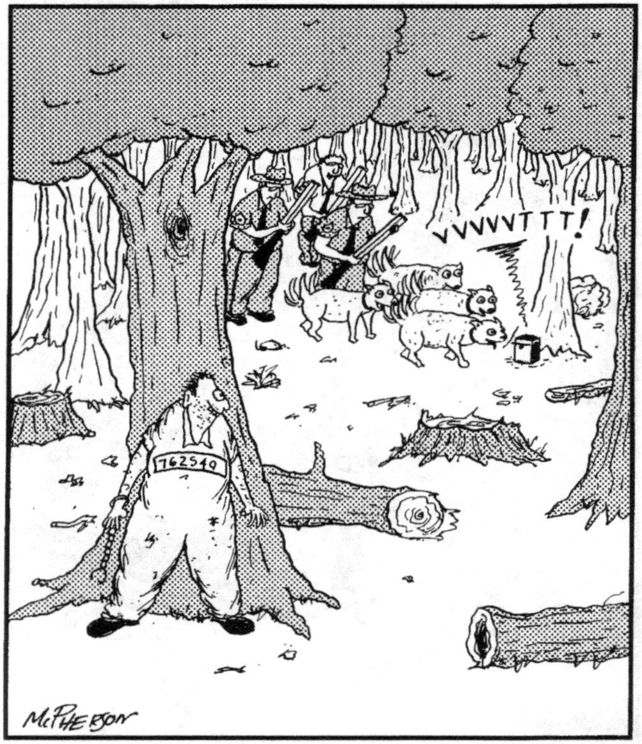
VVVVVTTT!
762540
McPHERSON

Having shrewdly placed a battery-operated can opener in the woods, Lyle was able to elude the search dogs.

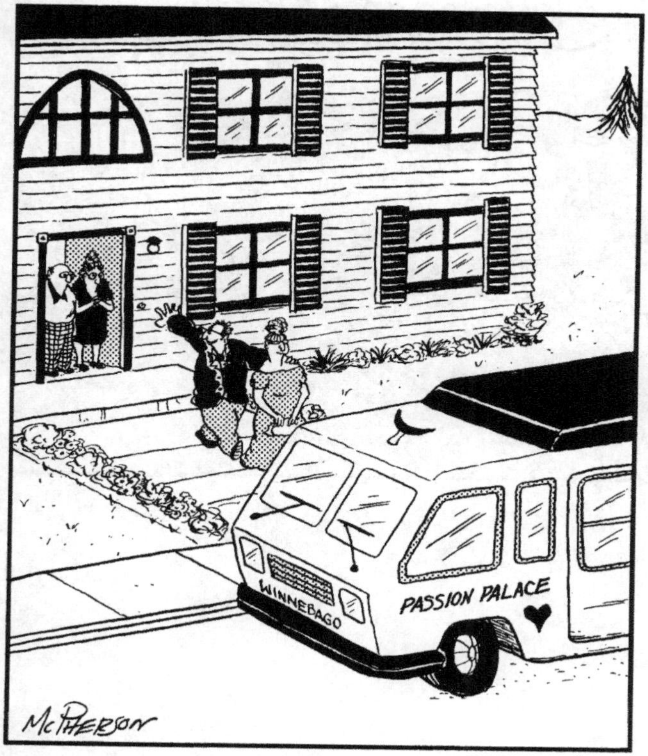
PASSION PALACE
WINNEBAGO

Despite Andy's convincing story that his parents' other car was in the shop, the Wilmers felt a twinge of apprehension as Amy headed off to the prom.

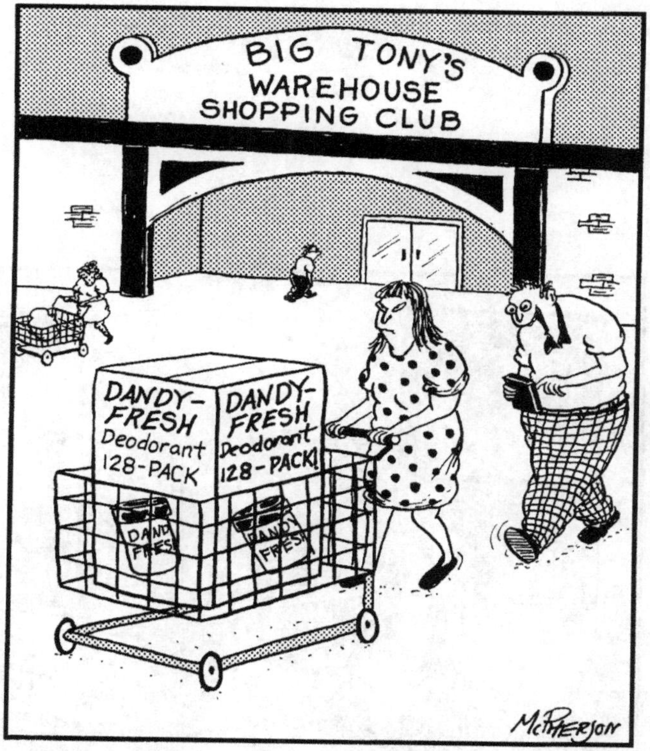
BIG TONY'S WAREHOUSE SHOPPING CLUB
DANDY-FRESH Deodorant 128-PACK
DANDY-FRESH Deodorant 128-PACK!
DANDY FRESH
DANDY FRESH

"... 128 sticks ... at $1.79 each ... regularly $2.39 each ... that's a savings of ... $76.80!"

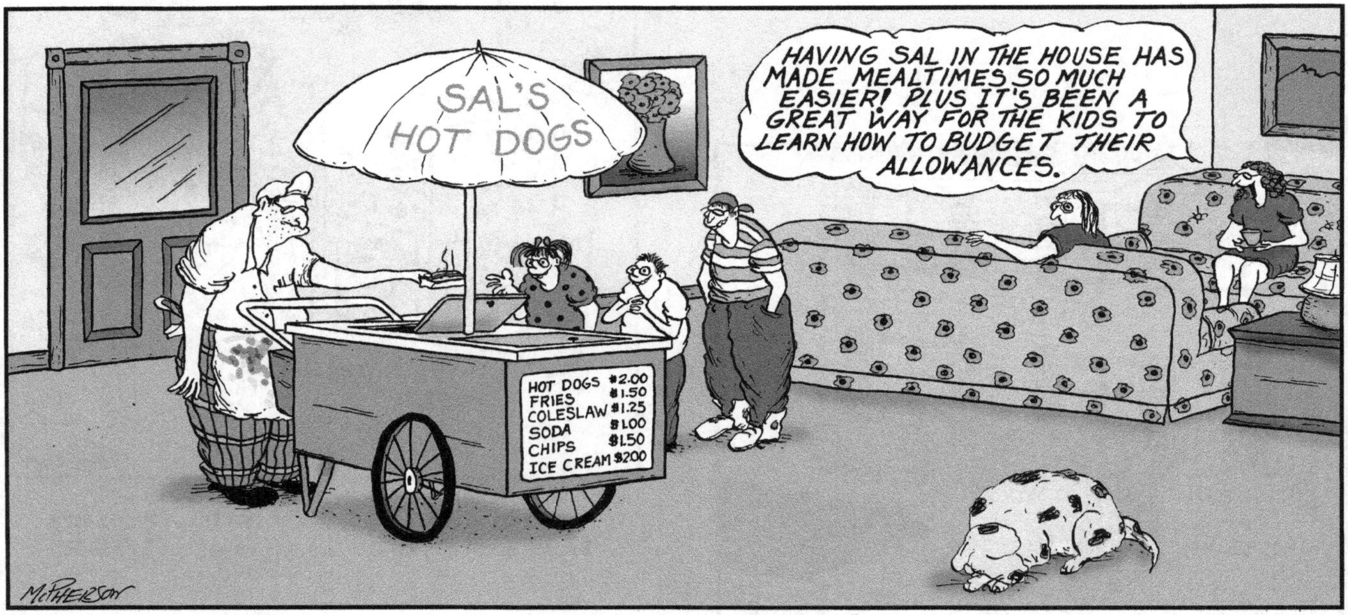
SAL'S HOT DOGS
HOT DOGS $2.00
FRIES $1.50
COLESLAW $1.25
SODA $1.00
CHIPS $1.50
ICE CREAM $2.00
HAVING SAL IN THE HOUSE HAS MADE MEALTIMES SO MUCH EASIER! PLUS IT'S BEEN A GREAT WAY FOR THE KIDS TO LEARN HOW TO BUDGET THEIR ALLOWANCES.
McPHERSON

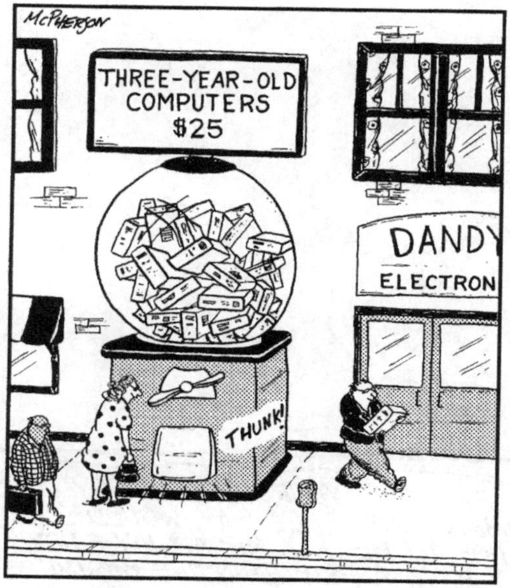
McPHERSON
THREE-YEAR-OLD COMPUTERS $25
DANDY
ELECTRON
THUNK!

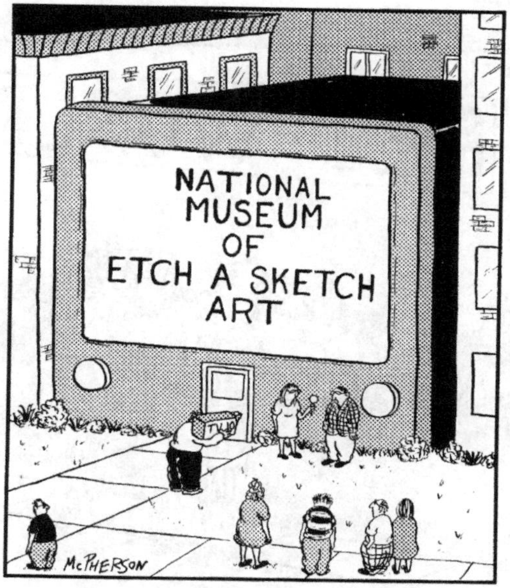
NATIONAL MUSEUM OF ETCH A SKETCH ART
McPHERSON

"Structurally, the building is fine. But sadly, the earthquake destroyed all of our art pieces."

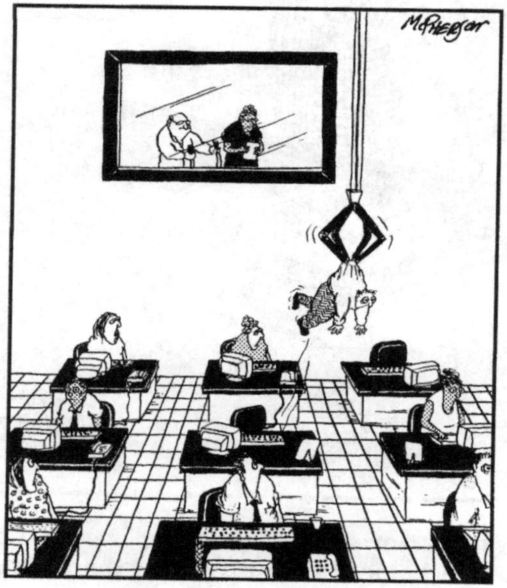
McPHERSON

Employees at Imperial Arcade Games brace themselves for another round of layoffs.

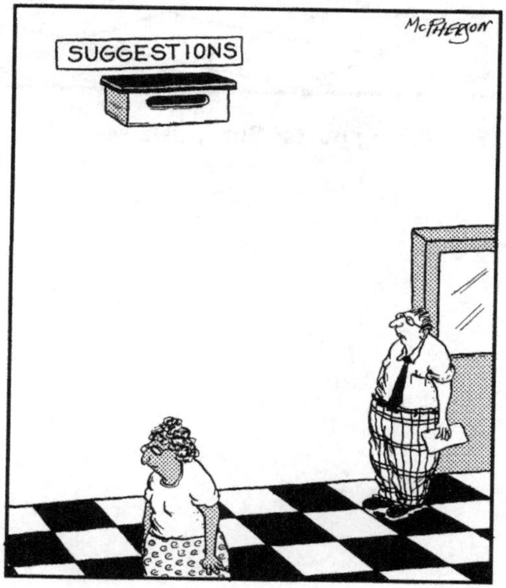
McPHERSON
SUGGESTIONS

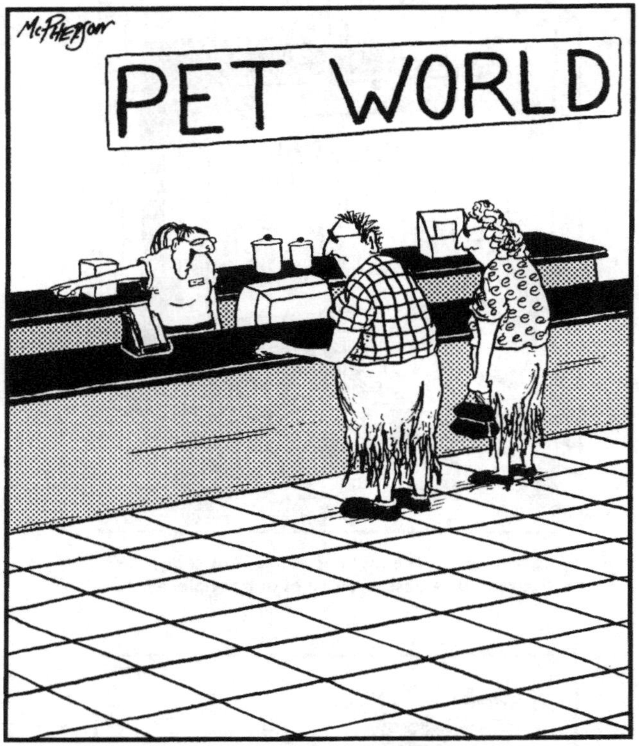
McPherson
PET WORLD

"Scratching posts? Sure, aisle seven."

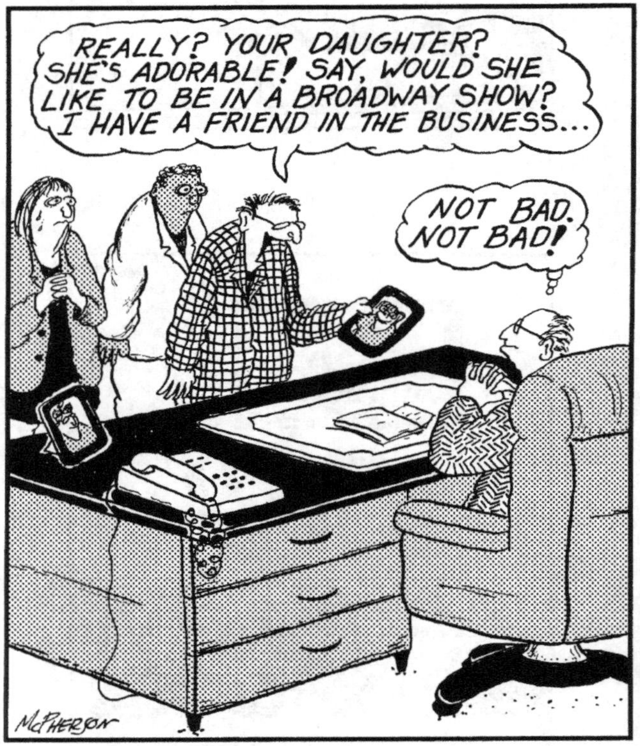
REALLY? YOUR DAUGHTER? SHE'S ADORABLE! SAY, WOULD SHE LIKE TO BE IN A BROADWAY SHOW? I HAVE A FRIEND IN THE BUSINESS...
NOT BAD. NOT BAD!
McPherson

Having narrowed the field of applicants to three, sales director Mark Sutton runs them through the critical brownnosing portion of the interview.

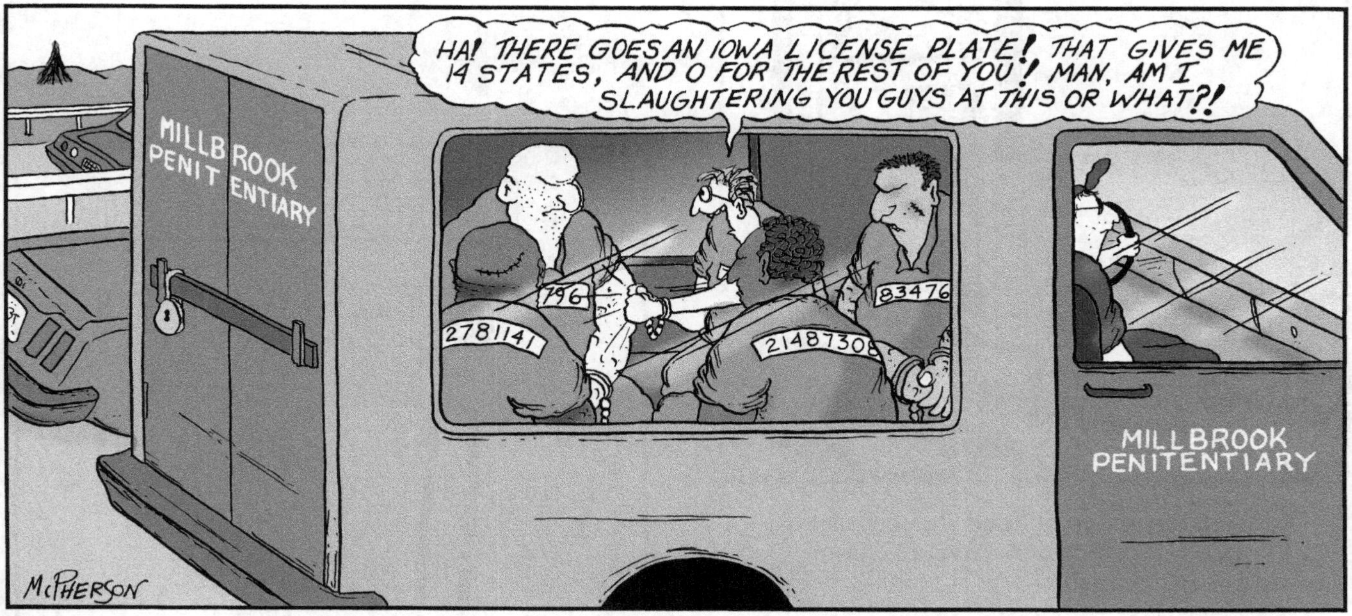
HA! THERE GOES AN IOWA LICENSE PLATE! THAT GIVES ME 14 STATES, AND 0 FOR THE REST OF YOU! MAN, AM I SLAUGHTERING YOU GUYS AT THIS OR WHAT?!
MILLBROOK PENITENTIARY
796
2781141
21487308
83476
MILLBROOK PENITENTIARY
McPHERSON

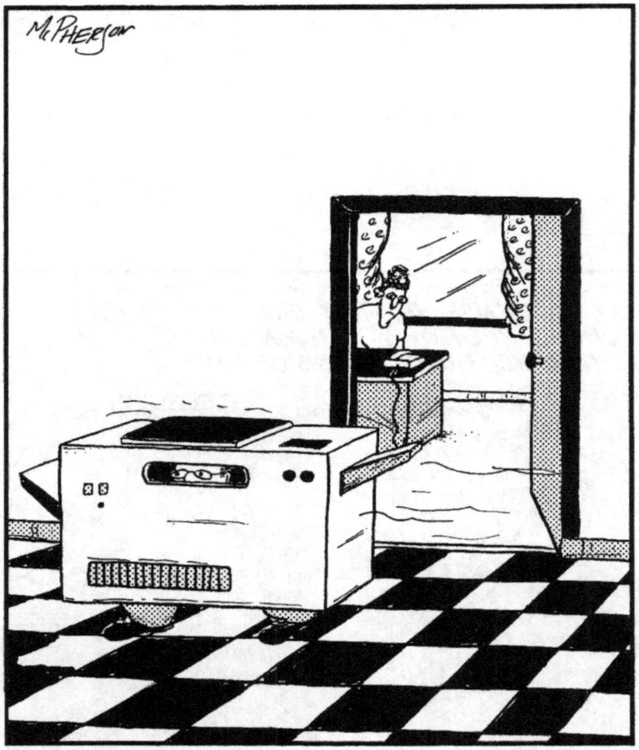

Running late as usual, Todd slipped past his manager's office in his new costume.

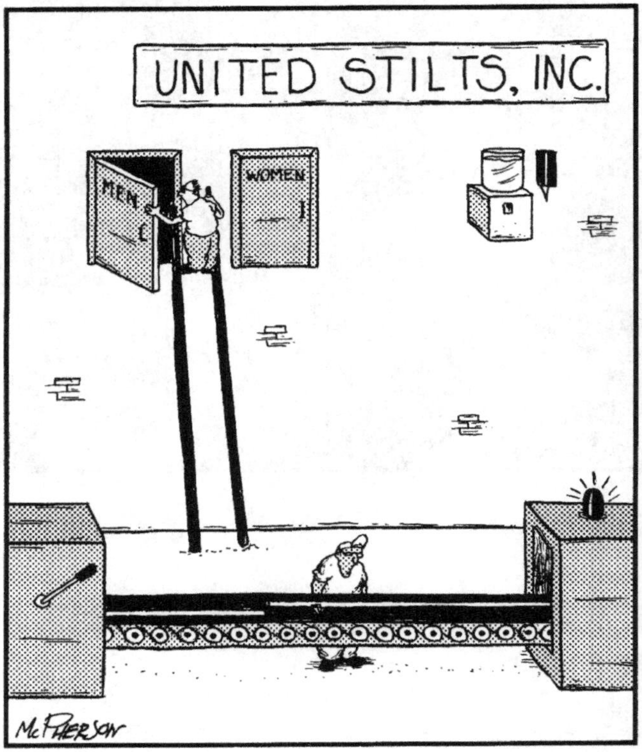
UNITED STILTS, INC.
MEN
WOMEN

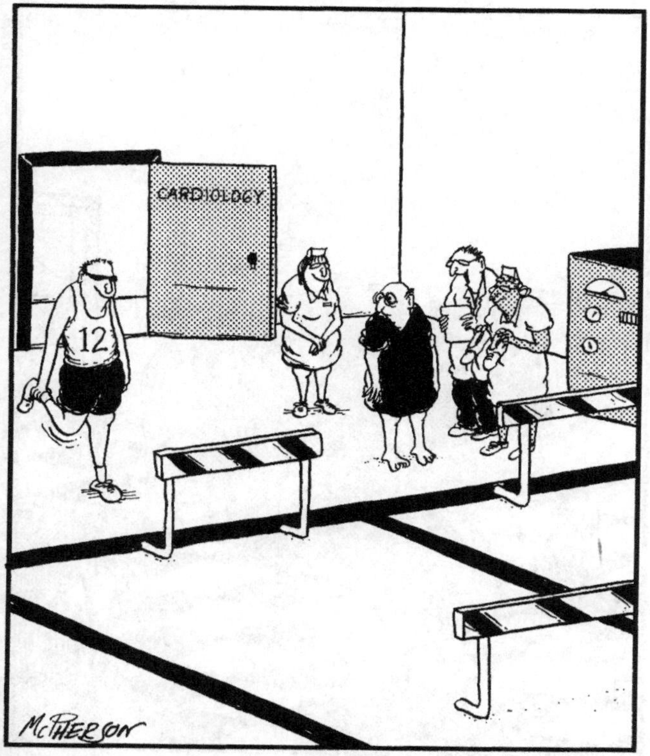
CARDIOLOGY
12
McPHERSON

"OK, Mr. Simms. Now it's time to test your pacemaker against a control subject."

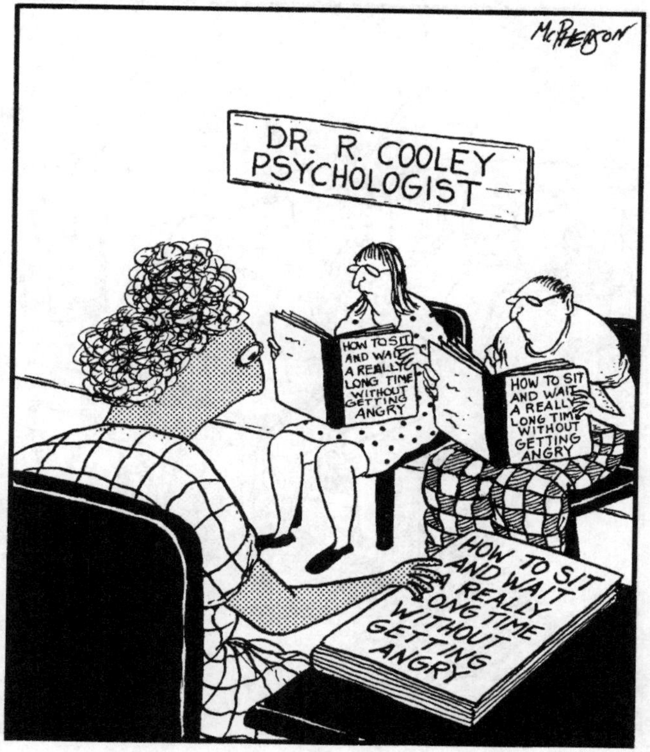
McPHERSON
DR. R. COOLEY PSYCHOLOGIST
HOW TO SIT AND WAIT A REALLY LONG TIME WITHOUT GETTING ANGRY
HOW TO SIT AND WAIT A REALLY LONG TIME WITHOUT GETTING ANGRY
HOW TO SIT AND WAIT A REALLY LONG TIME WITHOUT GETTING ANGRY

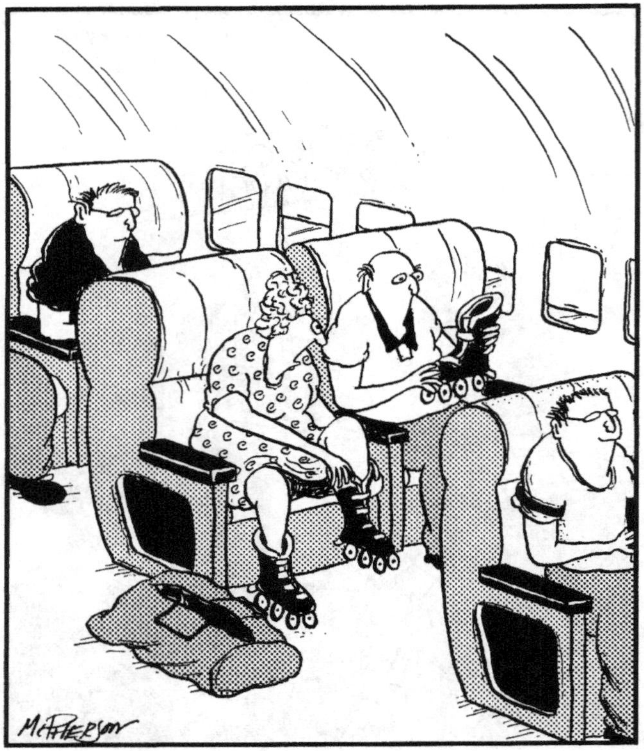
McPHERSON

"Quit whining and just put them on! Once we land we'll have three minutes, tops, to catch our connecting flight."

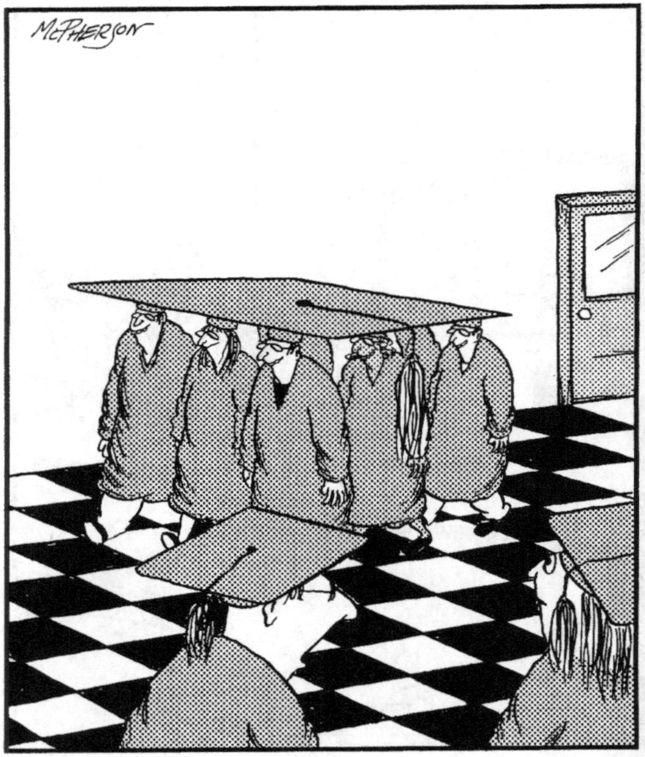
McPHERSON

"They always were a tight little clique."

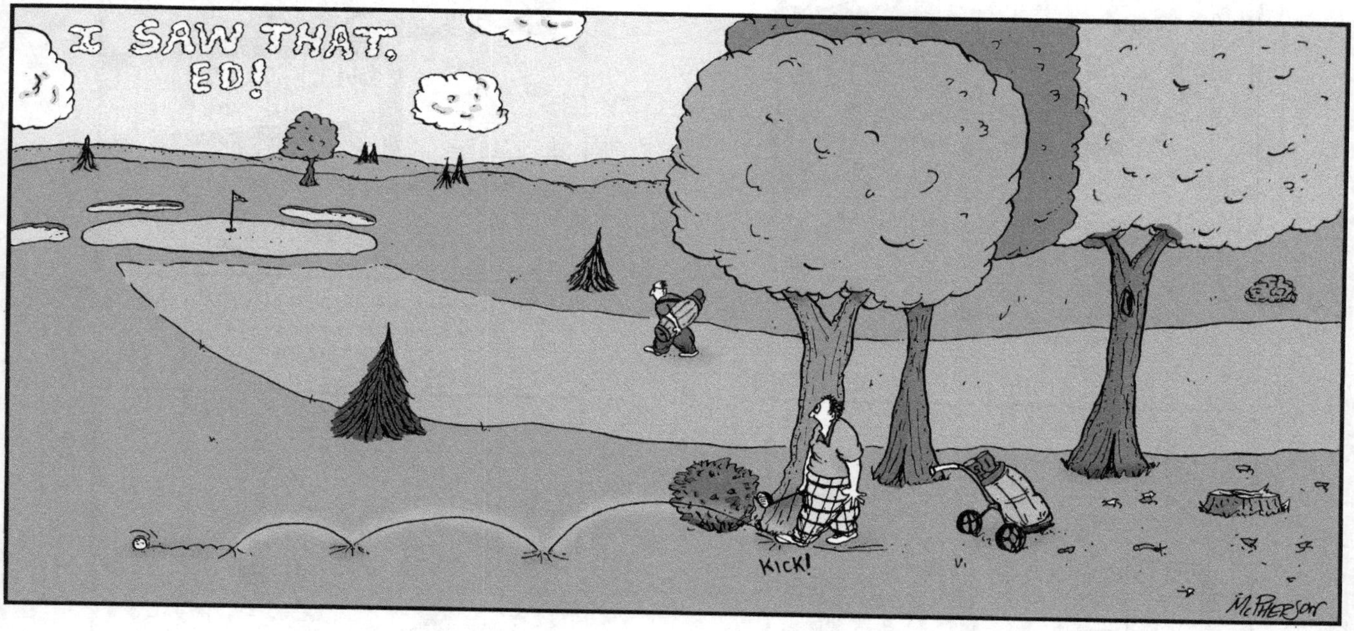
I SAW THAT, ED!
KICK!
McPherson

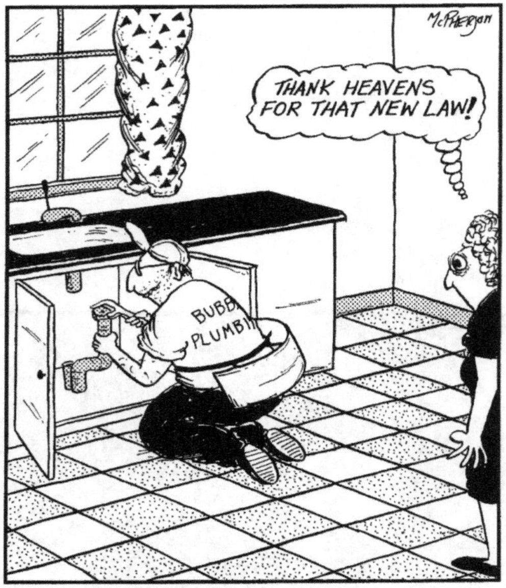
THANK HEAVENS FOR THAT NEW LAW!

A new federal law requires all on-site service technicians to wear low-riding-pants privacy shields.

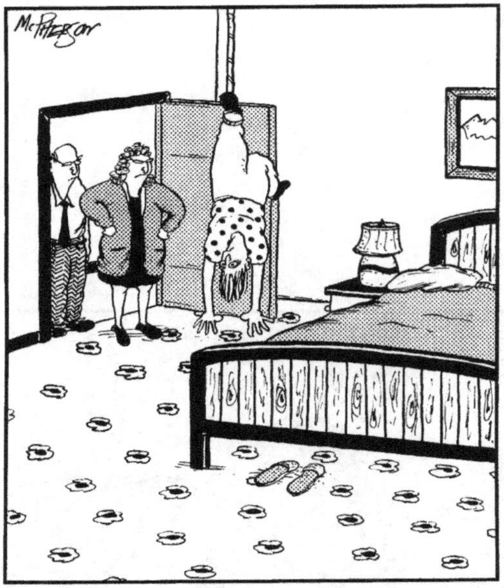

The Crowleys arrive home to discover that their babysitter has triggered their anti-snooping device.

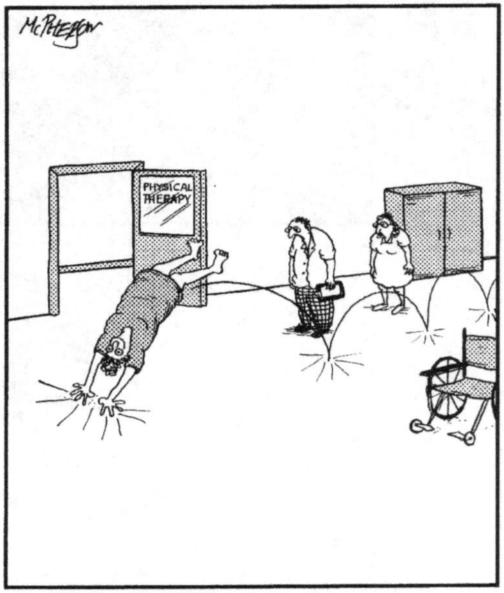
PHYSICAL THERAPY

"Now that is what I call a successful hip-replacement operation!"

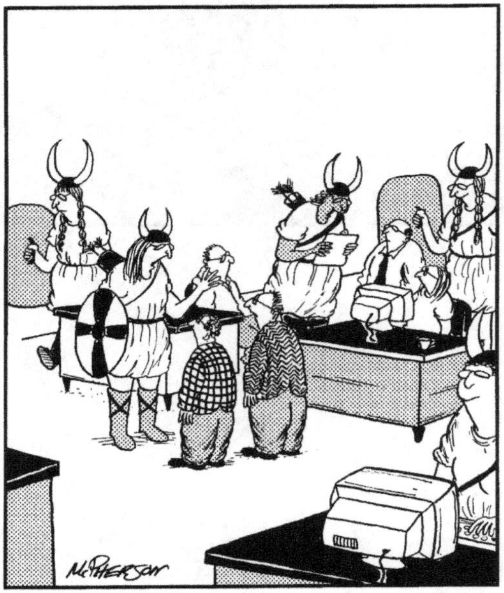

At the offices of Amazon.com.

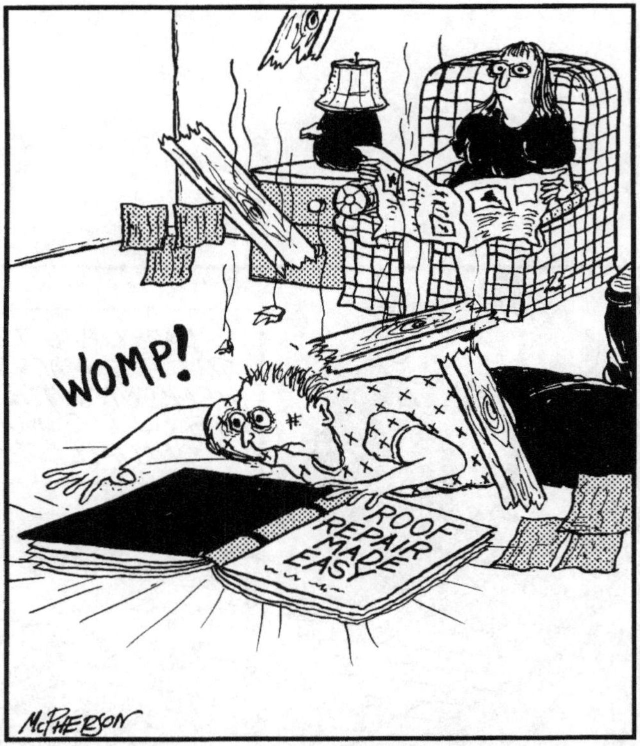
WOMP!
ROOF REPAIR MADE EASY
McPHERSON

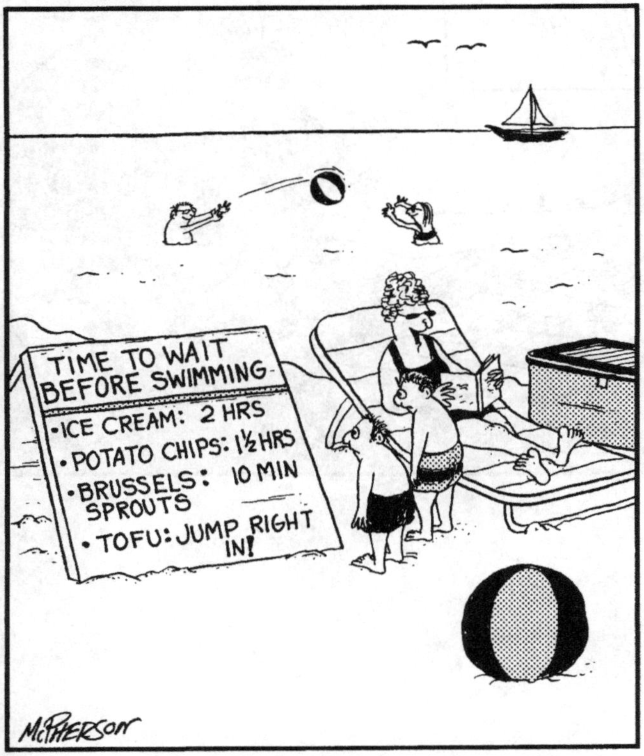
TIME TO WAIT BEFORE SWIMMING
•ICE CREAM: 2 HRS
•POTATO CHIPS: 1½ HRS
•BRUSSELS SPROUTS: 10 MIN
•TOFU: JUMP RIGHT IN!
McPHERSON

"It's your choice, kids."

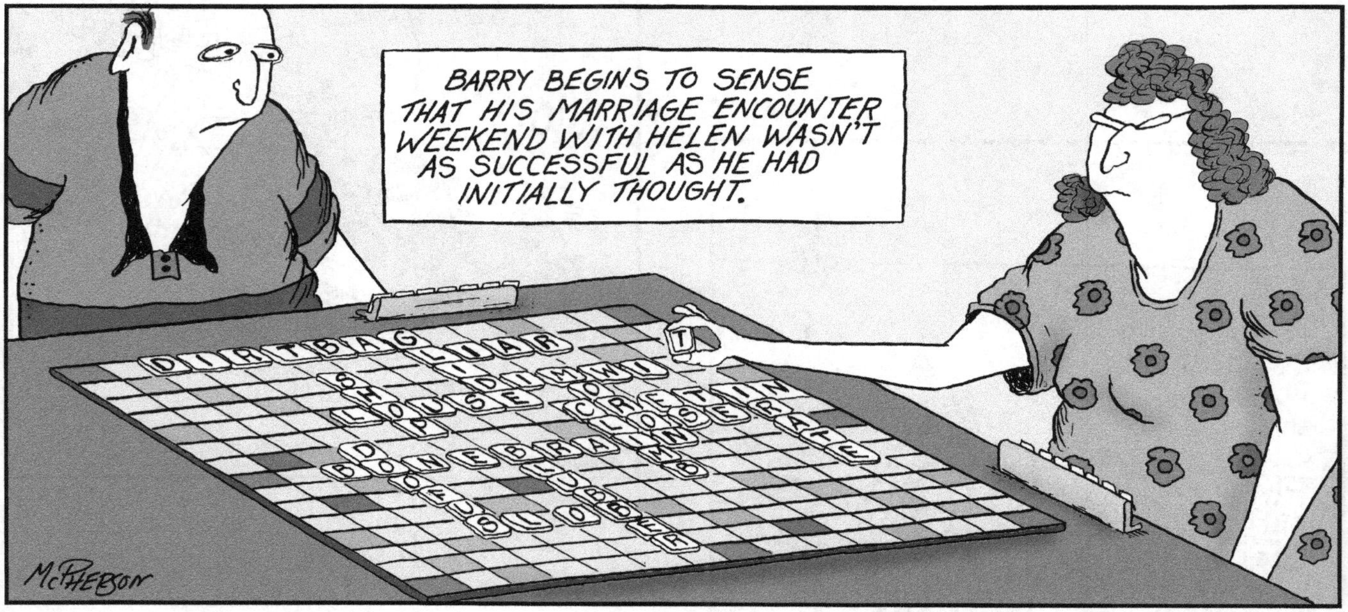
BARRY BEGINS TO SENSE THAT HIS MARRIAGE ENCOUNTER WEEKEND WITH HELEN WASN'T AS SUCCESSFUL AS HE HAD INITIALLY THOUGHT.
McPHERSON

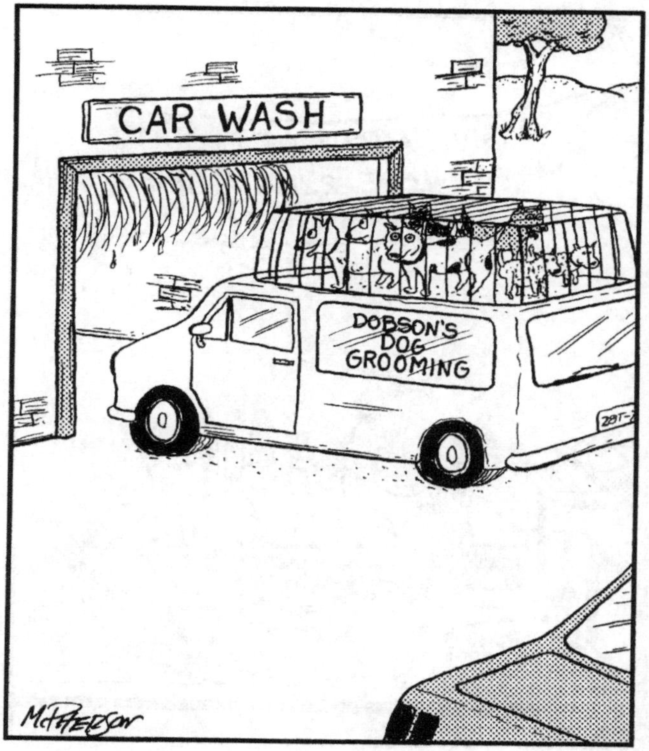
CAR WASH
DOBSON'S DOG GROOMING
McPHERSON

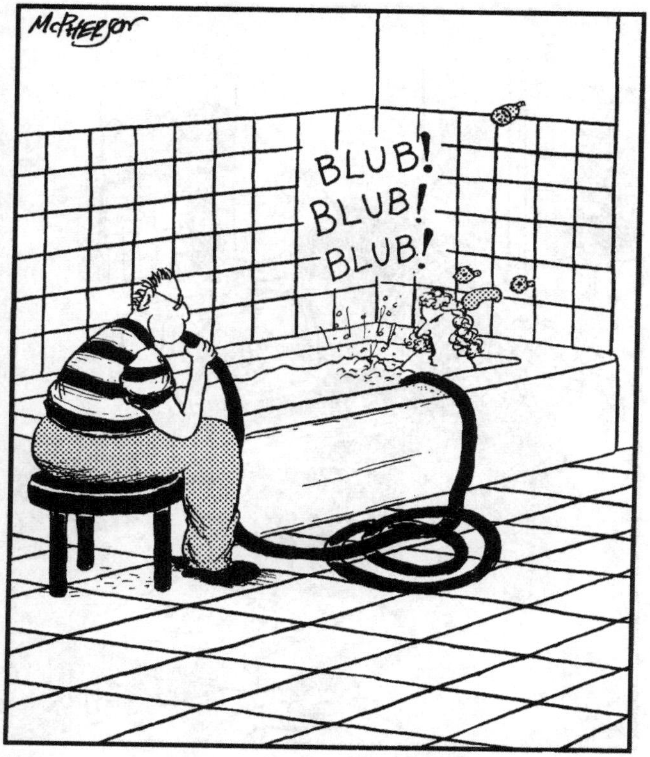
McPHERSON
BLUB!
BLUB!
BLUB!

"Don't think you can weasel out of buying me a Jacuzzi this easily!"

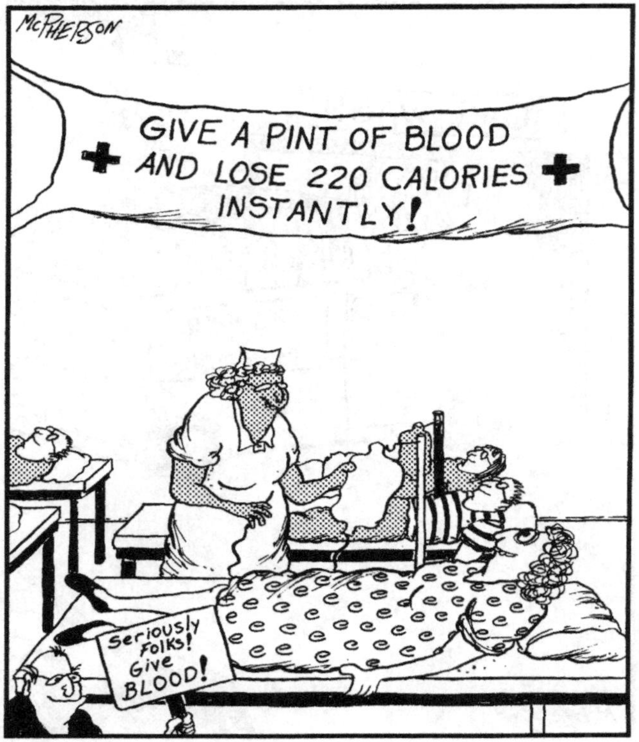
McPHERSON
GIVE A PINT OF BLOOD AND LOSE 220 CALORIES INSTANTLY!
Seriously Folks! Give BLOOD!

Thanks to an ingenious marketing ploy, the Red Cross embarks on its most successful blood drive ever.

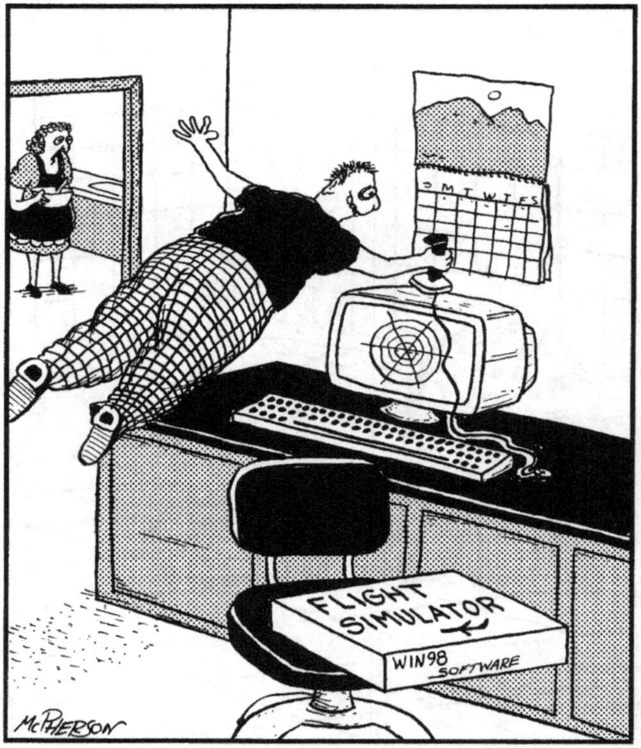
FLIGHT SIMULATOR
WIN98
SOFTWARE
McPHERSON

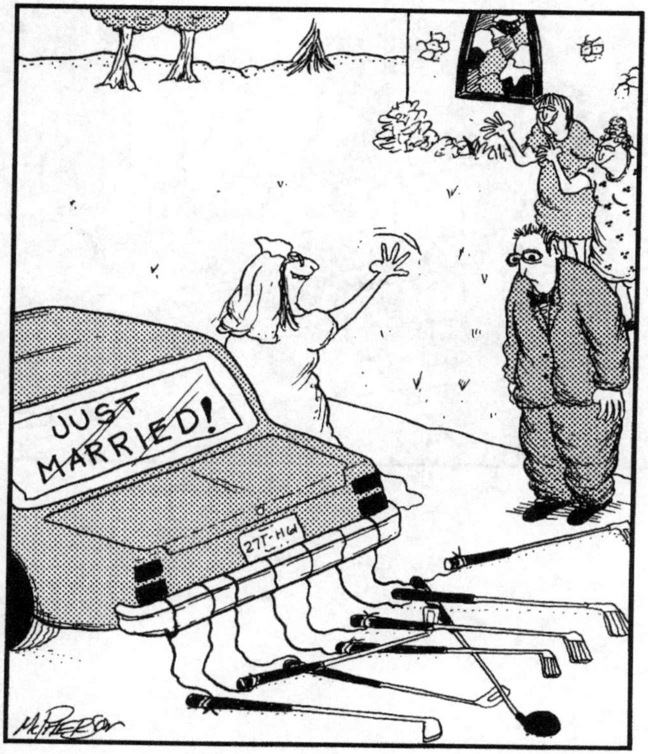
JUST MARRIED!
27T-HGI
McPHERSON

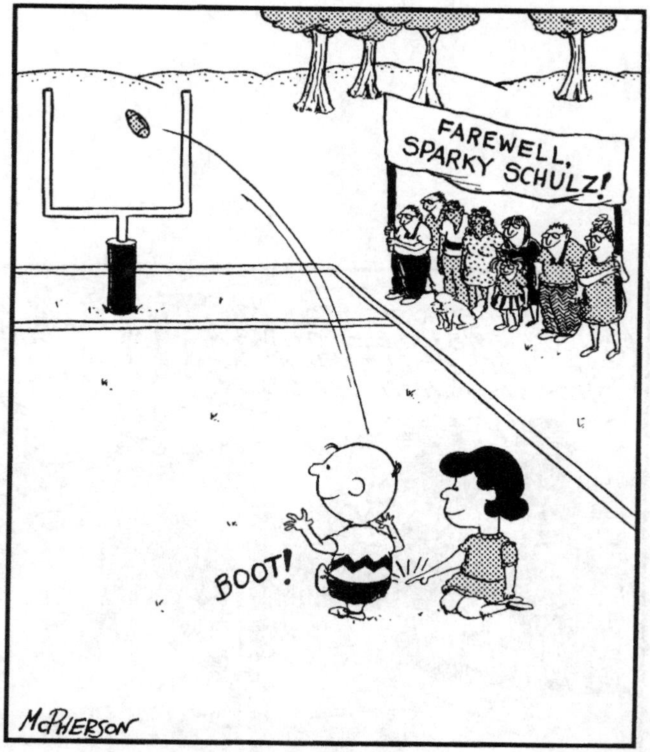
FAREWELL, SPARKY SCHULZ!
BOOT!
McPHERSON

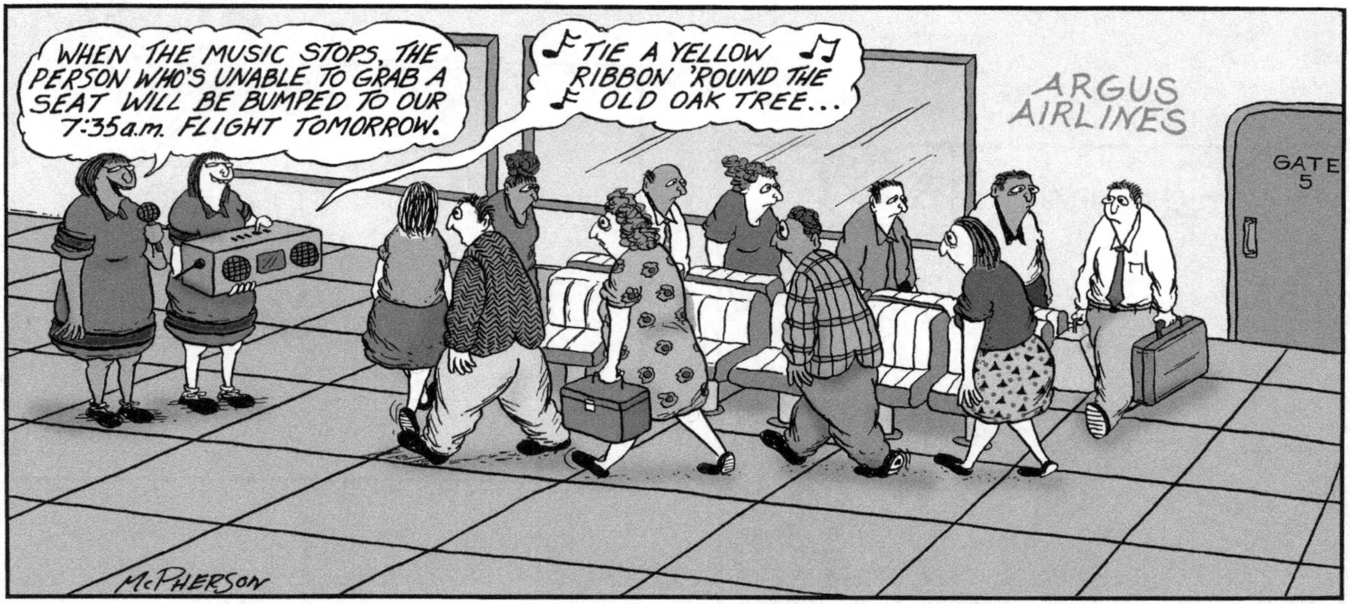
WHEN THE MUSIC STOPS, THE PERSON WHO'S UNABLE TO GRAB A SEAT WILL BE BUMPED TO OUR 7:35 a.m. FLIGHT TOMORROW.
TIE A YELLOW RIBBON 'ROUND THE OLD OAK TREE...
ARGUS AIRLINES
GATE 5
McPHERSON

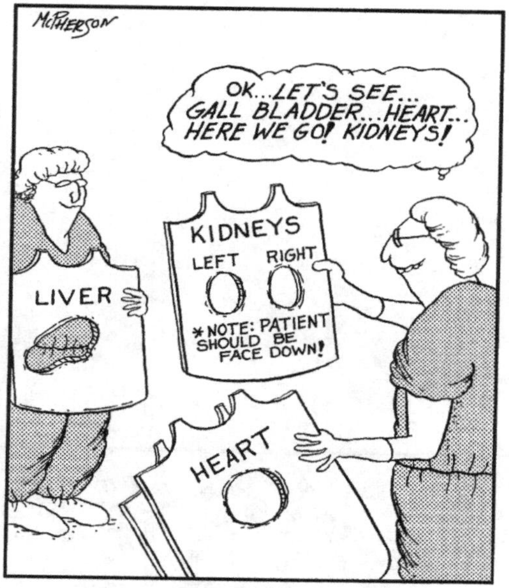
McPHERSON
OK...LET'S SEE...
GALL BLADDER...HEART...
HERE WE GO! KIDNEYS!
KIDNEYS
LEFT RIGHT
* NOTE: PATIENT SHOULD BE FACE DOWN!
LIVER
HEART

To avoid costly mistakes in the operating room, doctors at Oakmont Hospital relied on surgery templates.

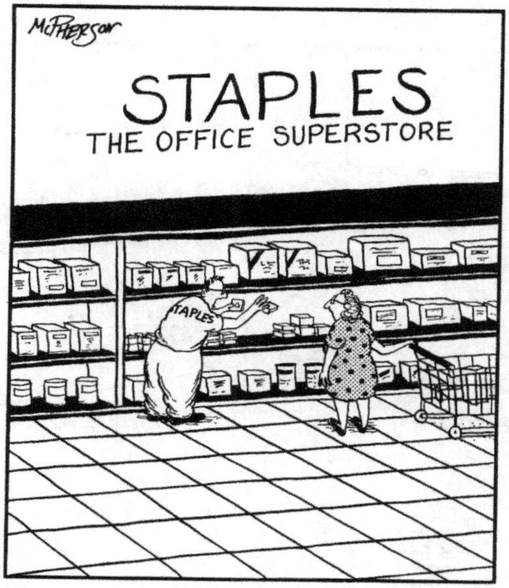
McPHERSON
STAPLES
THE OFFICE SUPERSTORE
STAPLES

"Well, let's see . . . paper clips . . . tape . . . glue . . . Oh, for cryin' out loud, you're right! We are out of staples!"

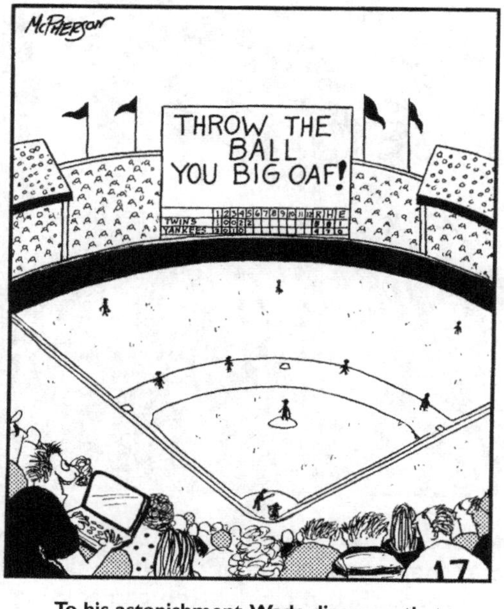
McPHERSON
THROW THE BALL YOU BIG OAF!
TWINS
YANKEES
17

To his astonishment, Wade discovers that he's able to send e-mail from his laptop to the stadium scoreboard.

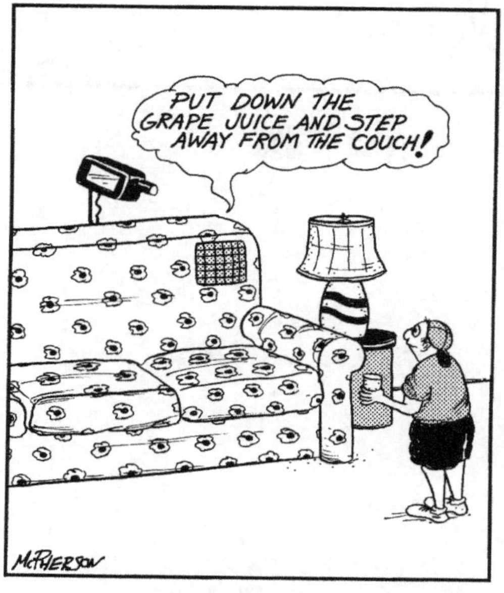
PUT DOWN THE GRAPE JUICE AND STEP AWAY FROM THE COUCH!
McPHERSON

Fortunately the Wagleys' new couch was equipped with Sof-Alarm 3000.

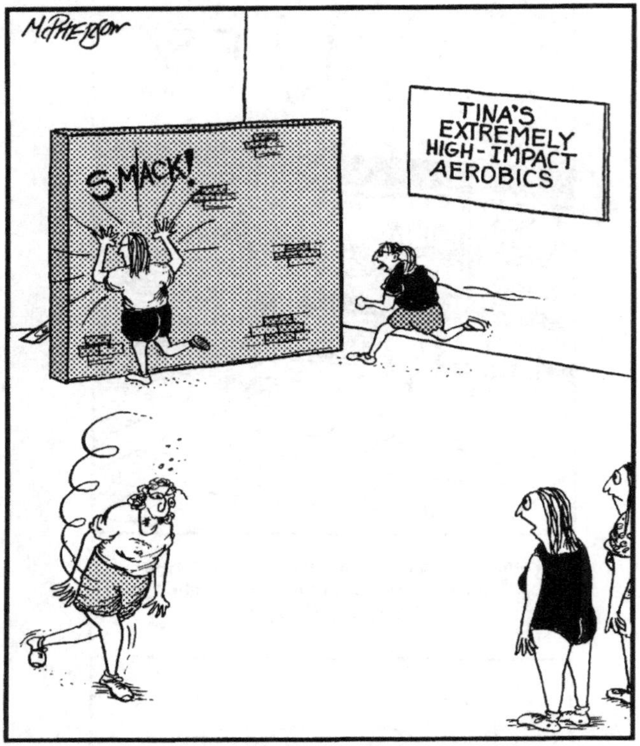
McPHERSON
TINA'S EXTREMELY HIGH-IMPACT AEROBICS
SMACK!

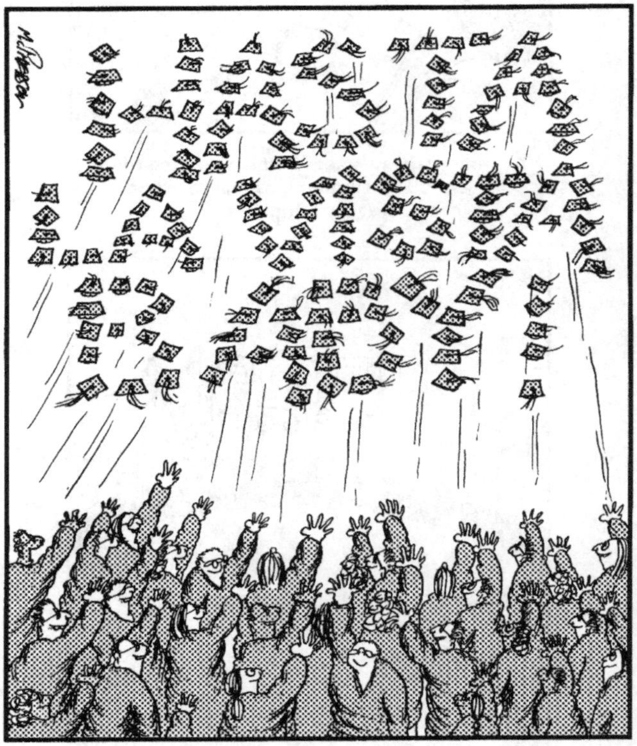
McPHERSON

The Creedmont High class of 2000 dazzles the commencement audience with a display of synchronized graduation cap tossing.

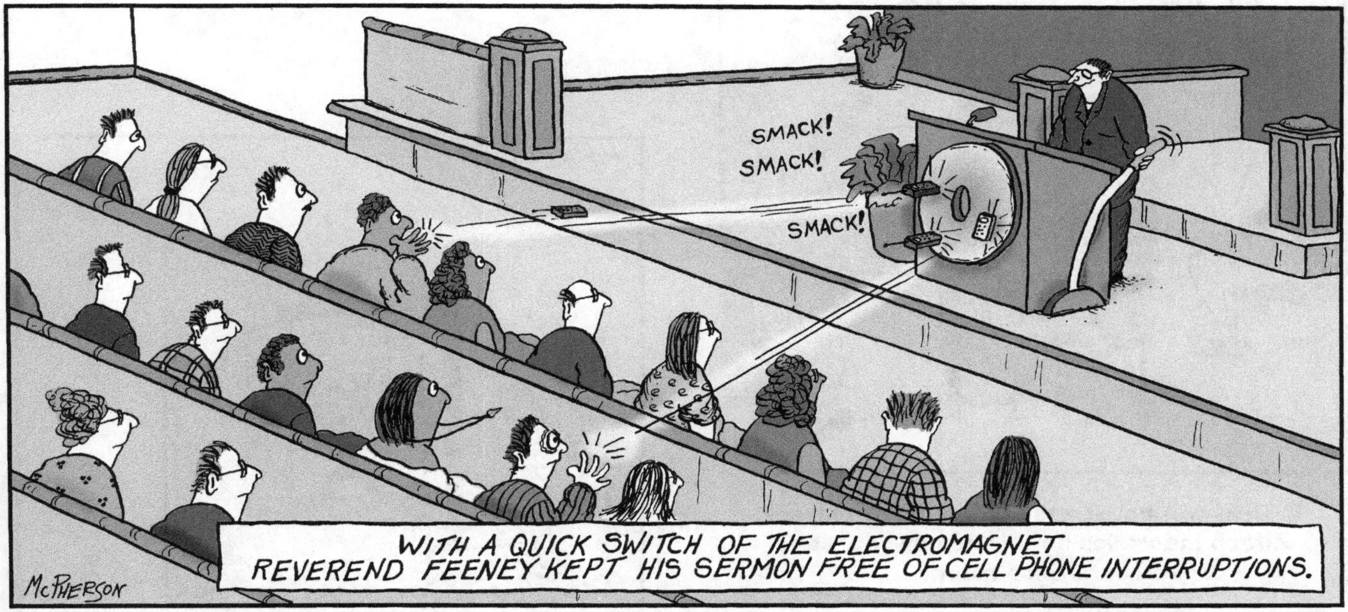
SMACK!
SMACK!
SMACK!
McPHERSON

WITH A QUICK SWITCH OF THE ELECTROMAGNET REVEREND FEENEY KEPT HIS SERMON FREE OF CELL PHONE INTERRUPTIONS.

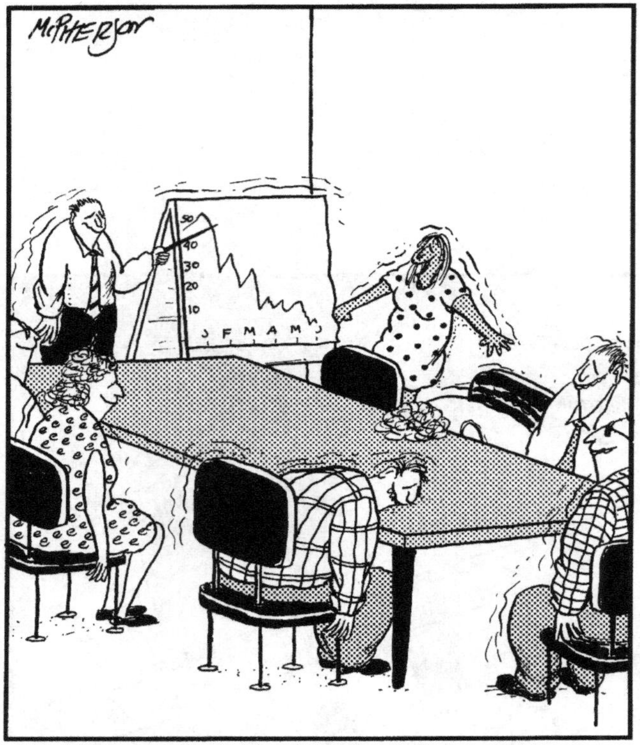
McPHERSON
50
40
30
20
10
J F M A M J

To help combat stress among its employees, Zitech Industries unveils its new vibrating conference room.

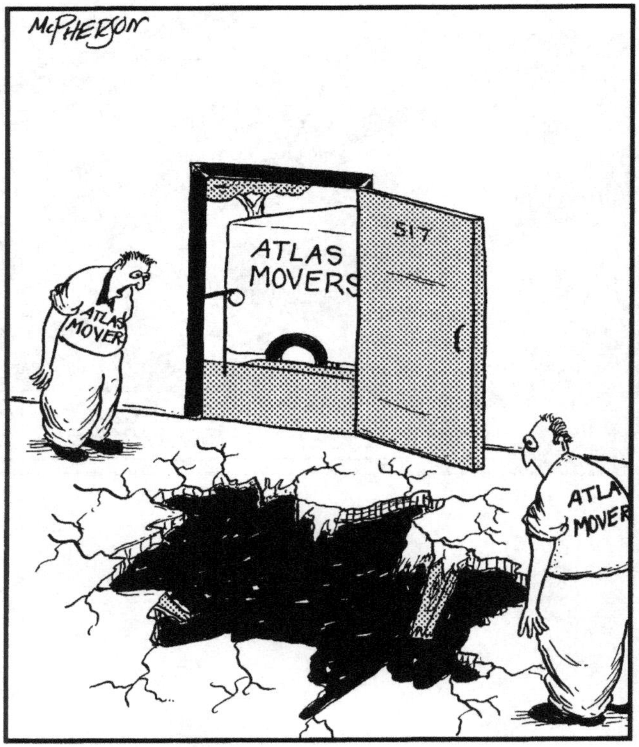
McPHERSON
517
ATLAS
MOVERS
ATLAS
MOVER
ATLA
MOVER

"I say we bring in that big Oriental rug next."

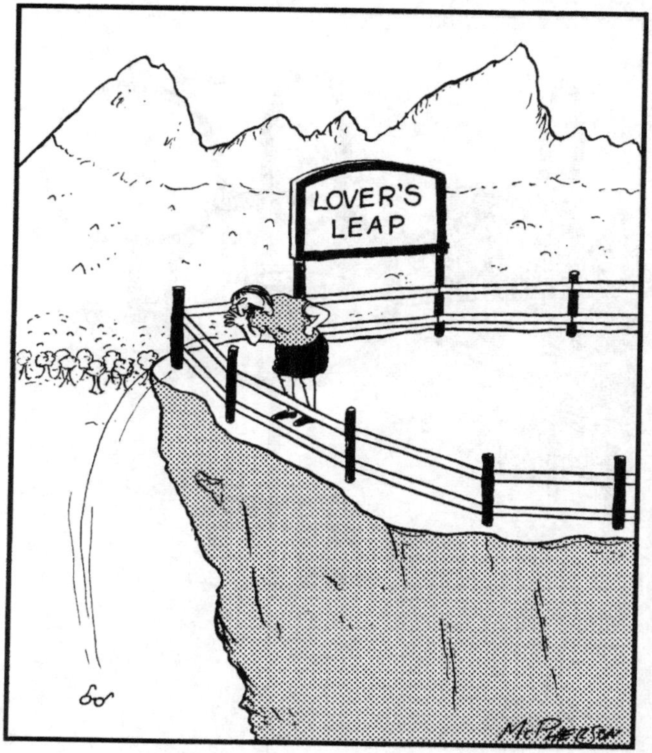
LOVER'S LEAP

"Who do you think you're fooling, Mr. Overdramatic? I know that backpack has a parachute in it!"

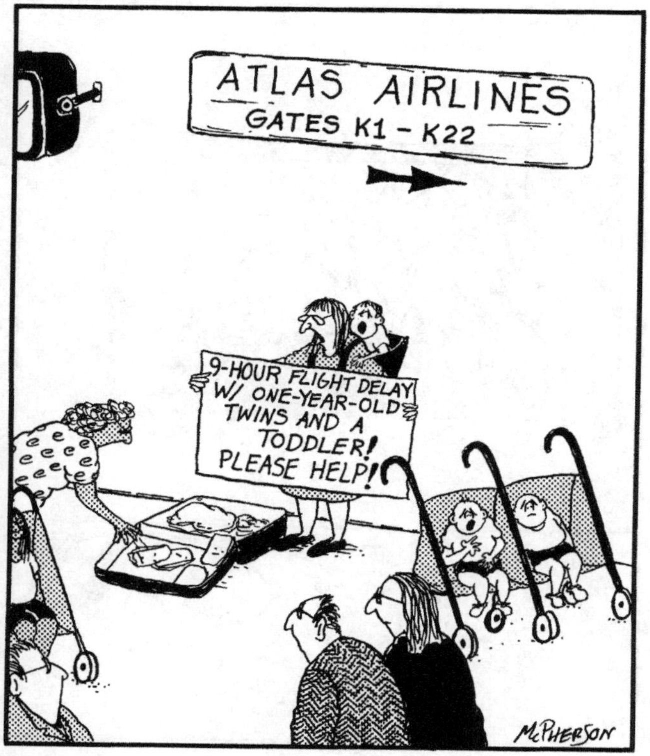
ATLAS AIRLINES
GATES K1 - K22
9-HOUR FLIGHT DELAY W/ ONE-YEAR-OLD TWINS AND A TODDLER! PLEASE HELP!

" . . . spare diaper, ma'am? Stage three or stage four? Bless you ma'am. Spare diaper? Spare diaper, sir?"

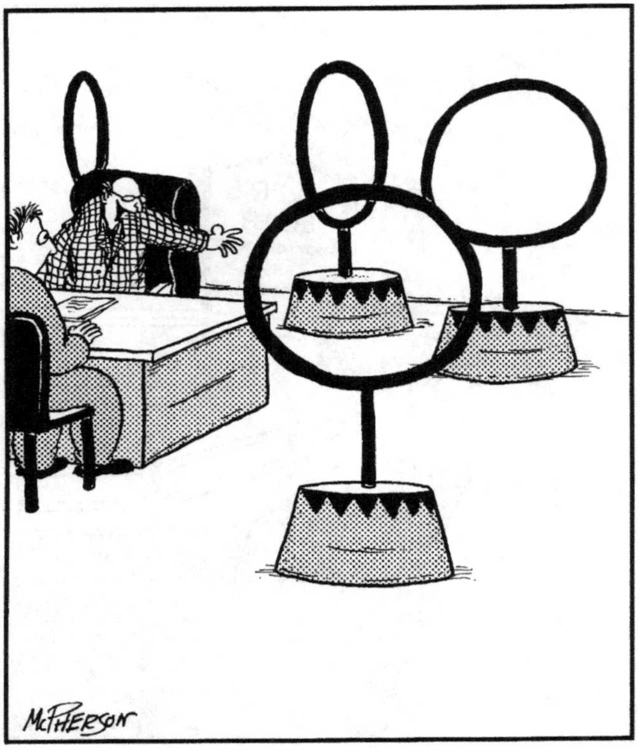
McPHERSON

"I'm happy to offer you the position of district manager, Ed. However, there's one symbolic gesture I'd like you to perform before we make it official."

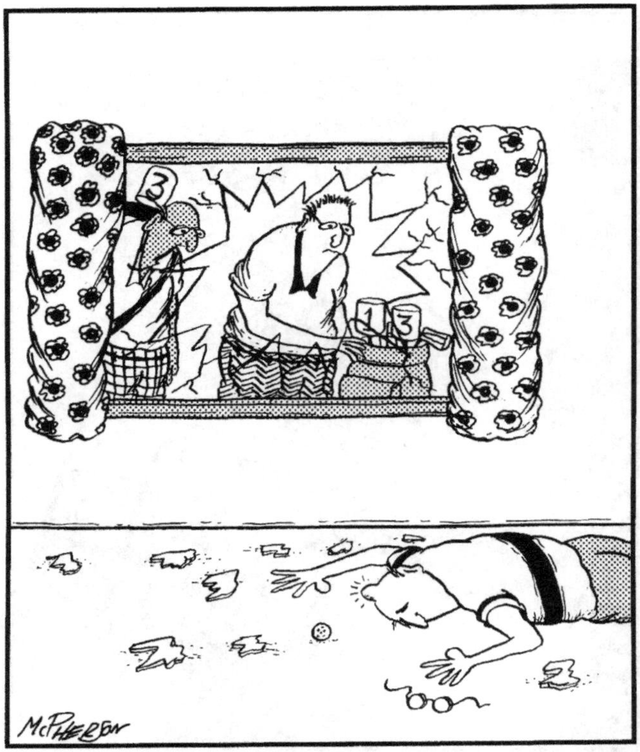
McPHERSON

"I don't see any out-of-bounds stakes. I say you play it."

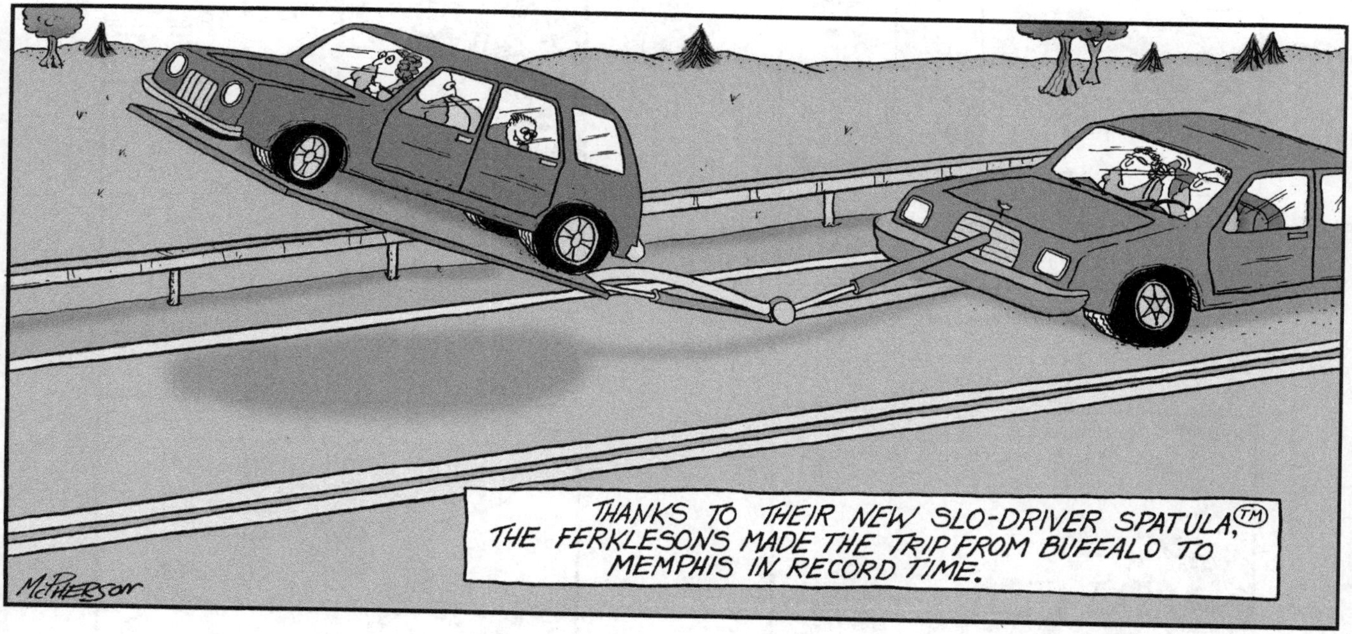
THANKS TO THEIR NEW SLO-DRIVER SPATULA,(TM) THE FERKLESONS MADE THE TRIP FROM BUFFALO TO MEMPHIS IN RECORD TIME.
McPHERSON

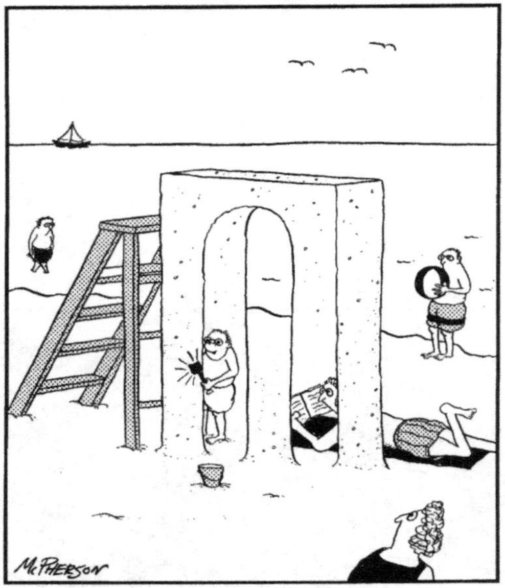
McPHERSON

M. C. Escher as a child.

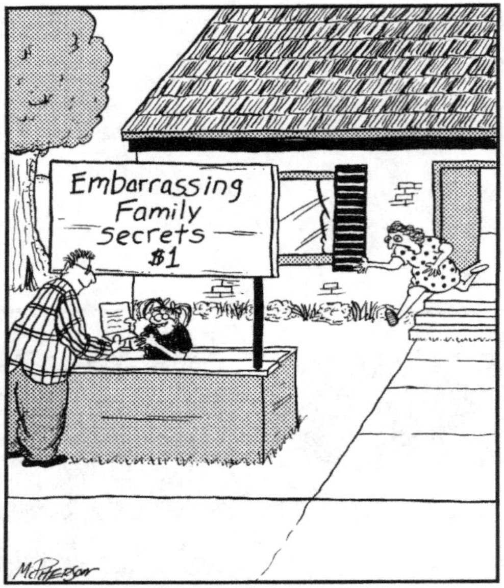
Embarrassing Family Secrets $1
McPHERSON

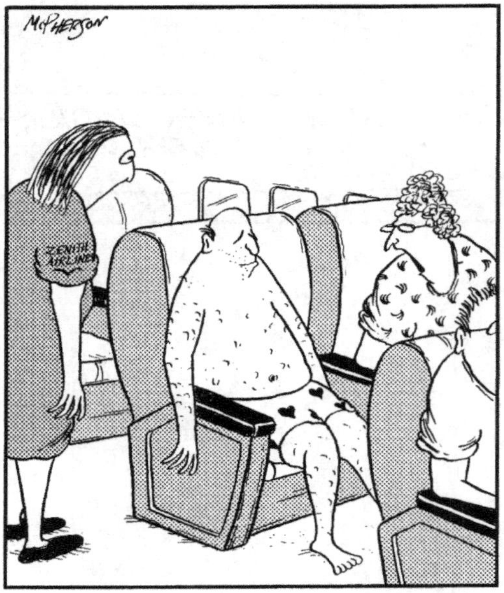
McPHERSON
ZENITH AIRLINES

"Well, I'm sorry if it bothers you, but my husband always sleeps in just his boxers."

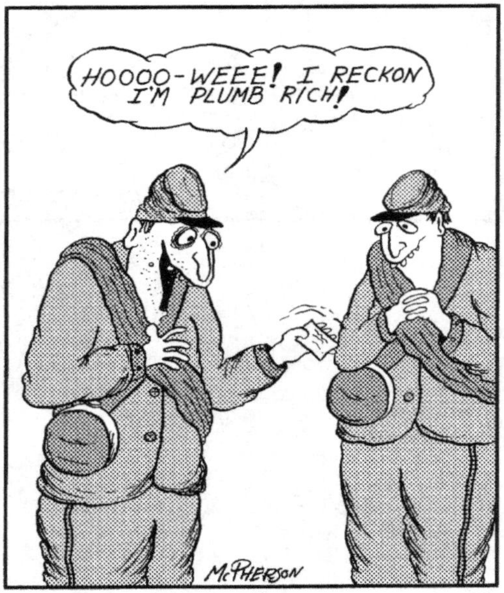
HOOOO-WEEE! I RECKON I'M PLUMB RICH!
McPHERSON

Big losers in U.S. history: Hiram Johnson wins the Confederate lottery on the same day that Lee surrenders at Appomattox.

"Ha! And you laughed when I bought this jackknife!"

"Gentleman, at last, my life's work is complete! It softens hands while you do the dishes!"

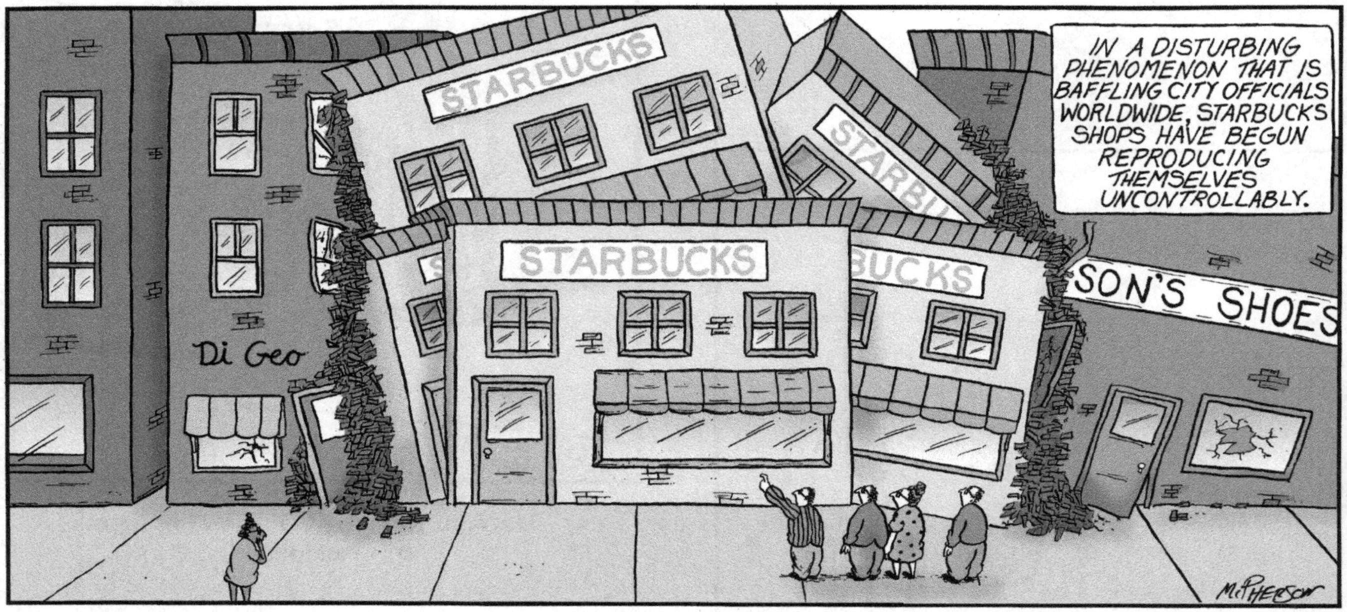
IN A DISTURBING PHENOMENON THAT IS BAFFLING CITY OFFICIALS WORLDWIDE, STARBUCKS SHOPS HAVE BEGUN REPRODUCING THEMSELVES UNCONTROLLABLY.
STARBUCKS
STARBUCKS
Di Geo
SON'S SHOES
McPHERSON

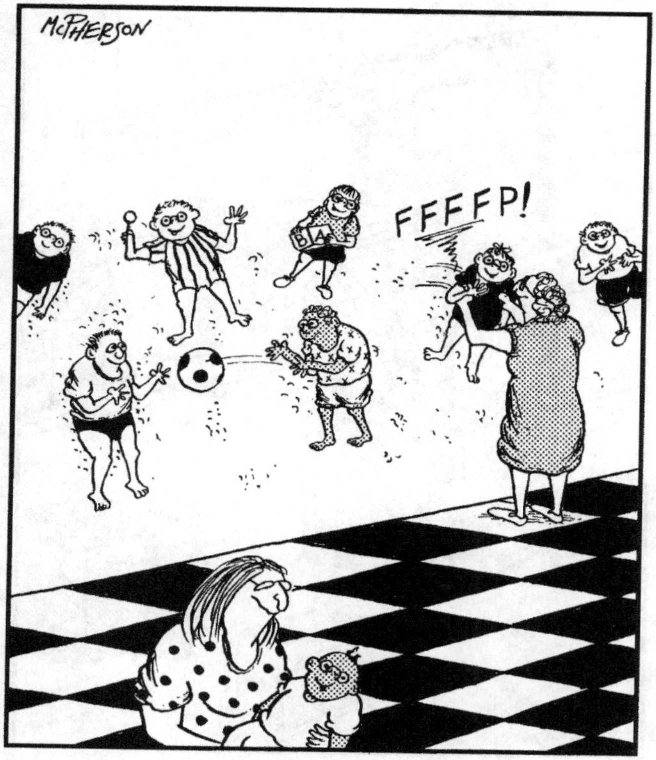
McPHERSON
FFFFP!
At the Velcro Corp. in-house day care.

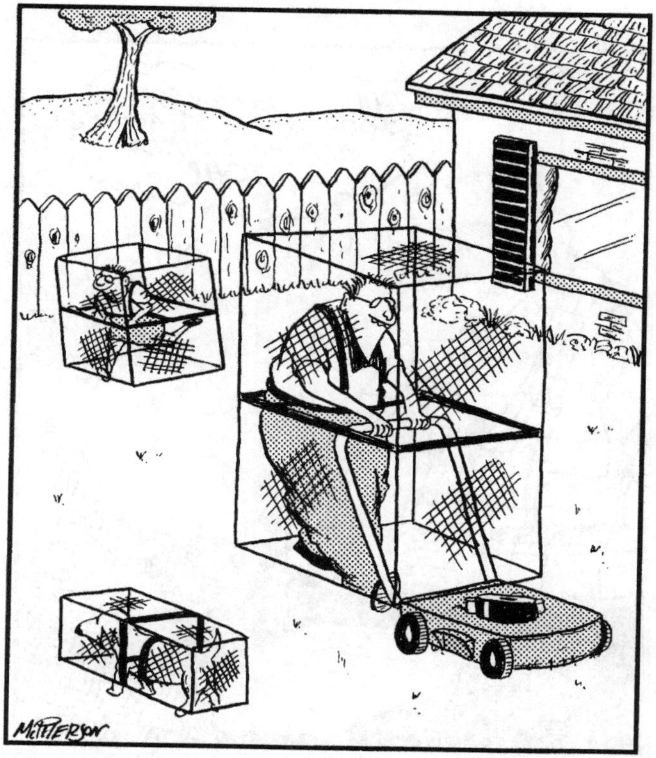
McPHERSON
Thanks to their new personal body screens, the Dempsters enjoyed a bug-free summer.

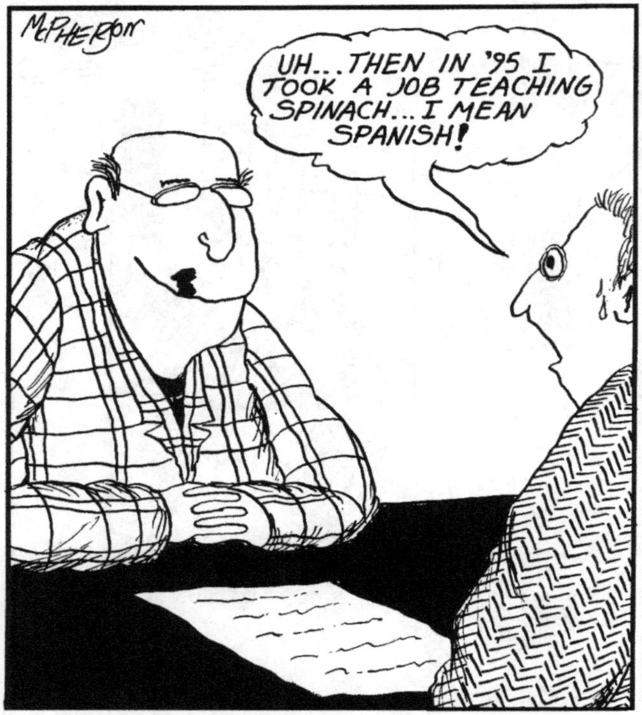
McPHERSON
UH...THEN IN '95 I TOOK A JOB TEACHING SPINACH...I MEAN SPANISH!

As a test of character, personnel manager Boyd Dinkins vowed to hire only those applicants who dared to tell him there was a piece of spinach on his lip.

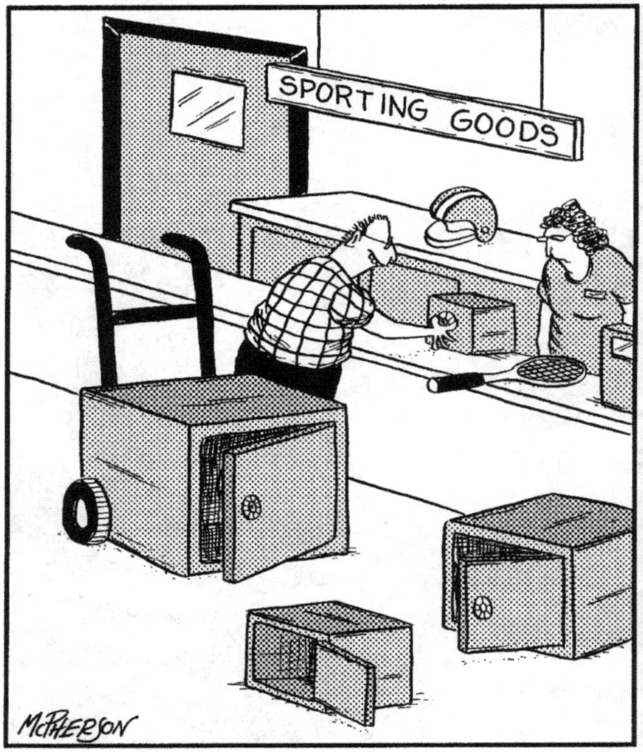
SPORTING GOODS
McPHERSON

To discourage frivolous purchases, Darren made sure his Visa card was as inaccessible as possible.

McPHERSON
UNITED DENTAL COLLEGE
DS 201: UNDERSTANDING MUMBLING PATIENTS
MMFBLGH! - My Arms are getting numb
PPPLBLZZ! - I swallowed some gauze
CRROGWLL! - AHH! Please, NO!

I'M PICKING UP A VERY STRONG SIGNAL! YES! I'VE FOUND ONE!
WAAA!
McPHERSON

For those desperate moments, the Nullmans relied on their pacifier detector.

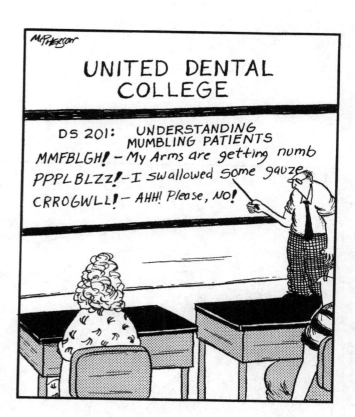

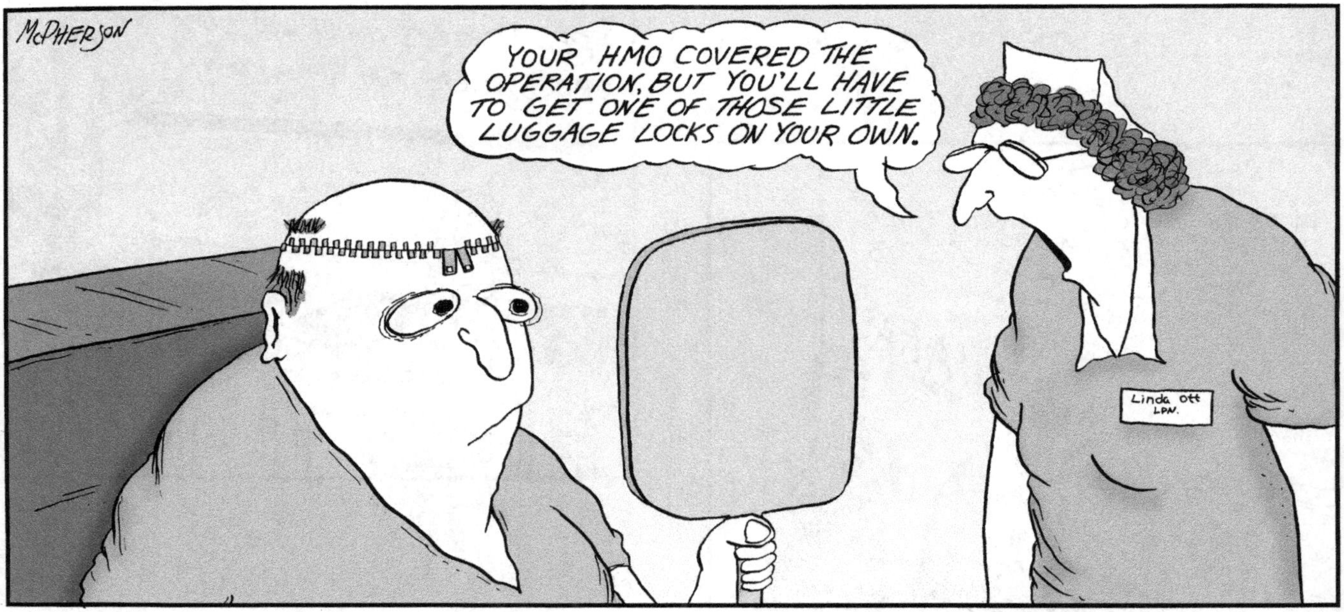
McPHERSON
YOUR HMO COVERED THE OPERATION, BUT YOU'LL HAVE TO GET ONE OF THOSE LITTLE LUGGAGE LOCKS ON YOUR OWN.
Linda Ott LPN.

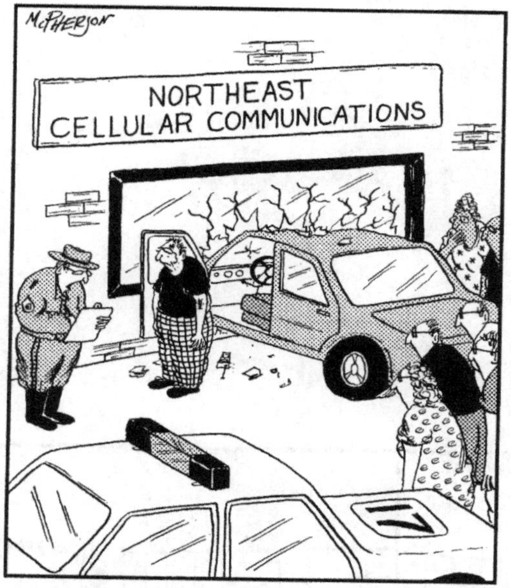
NORTHEAST
CELLULAR COMMUNICATIONS

"... distracted ... while ... talking ... on ... cell ... phone."

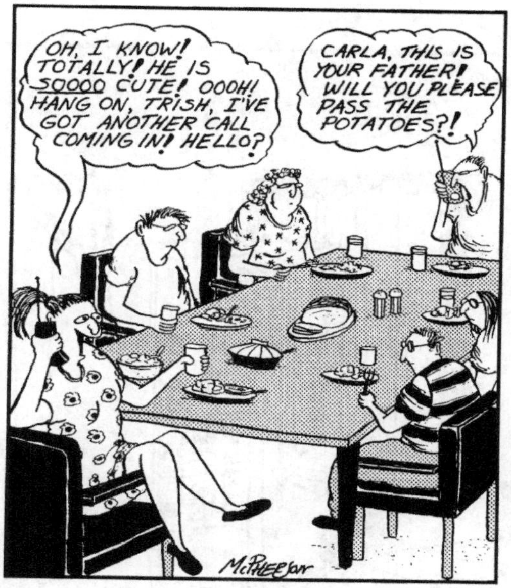
OH, I KNOW! TOTALLY! HE IS SOOOO CUTE! OOOH! HANG ON, TRISH, I'VE GOT ANOTHER CALL COMING IN! HELLO?
CARLA, THIS IS YOUR FATHER! WILL YOU PLEASE PASS THE POTATOES?!

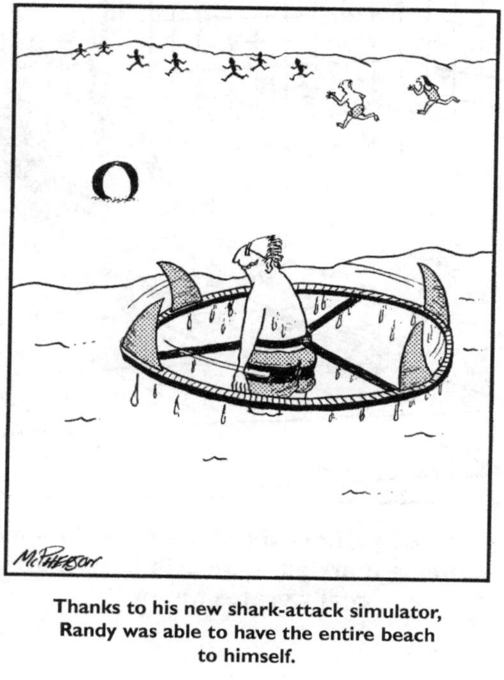

Thanks to his new shark-attack simulator, Randy was able to have the entire beach to himself.

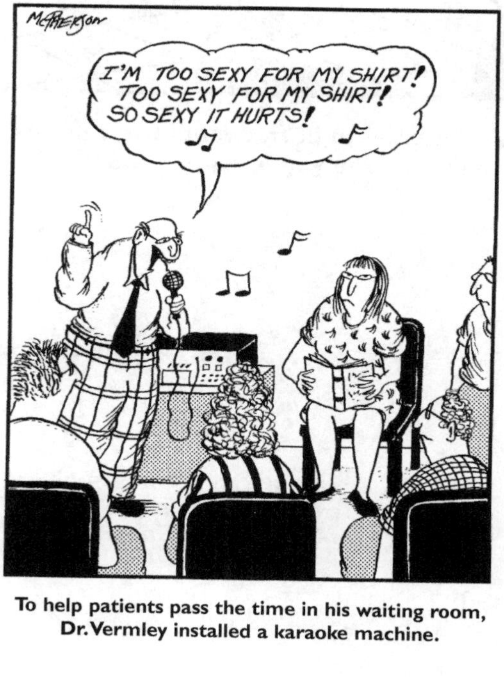
I'M TOO SEXY FOR MY SHIRT! TOO SEXY FOR MY SHIRT! SO SEXY IT HURTS!

To help patients pass the time in his waiting room, Dr. Vermley installed a karaoke machine.

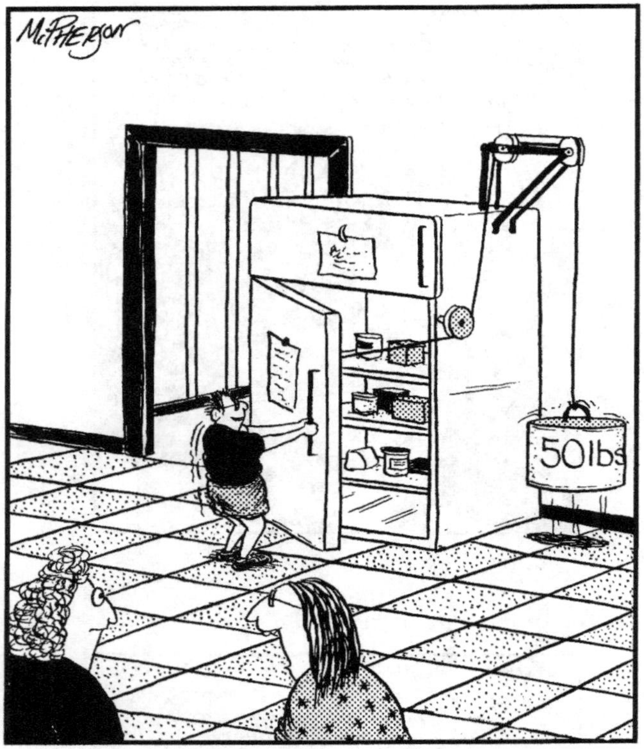
50lbs

"It's designed to burn twenty-five calories every time you open the door."

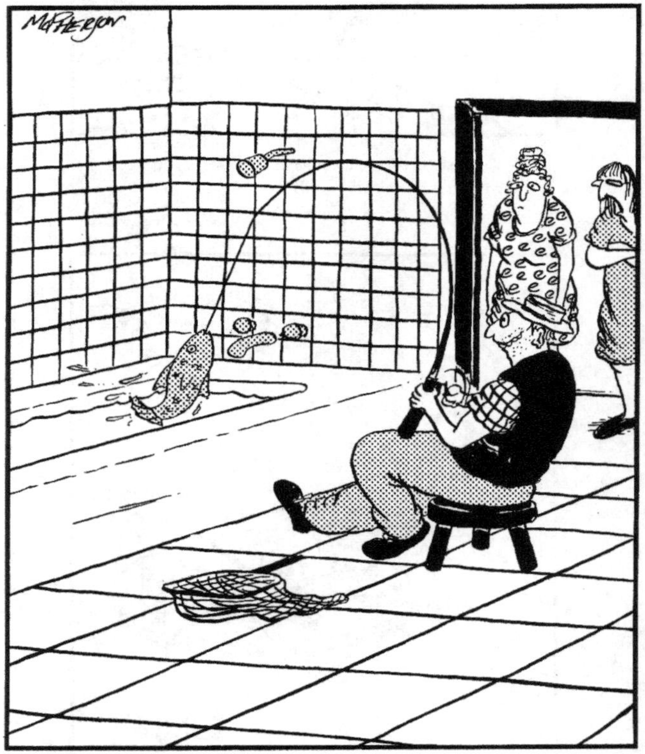

"I tell ya, Lois, there are times when being married to an avid fisherman really grates on me."

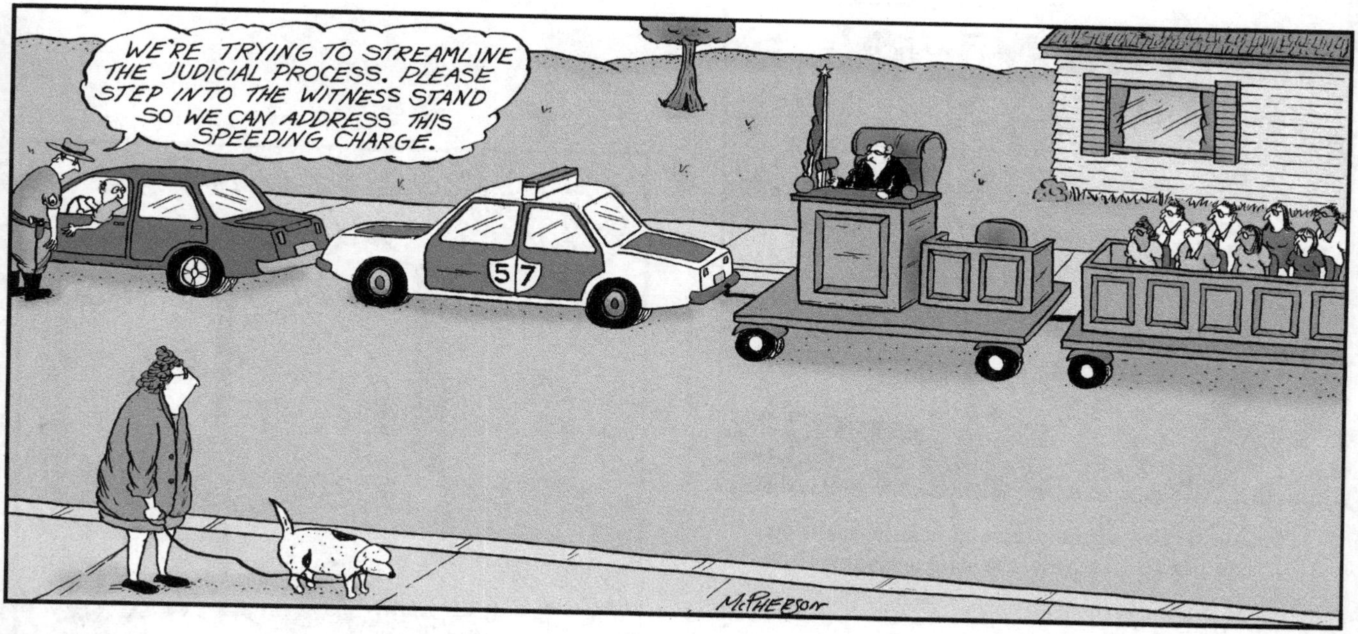
WE'RE TRYING TO STREAMLINE THE JUDICIAL PROCESS. PLEASE STEP INTO THE WITNESS STAND SO WE CAN ADDRESS THIS SPEEDING CHARGE.
57
McPHERSON

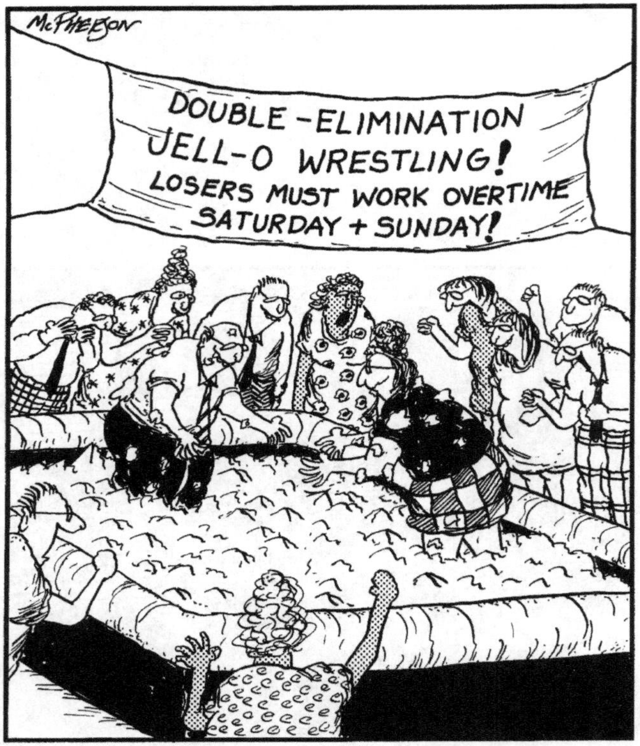
McPHERSON
DOUBLE-ELIMINATION JELL-O WRESTLING! LOSERS MUST WORK OVERTIME SATURDAY + SUNDAY!

Morale in the office was at an all-time high thanks to the new overtime system.

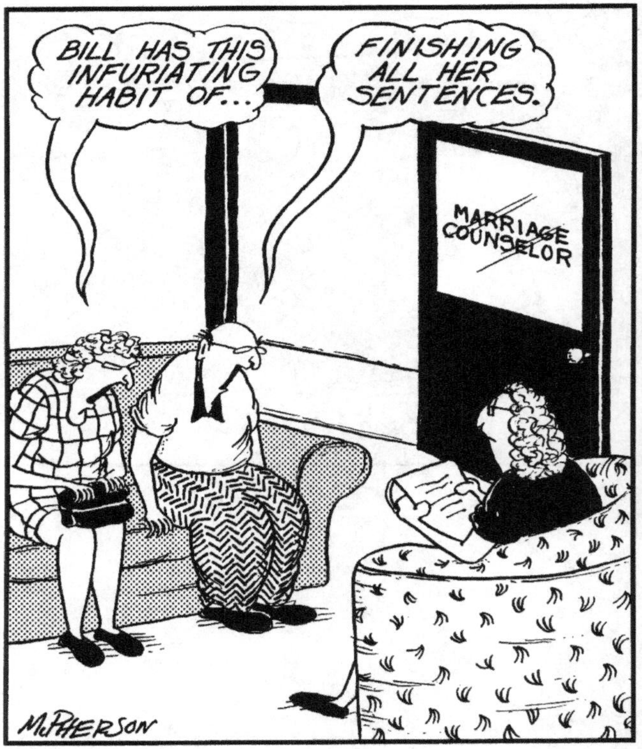
BILL HAS THIS INFURIATING HABIT OF...
FINISHING ALL HER SENTENCES.
MARRIAGE COUNSELOR
McPHERSON

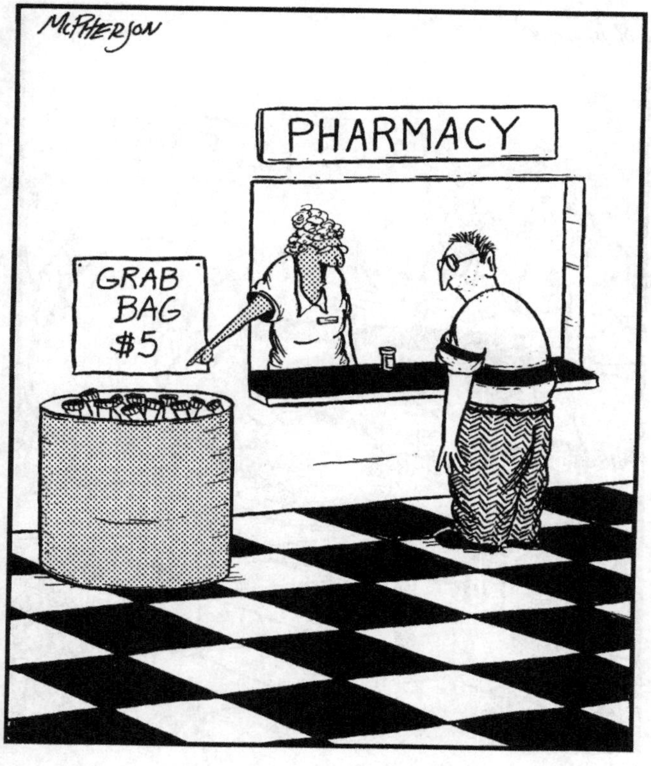
McPHERSON
PHARMACY
GRAB
BAG
$5

"Your prescription will be $90 or, if you prefer, you can try our grab bag and hope you get lucky."

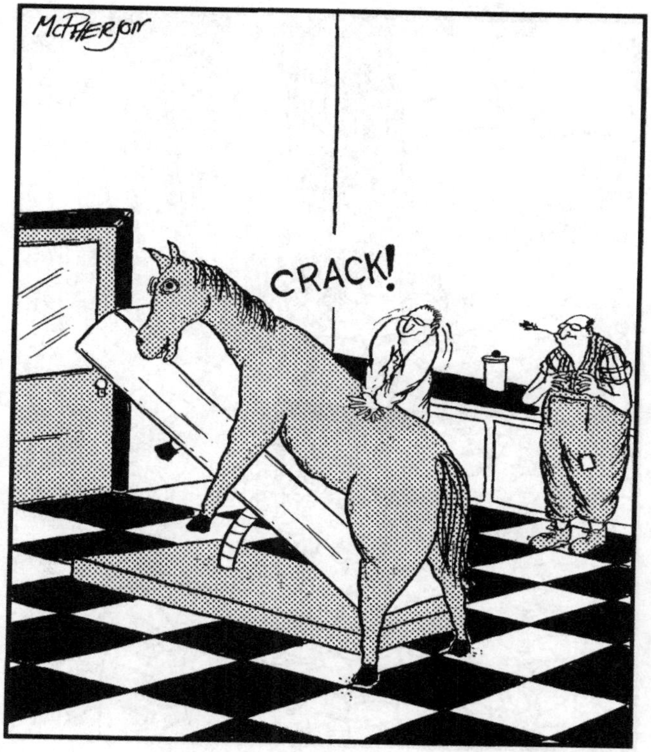
McPHERSON
CRACK!

Dr. Robert Slertman, bold pioneer in the emerging field of veterinary chiropractic.

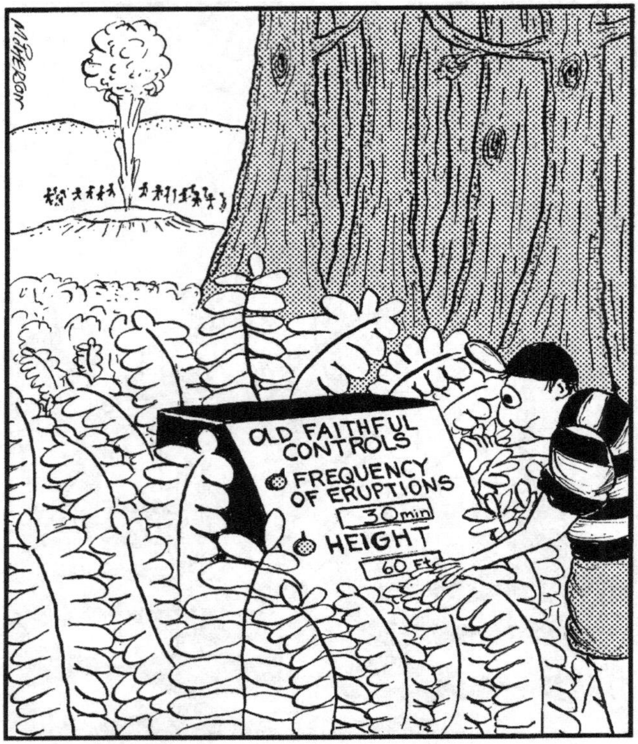
McPHERSON
OLD FAITHFUL CONTROLS
FREQUENCY OF ERUPTIONS
30min
HEIGHT
60 Ft

While collecting pinecones, eight-year-old Jimmy Rinaldi uncovers the biggest scandal in the history of the National Park Service.

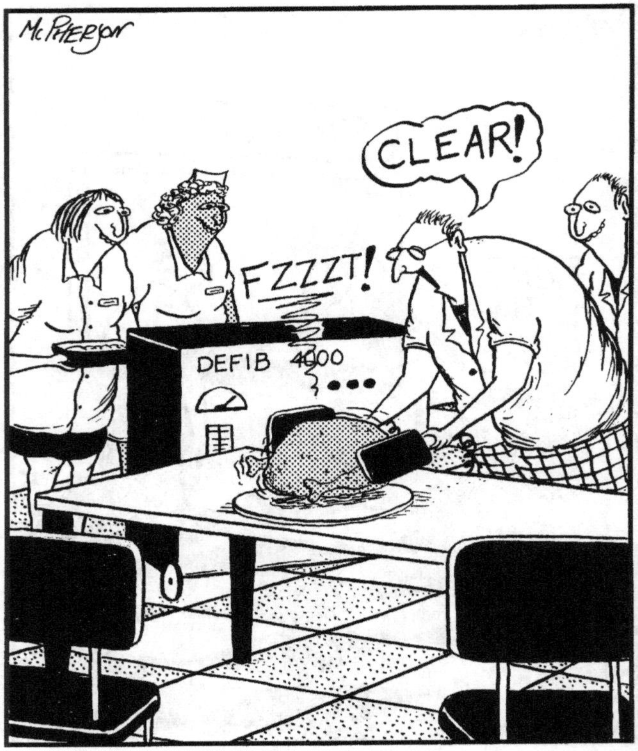
McPHERSON
CLEAR!
FZZZT!
DEFIB 4000

With the break room's microwave out of commission, resourceful doctors at Millmont Hospital improvised as best they could.

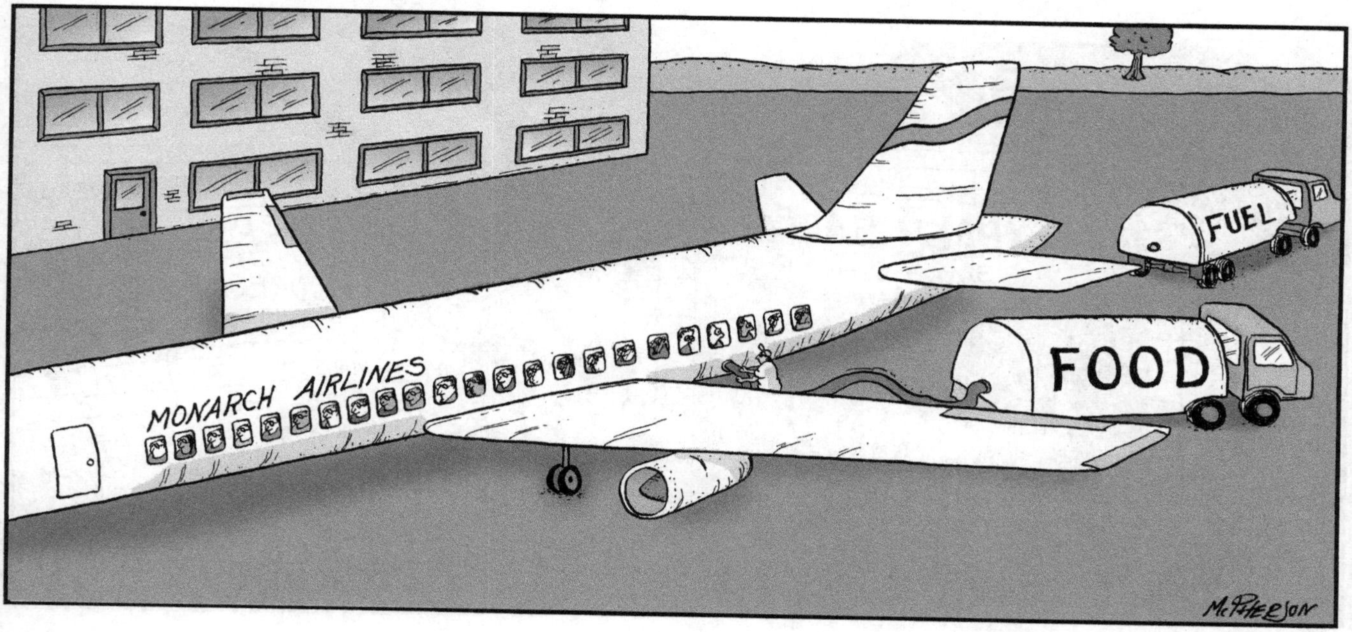
MONARCH AIRLINES
FUEL
FOOD
McPHERSON

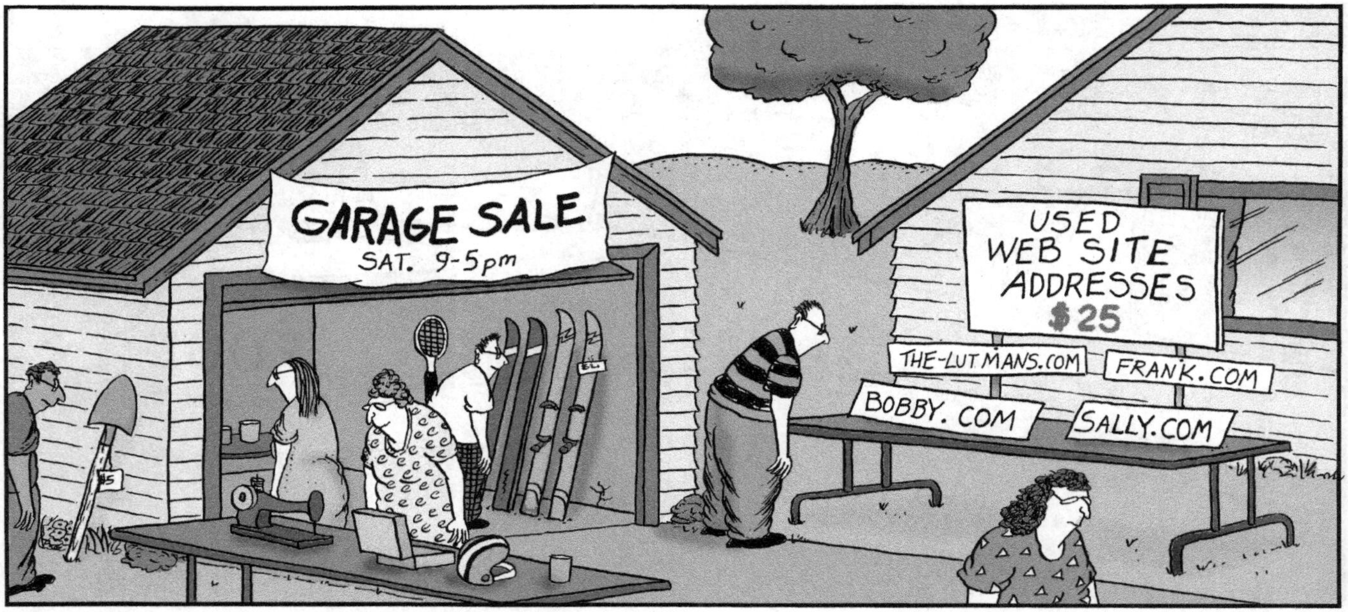
GARAGE SALE
SAT. 9-5pm
$5
USED
WEB SITE
ADDRESSES
$25
THE-LUTMANS.COM
FRANK.COM
BOBBY.COM
SALLY.COM

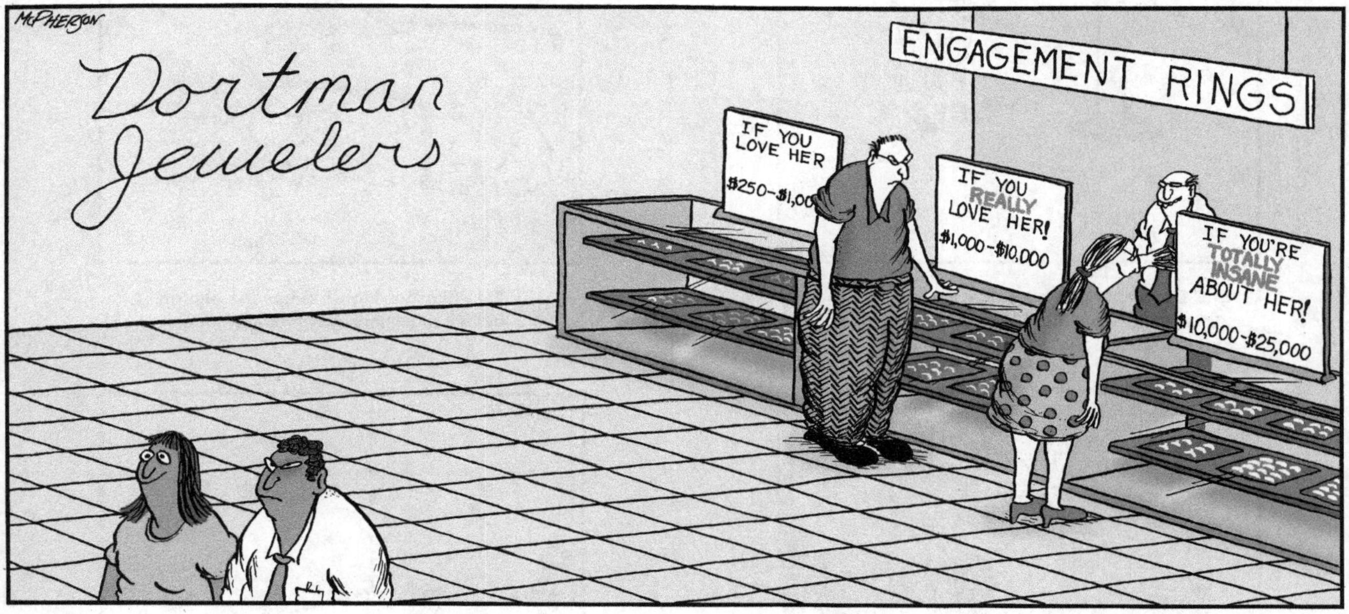
McPHERSON
Dortman Jewelers
ENGAGEMENT RINGS
IF YOU LOVE HER
IF YOU REALLY LOVE HER!
$1,000–$10,000
IF YOU'RE TOTALLY INSANE ABOUT HER!
$10,000–$25,000

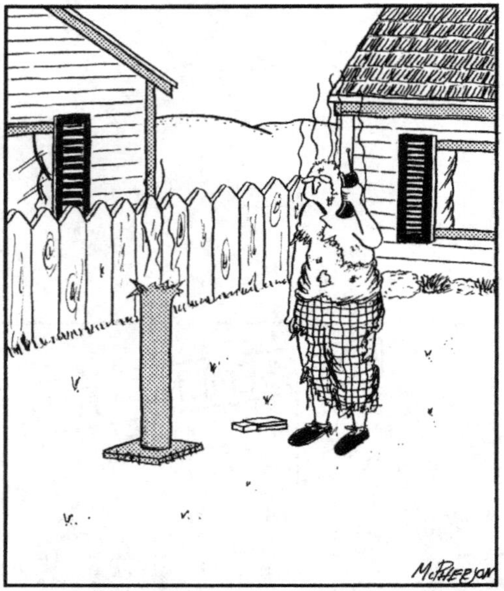
McPHERSON

"Bill? Dave Hawkins here. Say, you didn't happen to see a gas grill land in your yard or hear a loud thud on your roof, did you?"

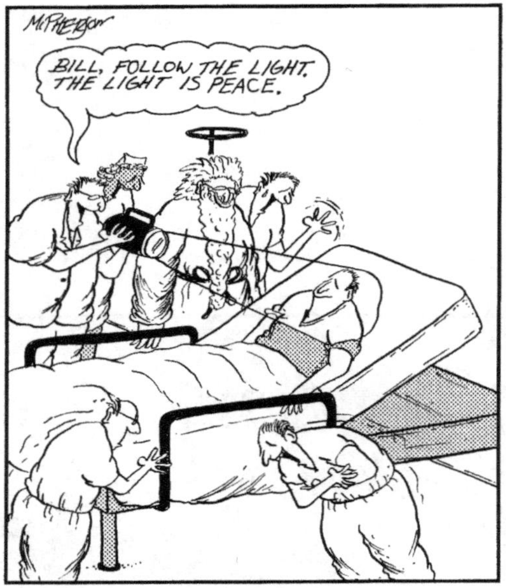
McPHERSON
BILL, FOLLOW THE LIGHT. THE LIGHT IS PEACE.

Why Philmont Hospital has the highest incidence of near-death experiences.

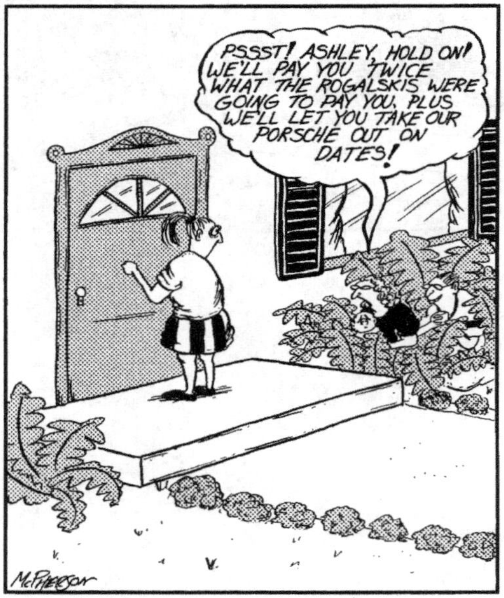
PSSST! ASHLEY, HOLD ON! WE'LL PAY YOU TWICE WHAT THE ROGALSKIS WERE GOING TO PAY YOU, PLUS WE'LL LET YOU TAKE OUR PORSCHE OUT ON DATES!
McPHERSON

Another shocking case of babysitter-jacking.

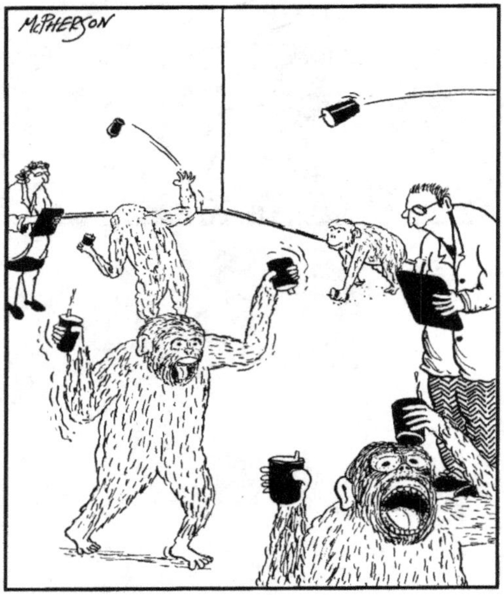
McPHERSON

At the National Sippy Cup Research Center.

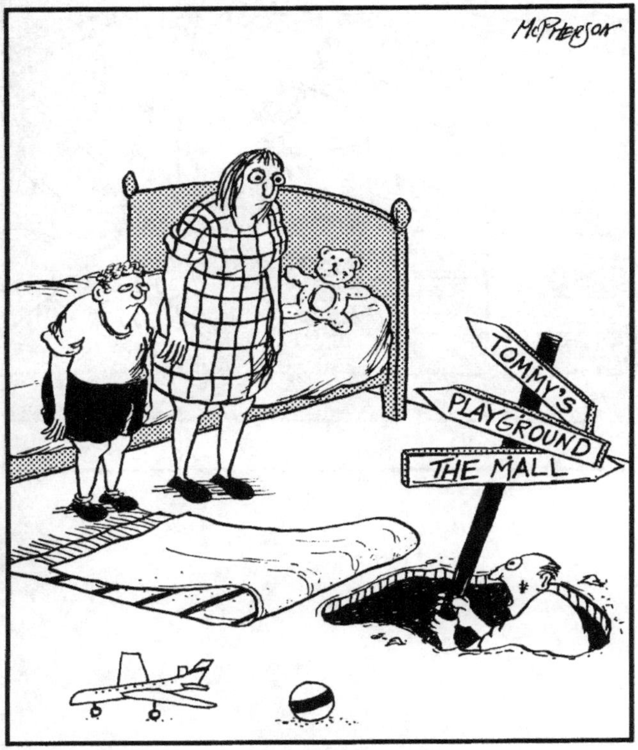
McPHERSON
TOMMY'S
PLAYGROUND
THE MALL

"I found this at an intersection about seventy-five yards down the tunnel!"

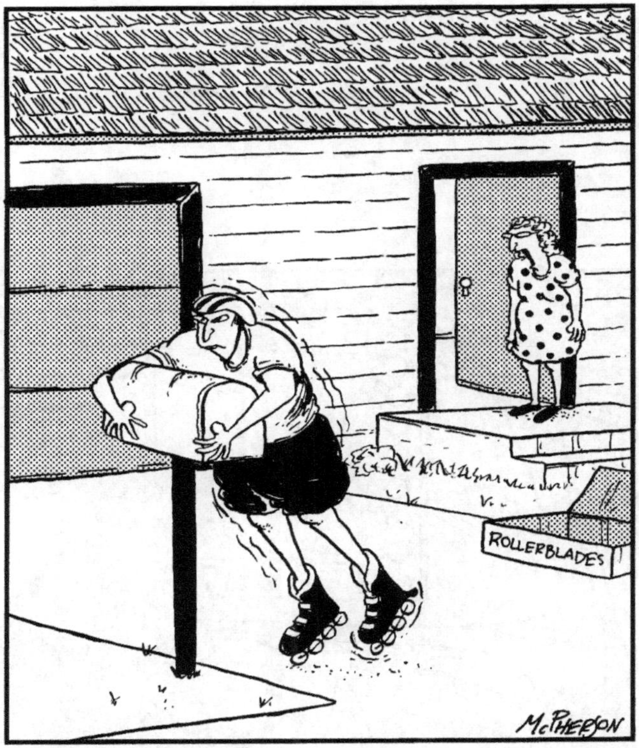
ROLLERBLADES
McPHERSON

"I made a five o'clock appointment for you at the emergency room!"

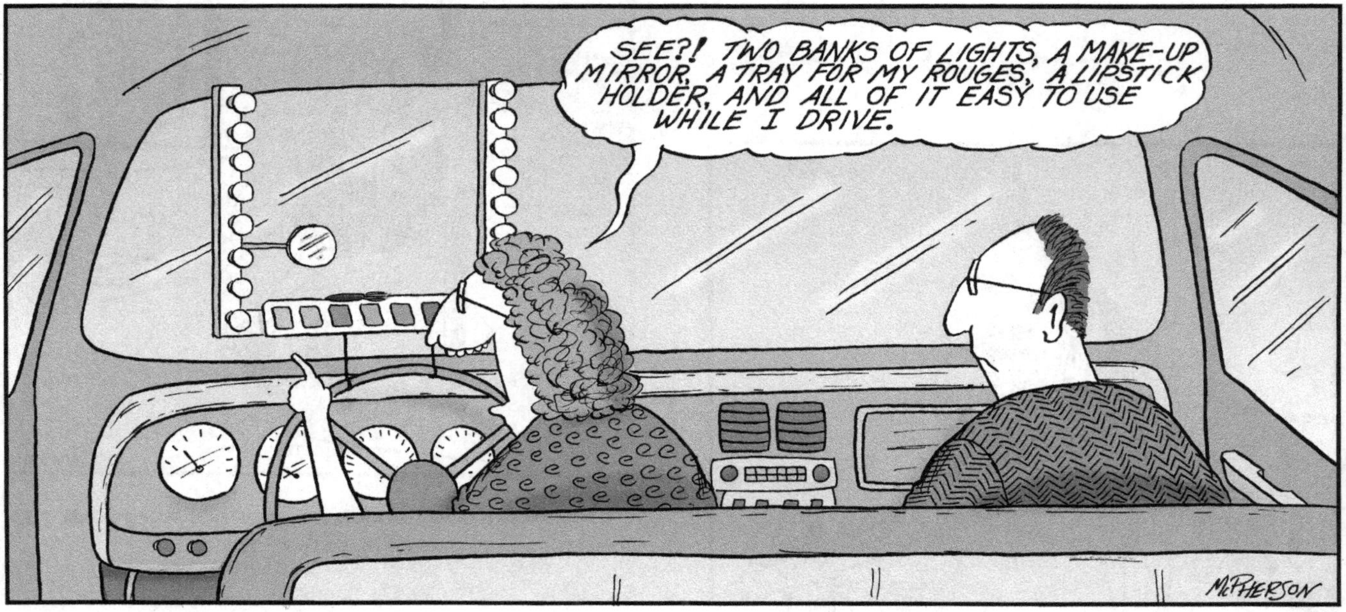
SEE?! TWO BANKS OF LIGHTS, A MAKE-UP MIRROR, A TRAY FOR MY ROUGES, A LIPSTICK HOLDER, AND ALL OF IT EASY TO USE WHILE I DRIVE.
McPHERSON

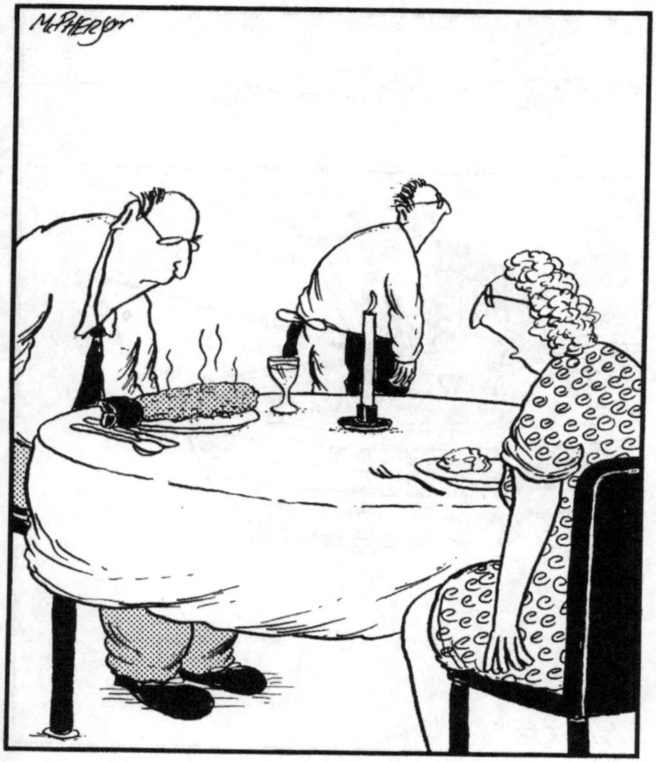

"I warned you not to order the prime rib this late in the evening."

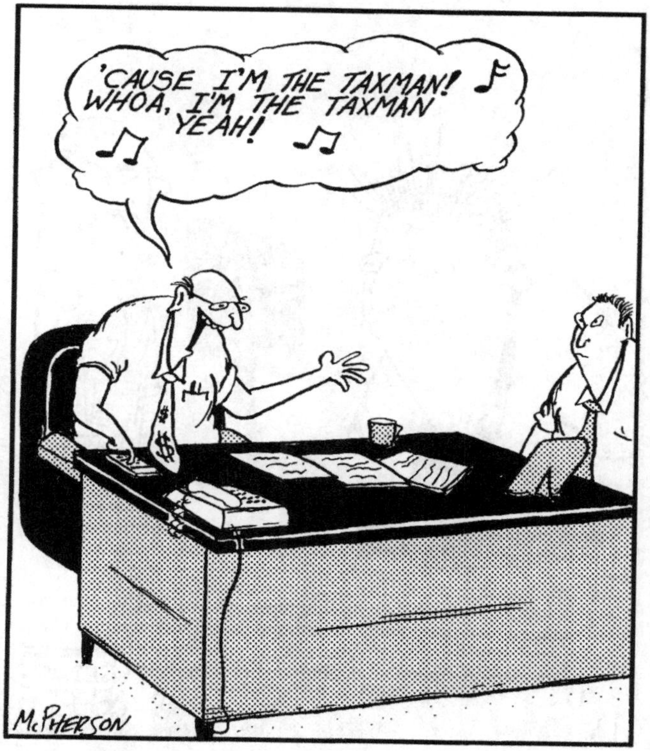
'CAUSE I'M THE TAXMAN! WHOA, I'M THE TAXMAN YEAH!

The IRS auditor quickly started to get on Ed's nerves.

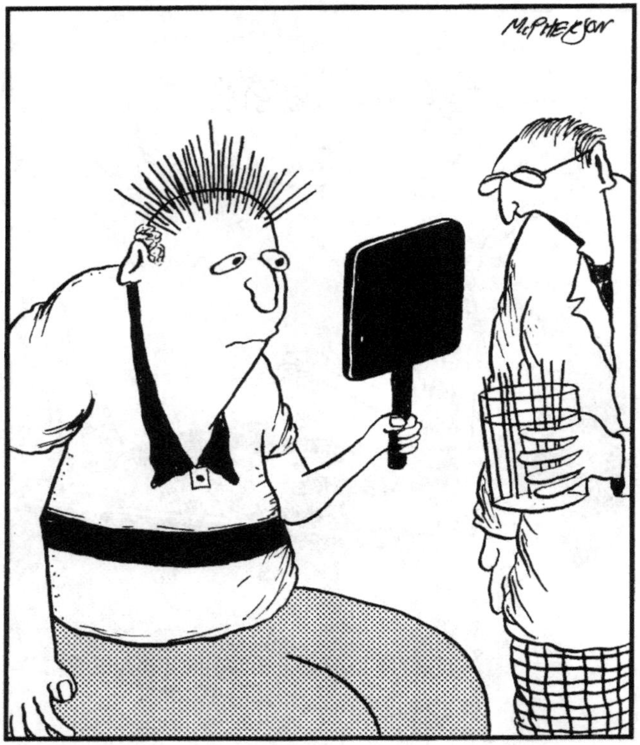
McPHERSON

"No, you misunderstood me. I said I could use acupuncture needles to simulate hair growth, not stimulate hair growth."

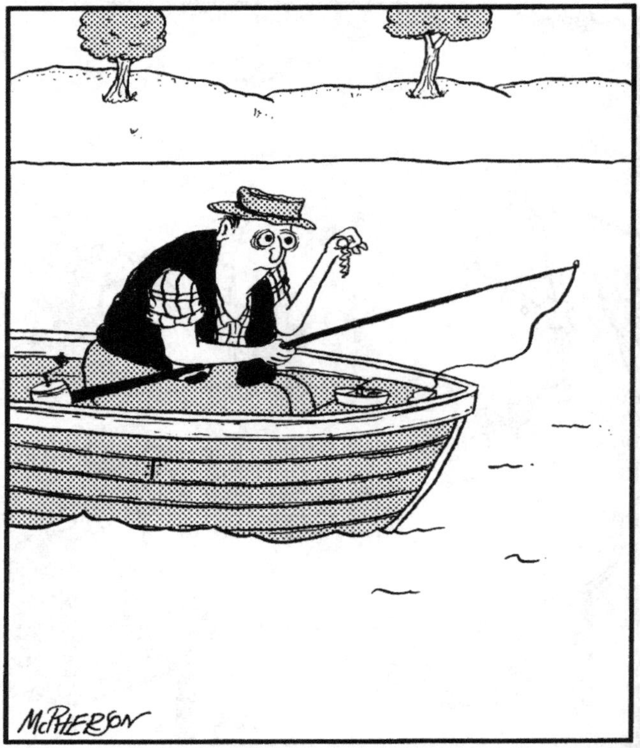
McPHERSON

Realizing that he was trying to bait his hook with a piece of his wife's pasta salad, it suddenly dawned on Dave why lunch had disagreed with him so much.

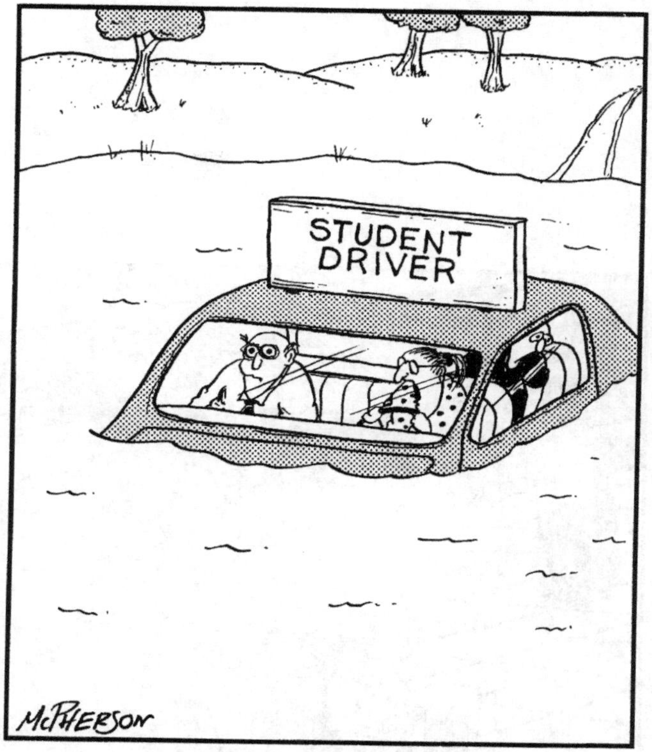
STUDENT DRIVER
McPHERSON

"In all fairness, you never covered 'Bridge out' signs in class."

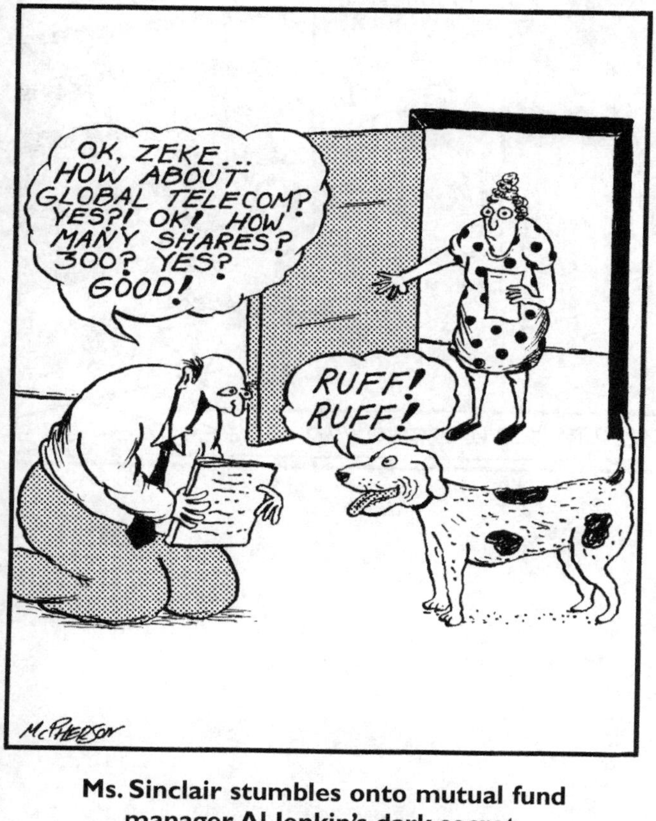
OK, ZEKE... HOW ABOUT GLOBAL TELECOM? YES?! OK! HOW MANY SHARES? 300? YES? GOOD!
RUFF! RUFF!
McPHERSON

Ms. Sinclair stumbles onto mutual fund manager Al Jenkin's dark secret.

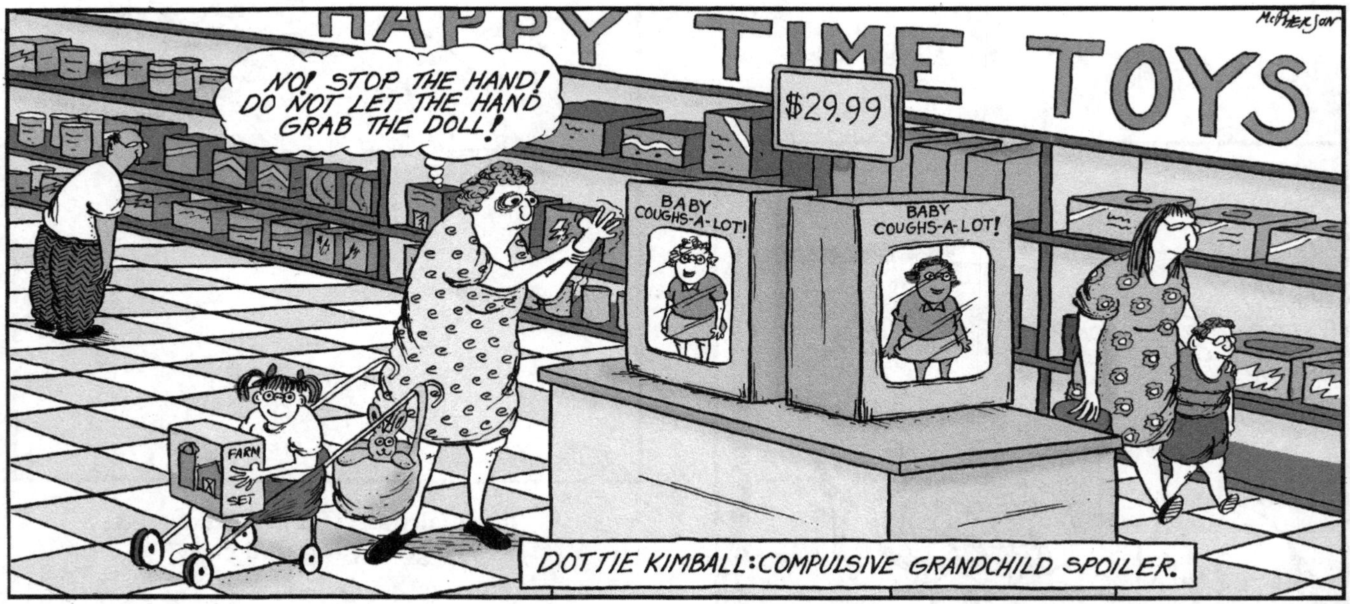
HAPPY TIME TOYS
NO! STOP THE HAND! DO NOT LET THE HAND GRAB THE DOLL!
$29.99
BABY COUGHS-A-LOT!
BABY COUGHS-A-LOT!
FARM SET
McPHERSON
DOTTIE KIMBALL: COMPULSIVE GRANDCHILD SPOILER.

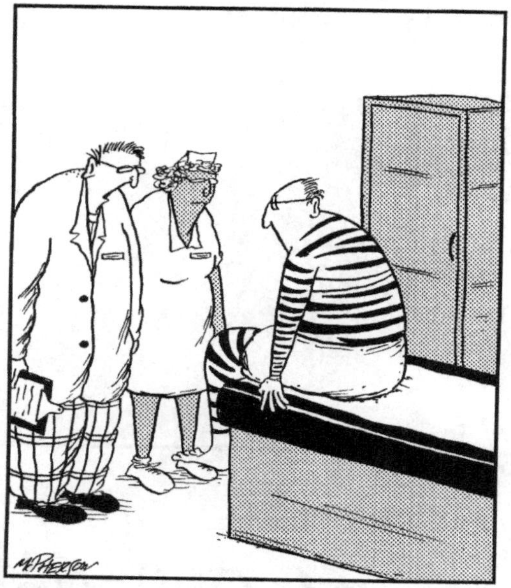
McPherson

"The bad news is we have no idea what's wrong with you. The good news is the Ringling Brothers wants to hire you."

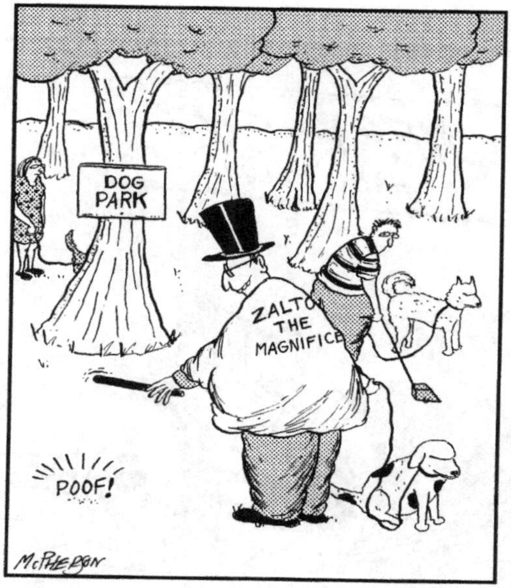
DOG PARK
ZALTO THE MAGNIFICE
POOF!
McPherson

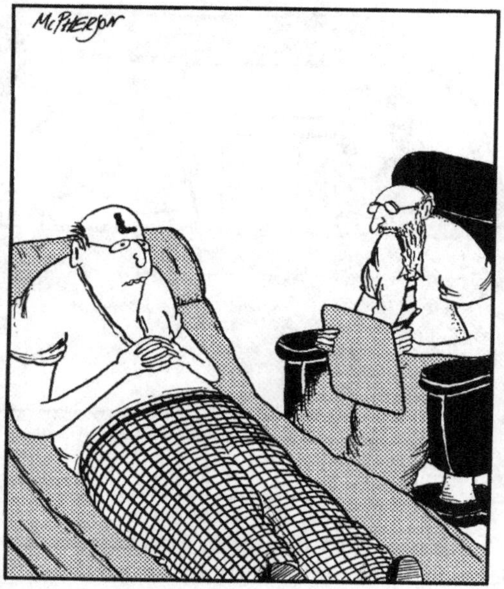
McPherson

"Have you ever considered the possibility that your feelings of inadequacy may be affected by the birth-mark on your forehead?"

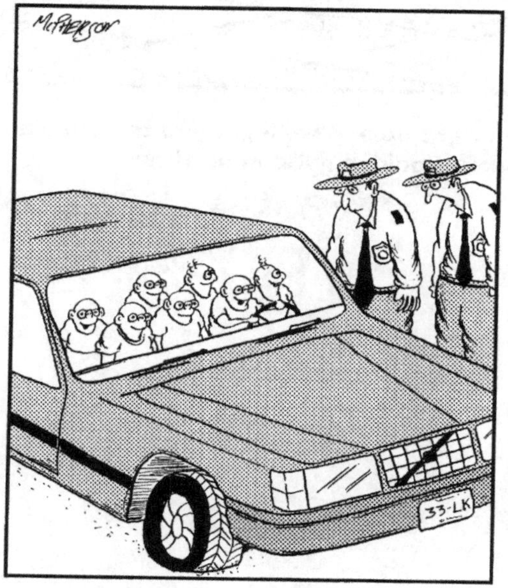
McPherson
33-LK

"I've got a hunch this ties in with those eleven cases of formula that were stolen from Food Baron."

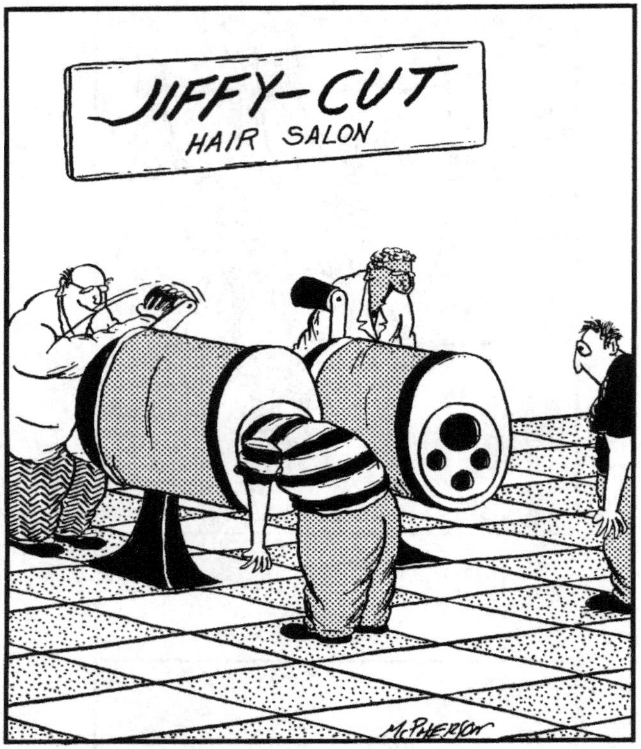
JIFFY-CUT
HAIR SALON

"Step right up and we'll get you trimmed and looking good in no time."

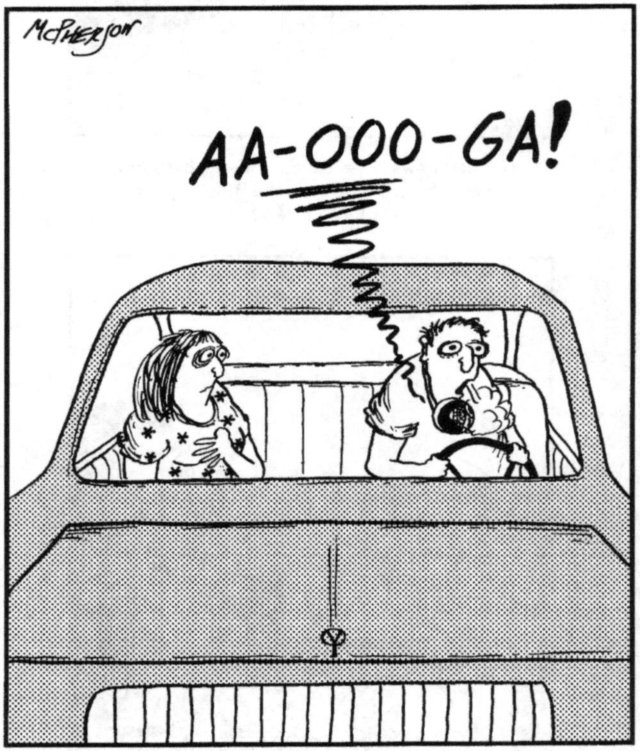
AA-OOO-GA!

Midway into the date, Brian's halitosis detector alerted him to a potential problem.

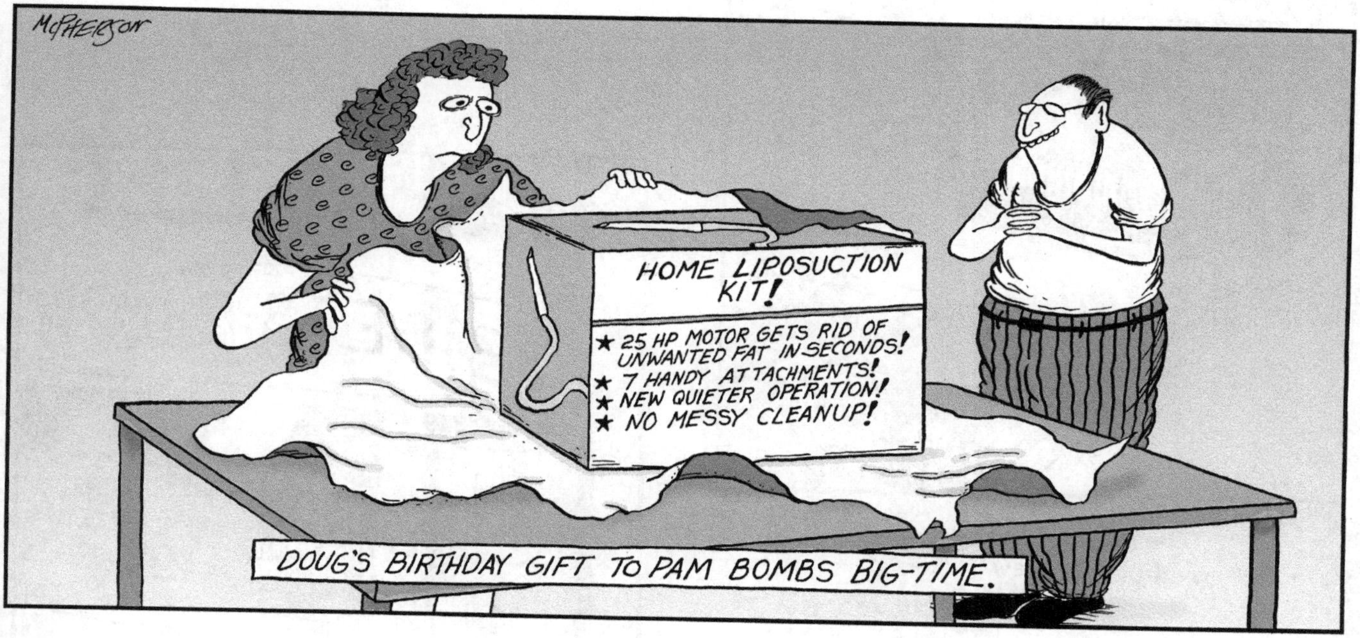
McPHERSON
HOME LIPOSUCTION KIT!
★ 25 HP MOTOR GETS RID OF UNWANTED FAT IN SECONDS!
★ 7 HANDY ATTACHMENTS!
★ NEW QUIETER OPERATION!
★ NO MESSY CLEANUP!
DOUG'S BIRTHDAY GIFT TO PAM BOMBS BIG-TIME.

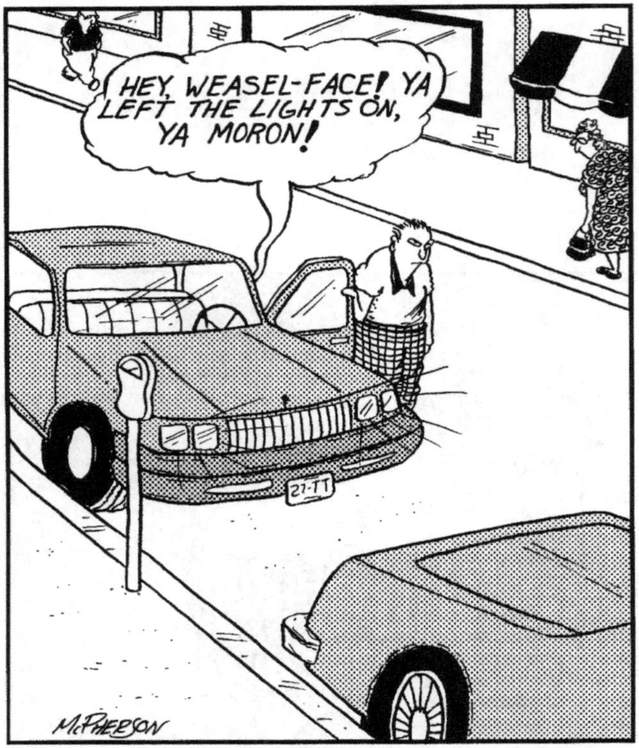
HEY, WEASEL-FACE! YA LEFT THE LIGHTS ON, YA MORON!
27-TT
McPHERSON

The downside of owning a Chrysler New Yorker.

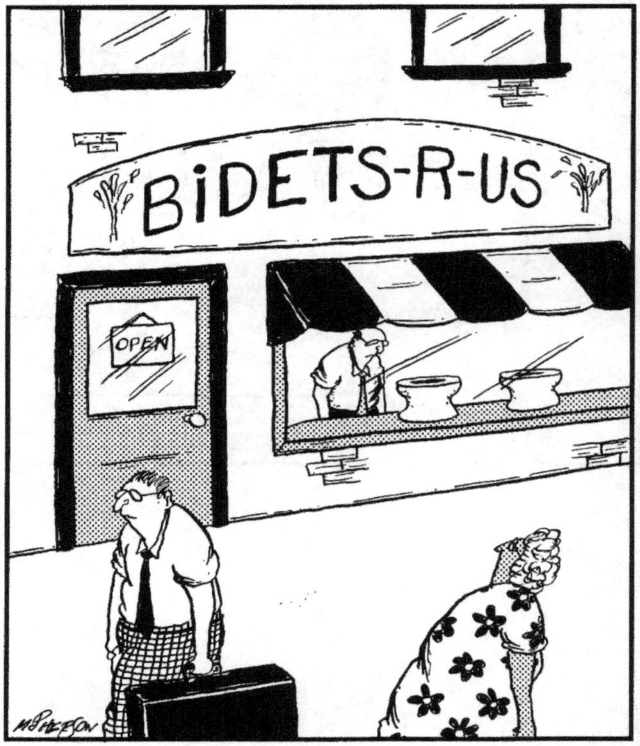
BIDETS-R-US
OPEN
McPHERSON

One of the top five worst franchises in America.

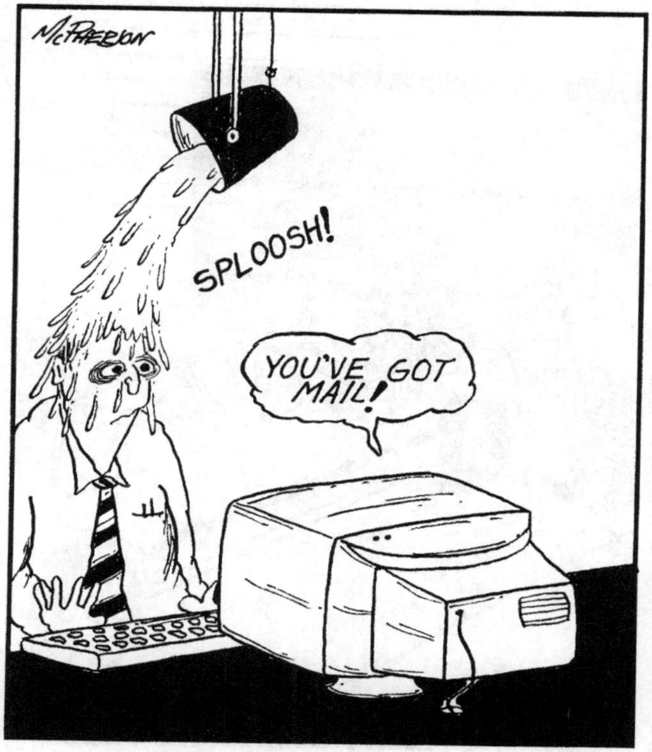
McPHERSON
SPLOOSH!
YOU'VE GOT MAIL!

At the National E-Mail Addiction Rehabilitation Center.

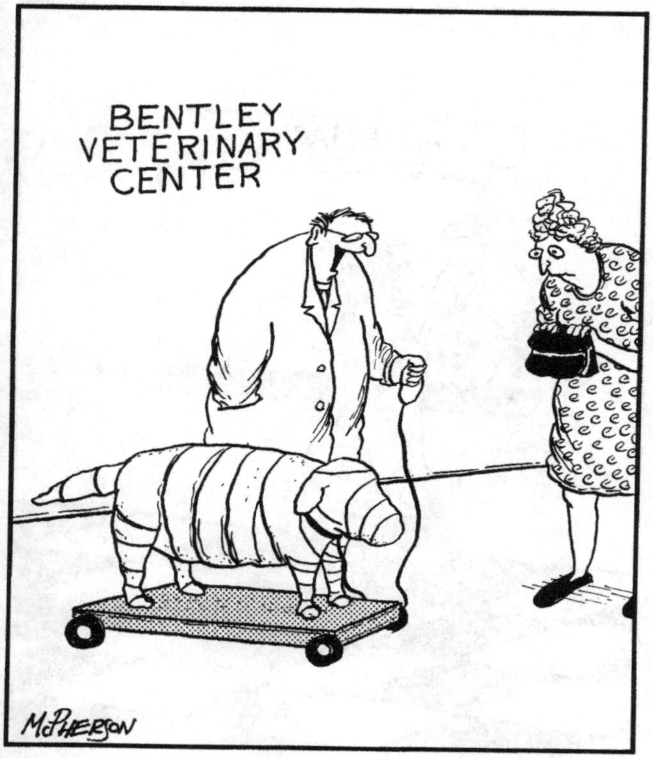
BENTLEY VETERINARY CENTER
McPHERSON

"There you go, Mrs. Keser! Good as new!"

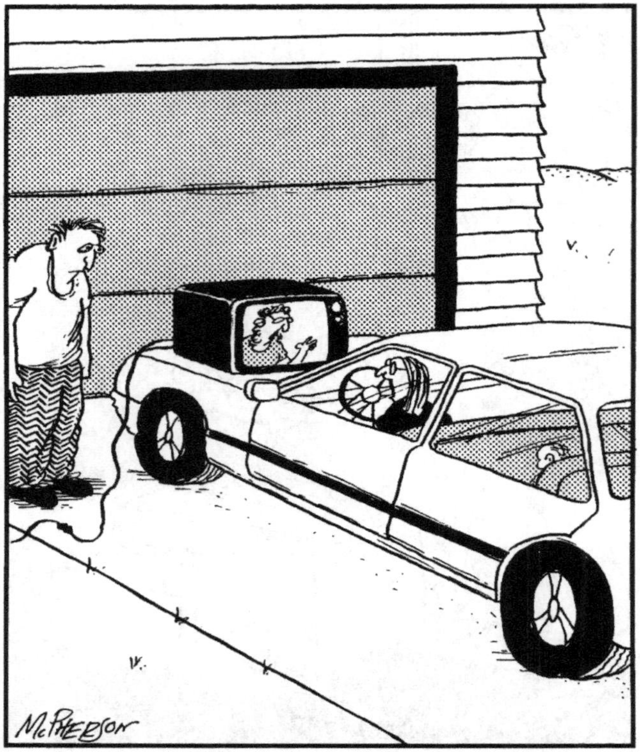

"The baby fell asleep just as I was pulling into the driveway, so I'm killing some time out here."

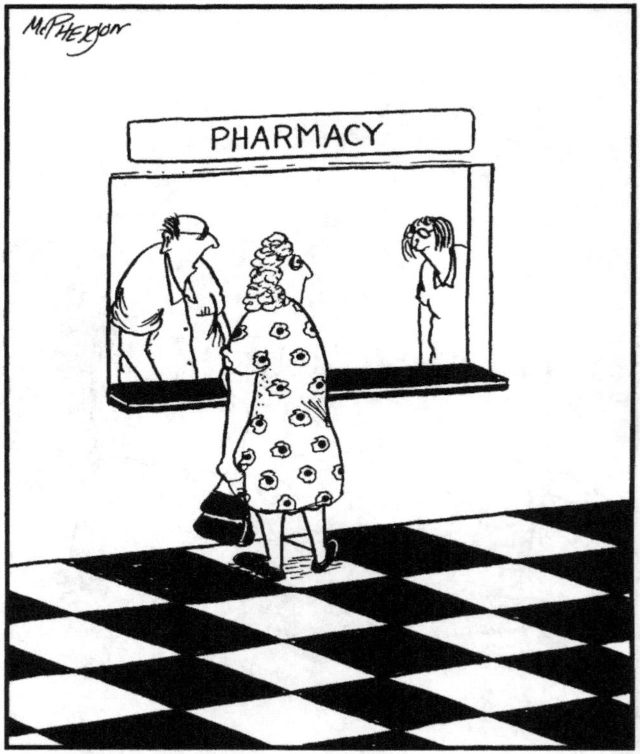
PHARMACY

"I'm gonna need some of that blue gunk mixed with a bottle of the red glop, and throw in a pinch of that stinky black goo while you're at it."

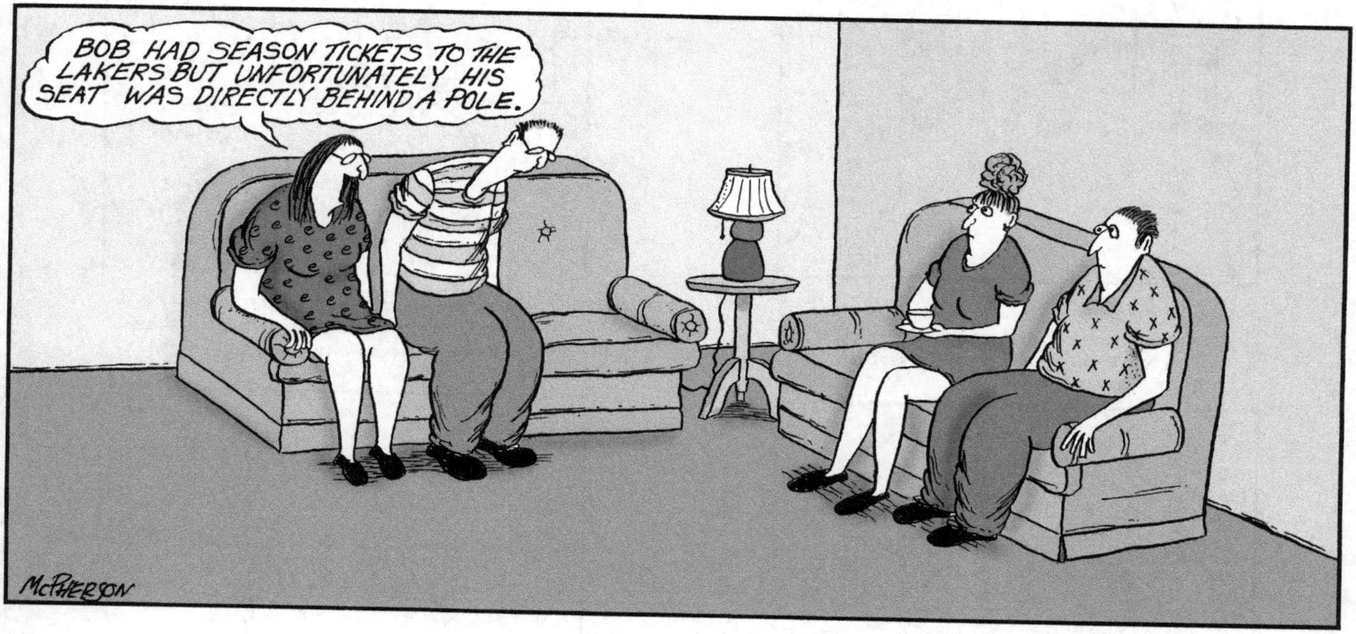
BOB HAD SEASON TICKETS TO THE LAKERS BUT UNFORTUNATELY HIS SEAT WAS DIRECTLY BEHIND A POLE.
McPHERSON

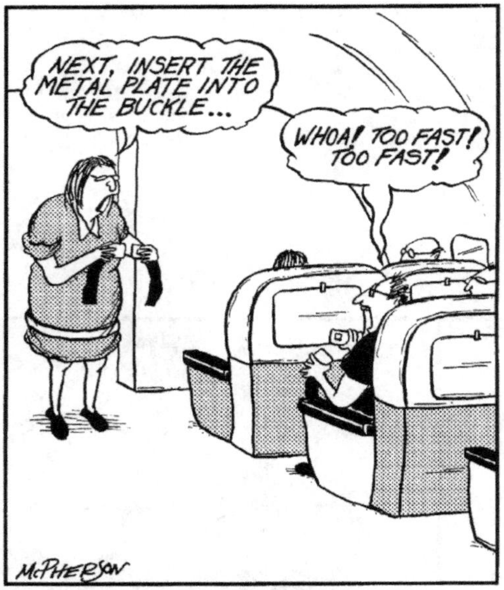
NEXT, INSERT THE METAL PLATE INTO THE BUCKLE...
WHOA! TOO FAST! TOO FAST!
MCPHERSON

August 21, 2000: Airline history is made when Dwayne Gertz becomes the first person to truly not know how to buckle a seatbelt.

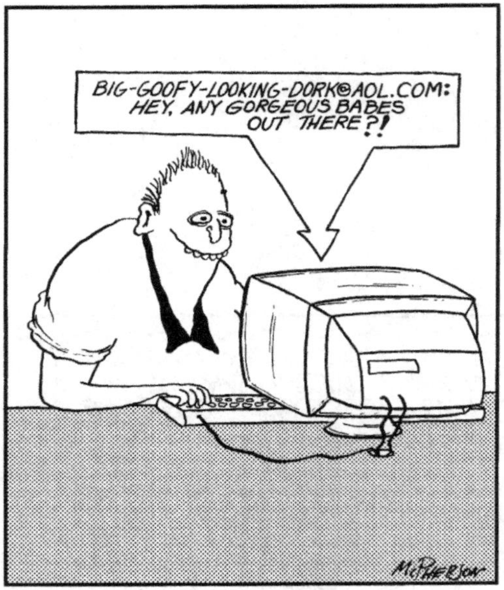
BIG-GOOFY-LOOKING-DORK@AOL.COM: HEY, ANY GORGEOUS BABES OUT THERE?!
MCPHERSON

It took Denny several months to make the connection between his screen name and his inability to meet women in chat rooms.

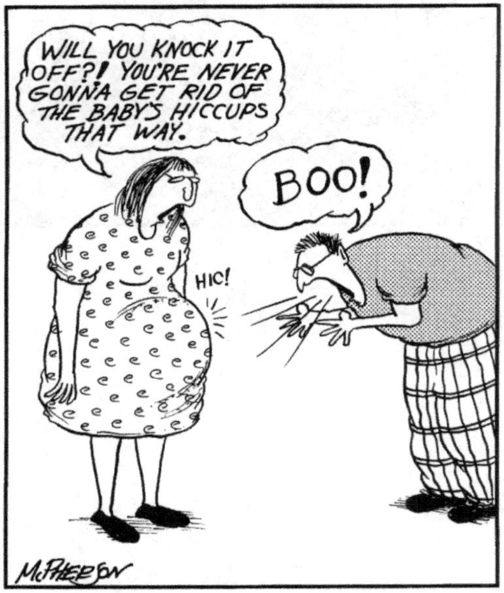
WILL YOU KNOCK IT OFF?! YOU'RE NEVER GONNA GET RID OF THE BABY'S HICCUPS THAT WAY.
BOO!
HIC!
MCPHERSON

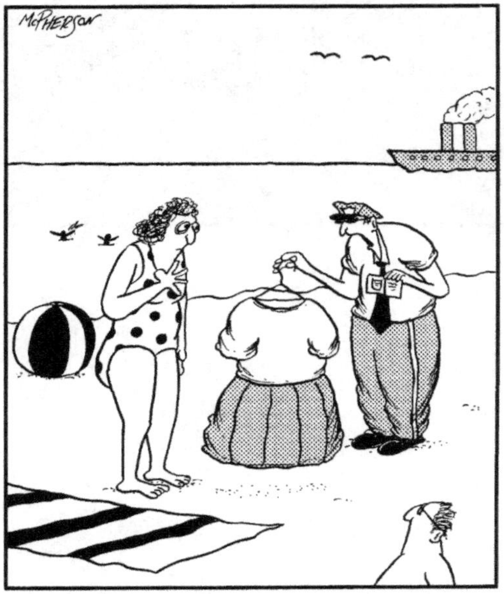
MCPHERSON

"Spandex Police, ma'am! I'm going to have to ask that you put this on immediately!"

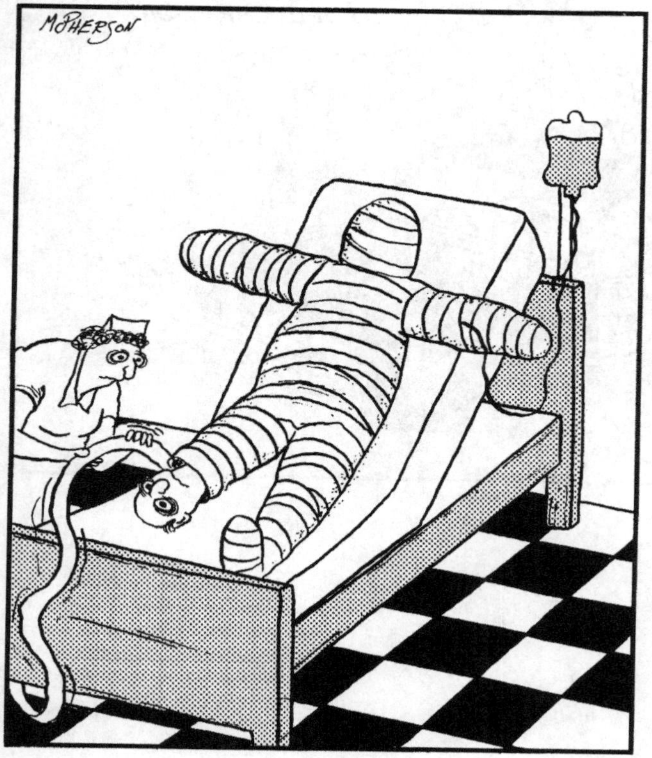
McPHERSON

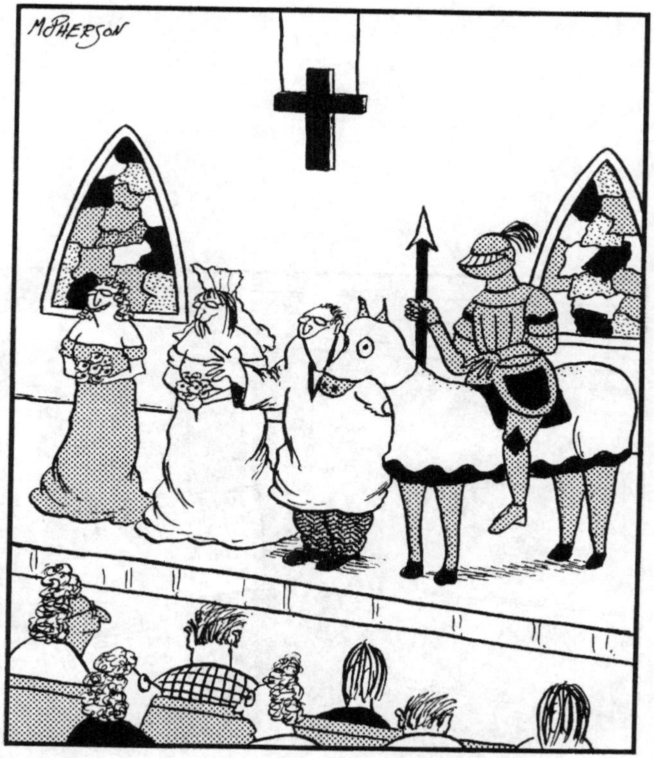
McPHERSON

"She kept raving about her knight in shining armor, but I just thought it was an expression."

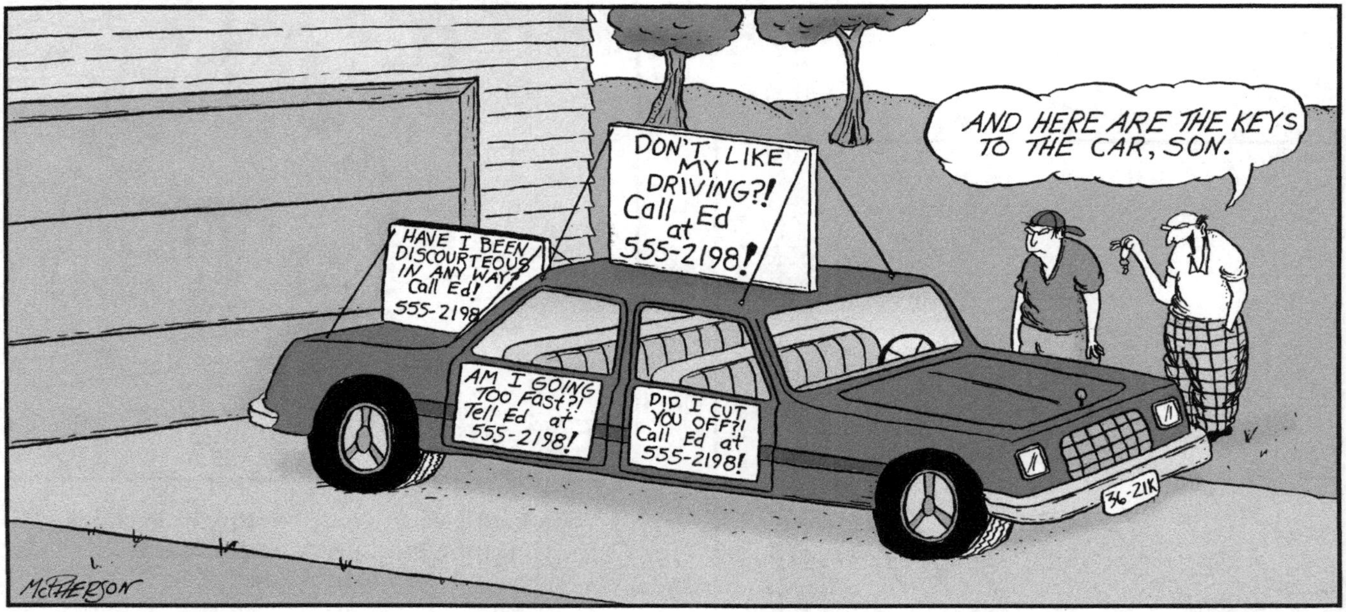
AND HERE ARE THE KEYS TO THE CAR, SON.
DON'T LIKE MY DRIVING?! Call Ed at 555-2198!
HAVE I BEEN DISCOURTEOUS IN ANY WAY? Call Ed! 555-2198
AM I GOING TOO Fast?! Tell Ed at 555-2198!
DID I CUT YOU OFF?! Call Ed at 555-2198!
36-21K
McPHERSON

McPHERSON
ZIPPY-FREEZE
CRYOGENICS
ZEFFLE
MERKLE

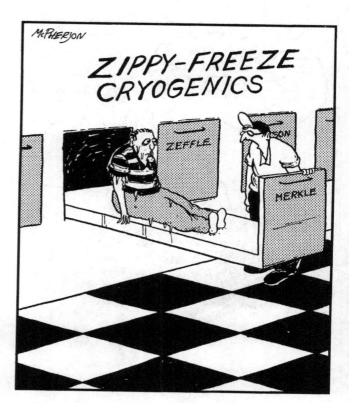

"The good news is they finally found a cure for you. The bad news is you owe $276,000 for an overdue library book."

McPHERSON
CONQUER YOUR FEAR OF HEIGHTS
SELF HELP

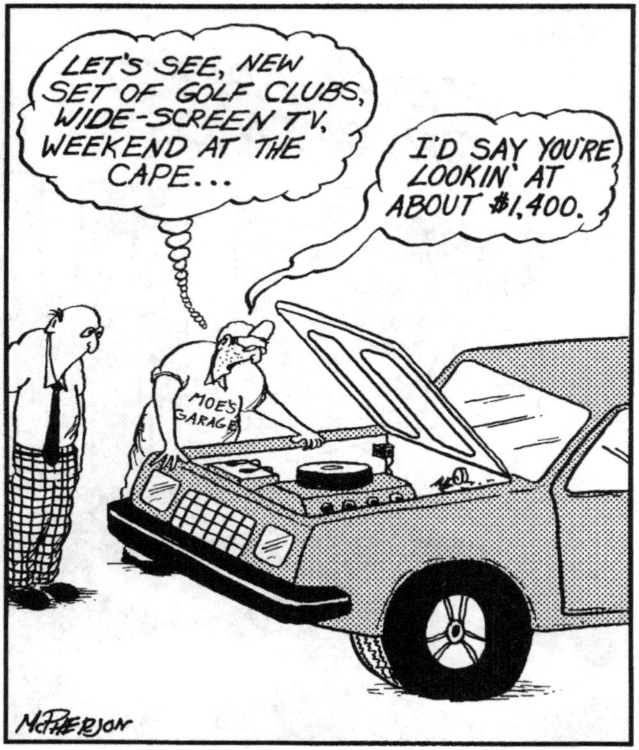
LET'S SEE, NEW SET OF GOLF CLUBS, WIDE-SCREEN TV, WEEKEND AT THE CAPE...
I'D SAY YOU'RE LOOKIN' AT ABOUT $1,400.
MOE'S GARAGE
MCPHERSON

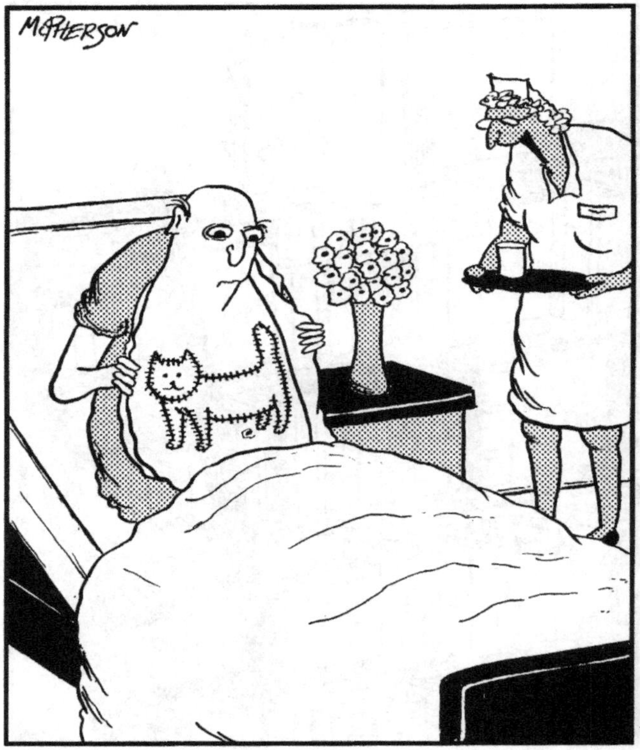
MCPHERSON

"The surgeon who worked on you is an avid cross-stitcher."

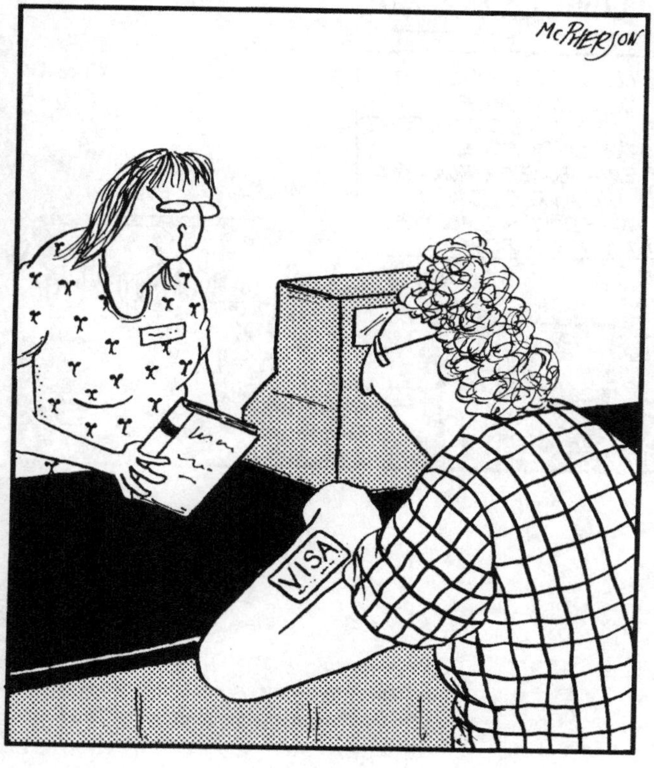
McPHERSON
VISA

To help combat fraud, many credit card companies are turning to implants.

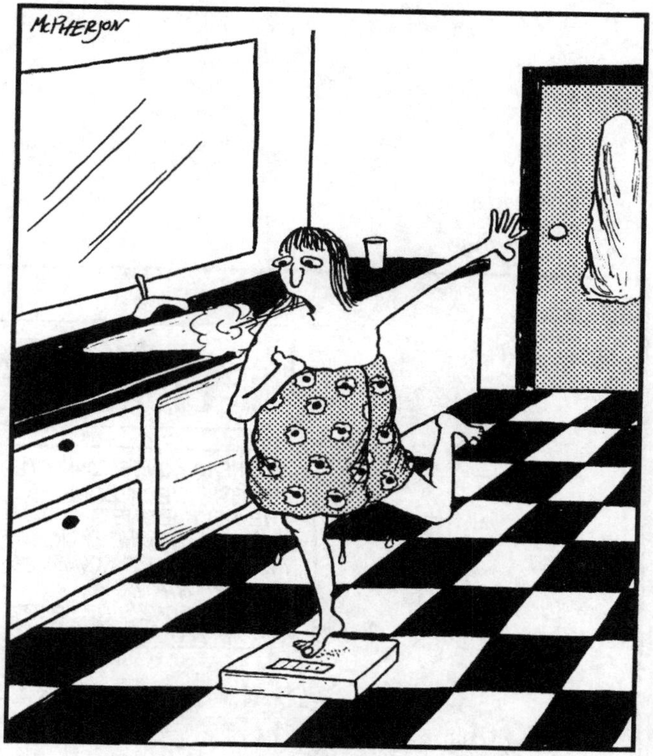
McPHERSON

By standing on one foot, holding her left arm at a fifty-two-degree angle, and exhaling, Carol was able to get the scale to read a half-pound lighter.

McPHERSON
NORTHEAST MEDICAL SKELETON CO.
• THE HEAD BONE'S CONNECTED TO THE NECK BONE.
• THE NECK BONE'S CONNECTED TO THE BACKBONE
• THE BACKBONE'S CONNECTED TO THE HIP BONE.
• THE HIP BONE'S CONNECTED TO THE LEG BONE.
• THE LEG BONE'S CONNECTED TO THE KNEE BONE
• THE KNEE BONE'S CONNECTED TO THE SHIN BONE.
• THE SHIN BONE'S CONNECTED TO THE ANKLE BONE.
• THE ANKLE BONE'S CONNECTED TO THE FOOT BONE.
HEAD BONES

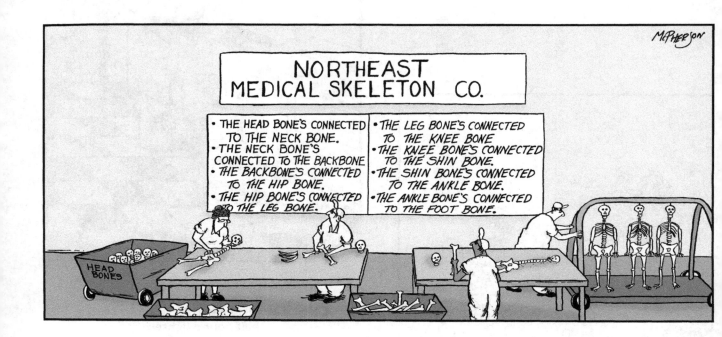

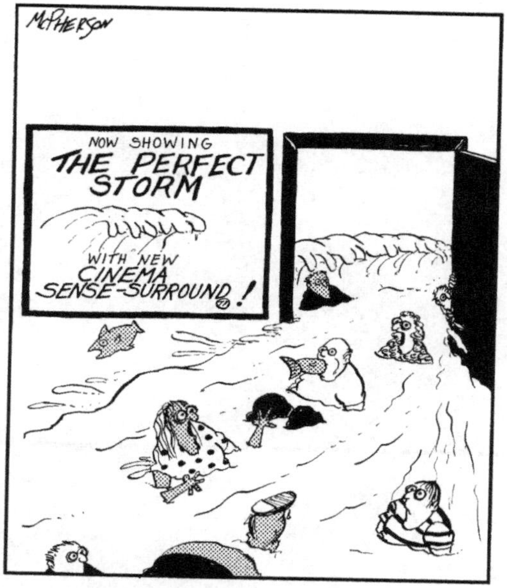
McPHERSON
NOW SHOWING
THE PERFECT STORM
WITH NEW CINEMA SENSE-SURROUND!

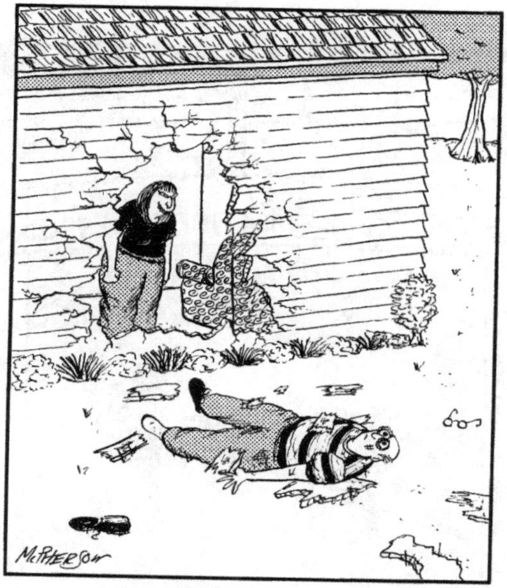
McPHERSON

Carl makes a mental note to never again make snide remarks about Barbara's aerobic kickboxing class.

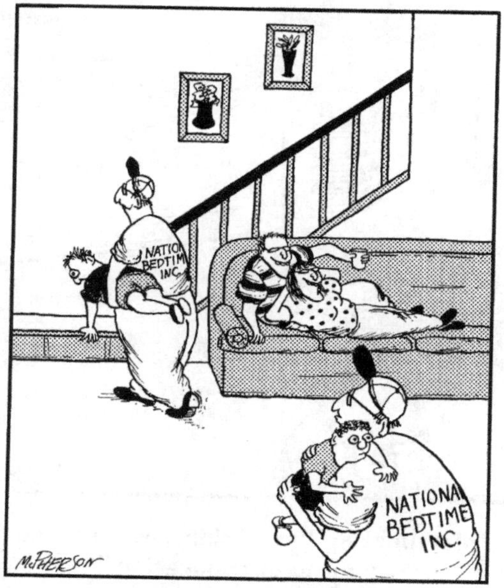
NATIONAL BEDTIME INC.
McPHERSON

Evenings became much more serene for the Wertners once they hired a professional bedtime service.

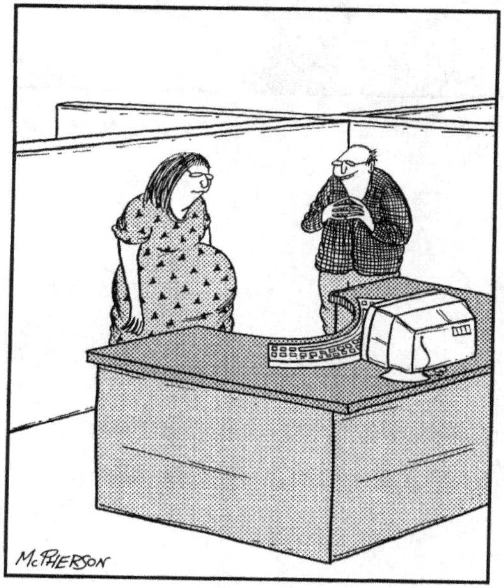
McPHERSON

Managers at Gilmont Industries prided themselves in going all out to accommodate pregnant employees.

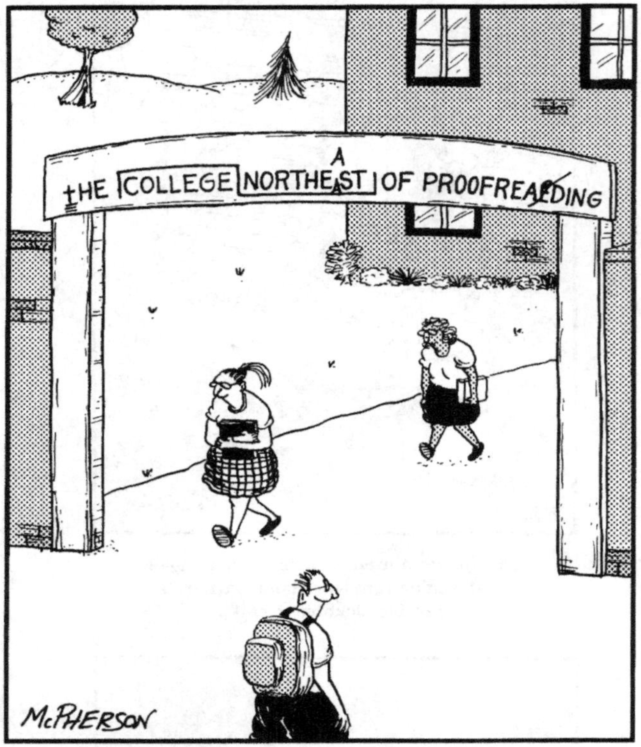
tHE COLLEGE NORTHEAST OF PROOFREADING
McPHERSON

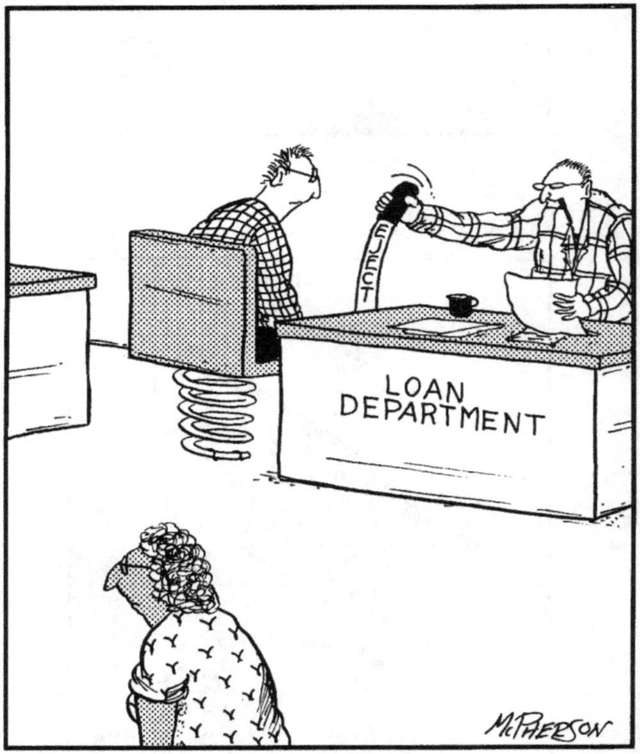
EJECT
LOAN DEPARTMENT
McPHERSON

"Unfortunately, Mr. Simkins, we must decline your loan application."

AS USUAL, THE FERGUSONS DECOY PICNIC WORKED TO PERFECTION.

McPHERSON

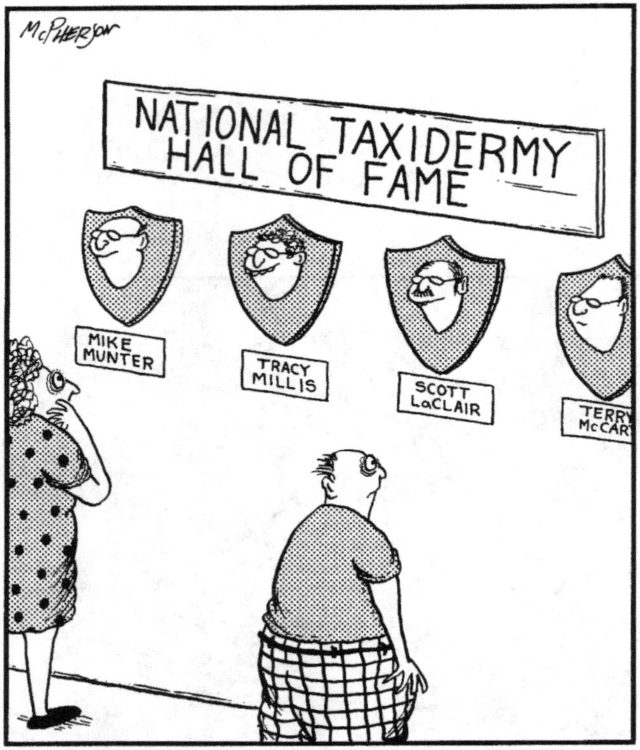
McPHERSON
NATIONAL TAXIDERMY HALL OF FAME
MIKE MUNTER
TRACY MILLIS
SCOTT LaCLAIR

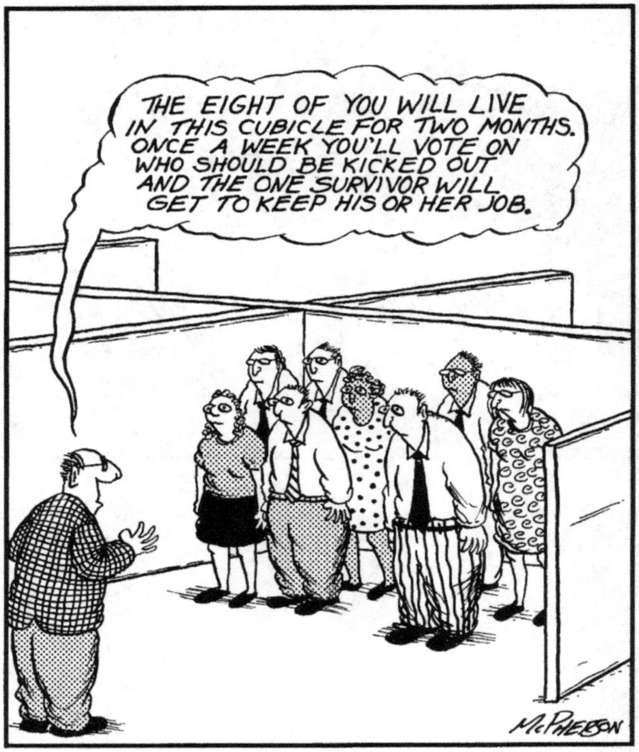
THE EIGHT OF YOU WILL LIVE IN THIS CUBICLE FOR TWO MONTHS. ONCE A WEEK YOU'LL VOTE ON WHO SHOULD BE KICKED OUT AND THE ONE SURVIVOR WILL GET TO KEEP HIS OR HER JOB.
McPHERSON

Inspired by recent television events, Millis Industries devised a new way to downsize.

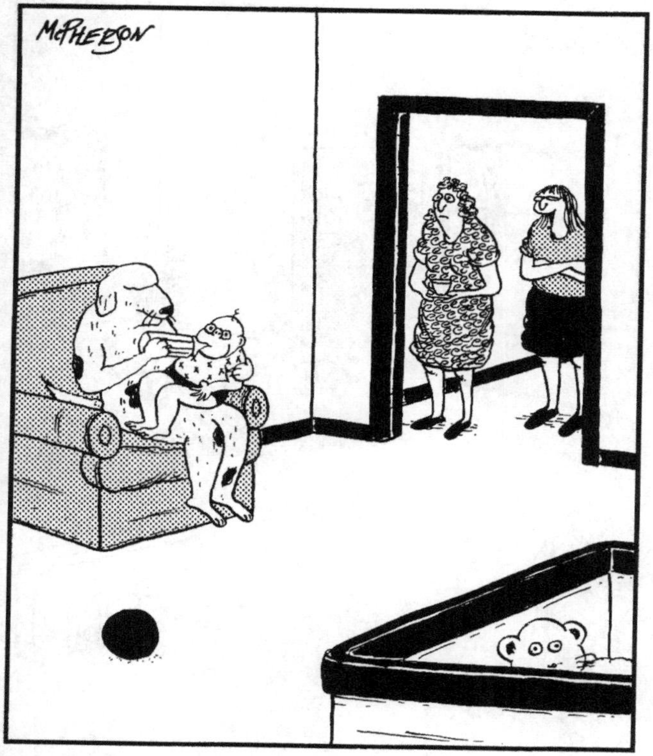
McPHERSON

"We had heard that this breed was good with kids, but I just had no idea!"

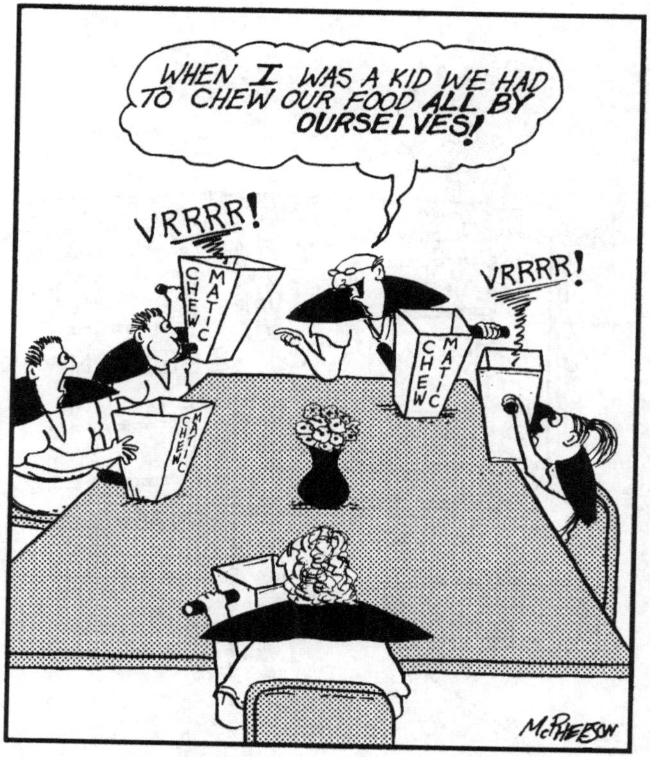
WHEN I WAS A KID WE HAD TO CHEW OUR FOOD ALL BY OURSELVES!
VRRRR!
CHEW MATIC
VRRRR!
CHEW MATIC
CHEW MATIC
McPHERSON

Grandfather stories in 2080.

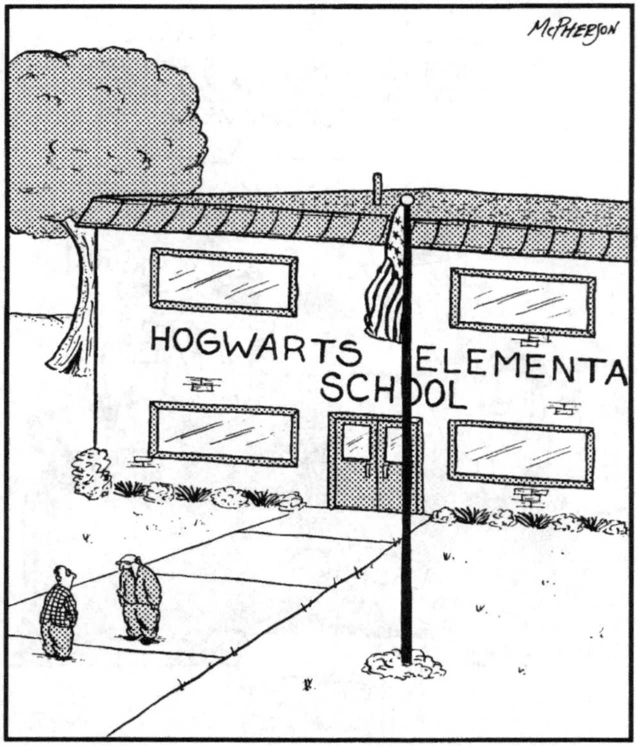
McPHERSON
HOGWARTS ELEMENTA
SCHOOL

"The school board voted to change the name from Erwin Valley to Hogwarts Elementary, and we've had perfect attendance ever since."

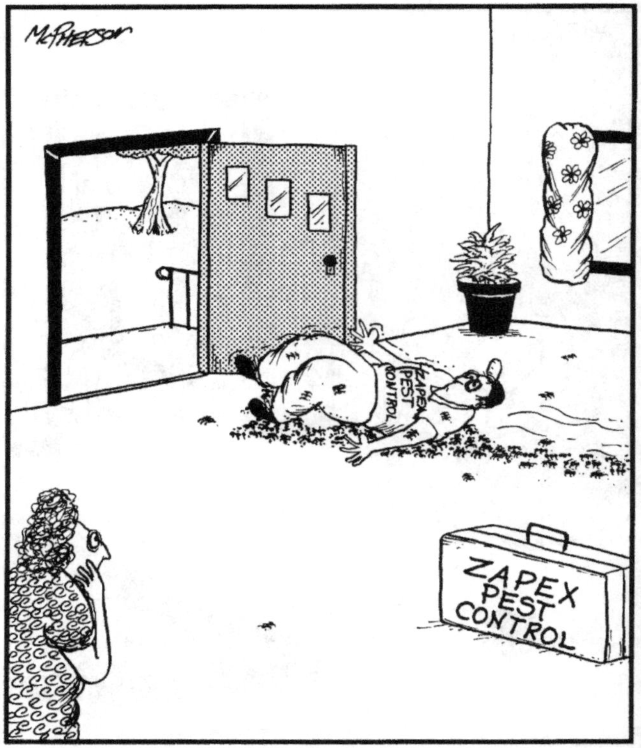
McPHERSON
ZAPEX PEST CONTROL
ZAPEX PEST CONTROL

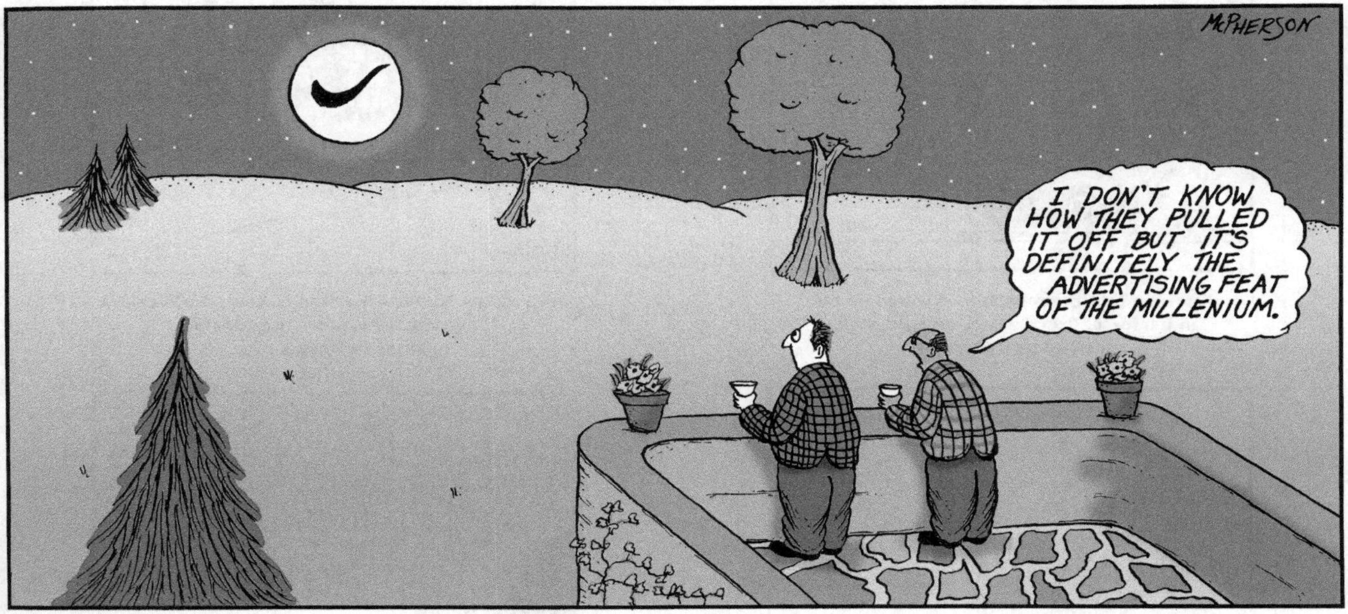
McPHERSON
I DON'T KNOW HOW THEY PULLED IT OFF BUT IT'S DEFINITELY THE ADVERTISING FEAT OF THE MILLENIUM.

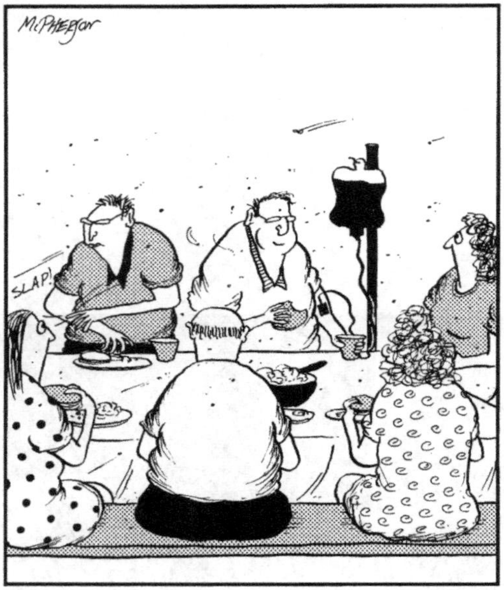
SLAP!

Knowing that the mosquitoes would be out in full force, Bruce wisely brought along a spare pint of blood.

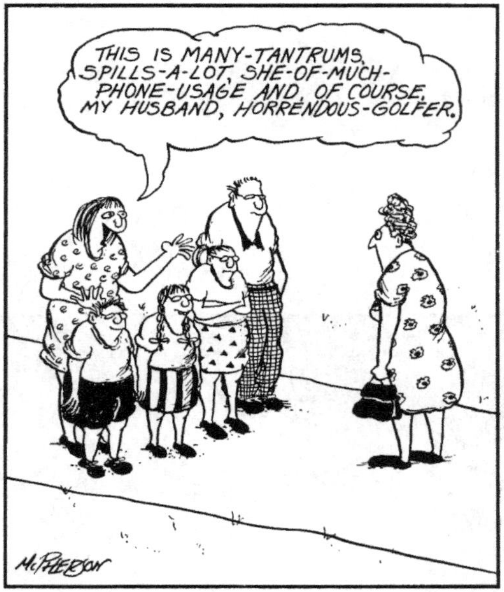
THIS IS MANY-TANTRUMS, SPILLS-A-LOT, SHE-OF-MUCH-PHONE-USAGE AND, OF COURSE, MY HUSBAND, HORRENDOUS-GOLFER.

Inspired by Native American culture, the Waxleys adopted new, more meaningful names for themselves.

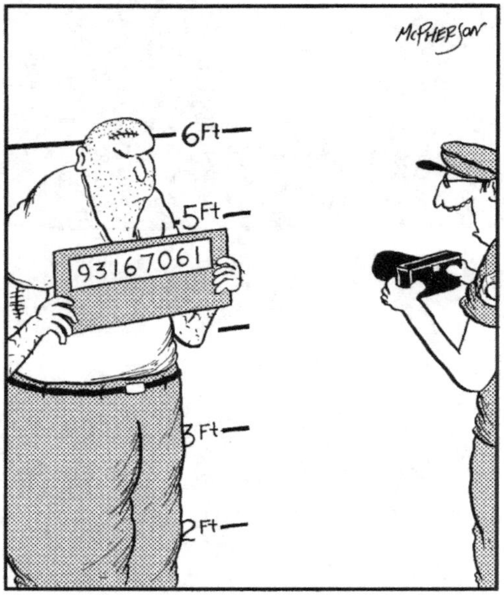
6Ft
5Ft
93167061
3Ft
2Ft

"Would you like some extra copies to give to friends and relatives?"

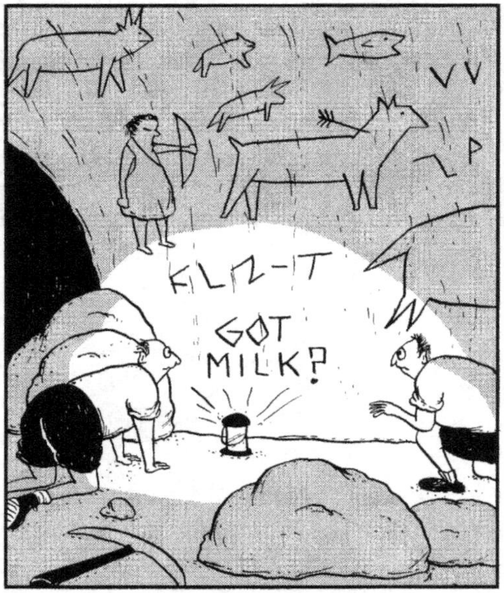
GOT MILK?

Out of concern for the ninety-seven-year-old bride and groom's health, the wedding goers wisely threw the birdseed underhand.

The downside of wearing diapers to the beach.

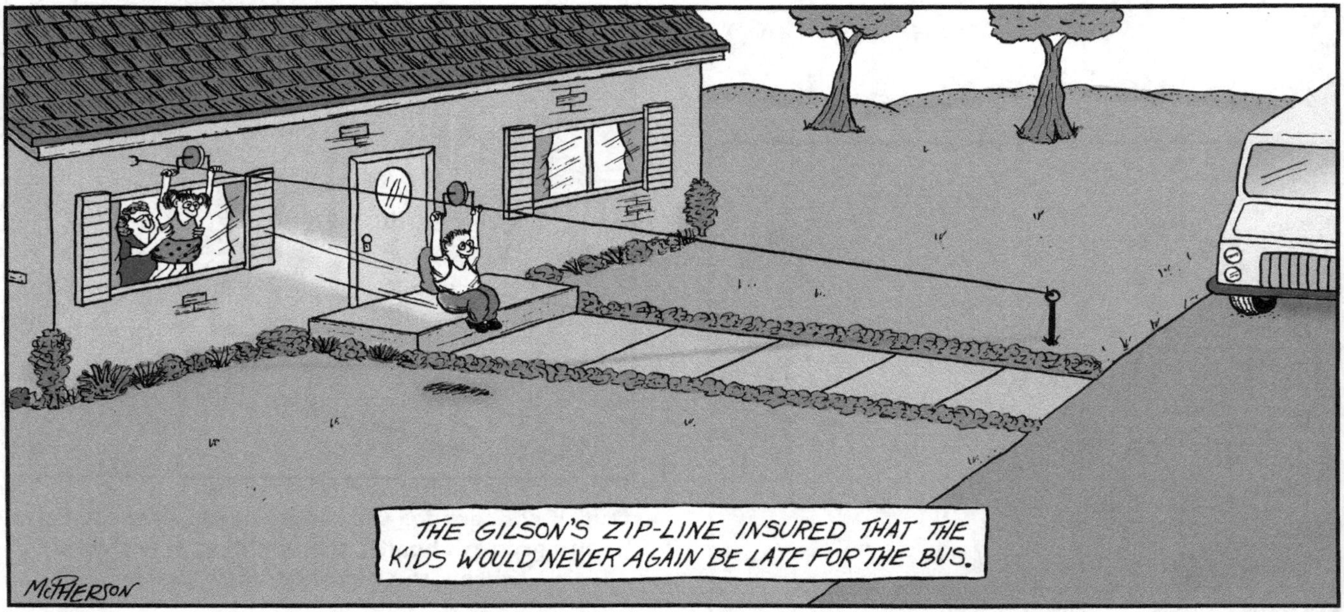
THE GILSON'S ZIP-LINE INSURED THAT THE KIDS WOULD NEVER AGAIN BE LATE FOR THE BUS.
MCPHERSON

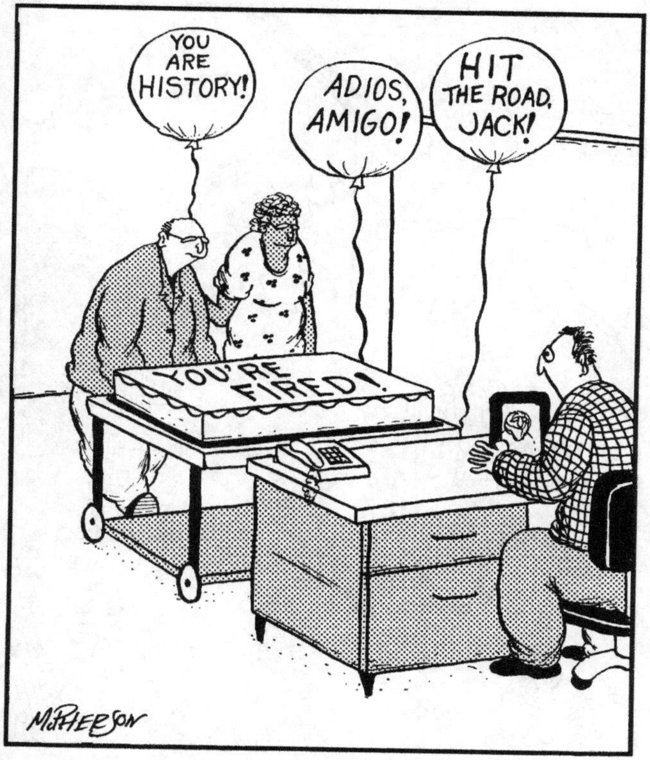
YOU ARE HISTORY!
ADIOS, AMIGO!
HIT THE ROAD, JACK!
YOU'RE FIRED!
McPHERSON

Loathing the task of letting employees go, managers at Eckford Industries did their best to soften the blow.

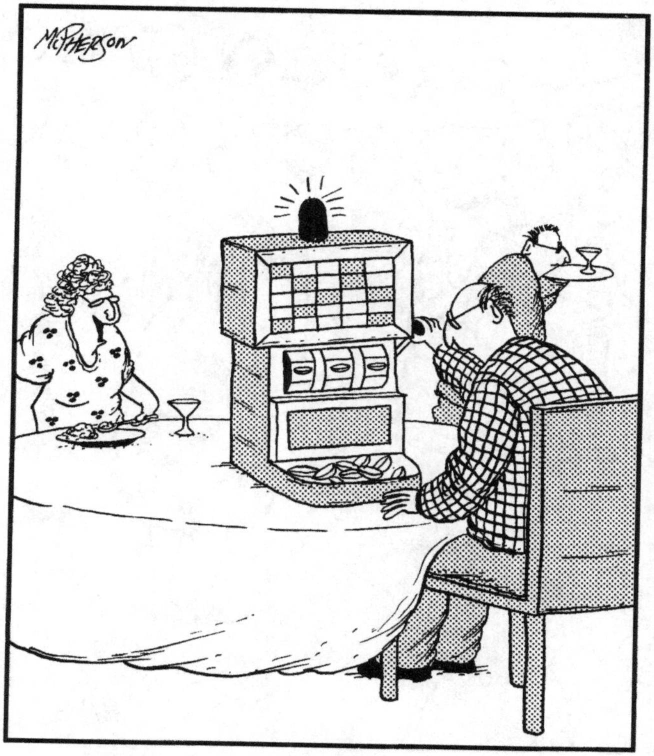
McPHERSON

"How are your clams casino, dear?"

"Me? I worked in an ice cream parlor all summer. How about you? What did you do this summer?"

"It's OK. I saved the receipt!"

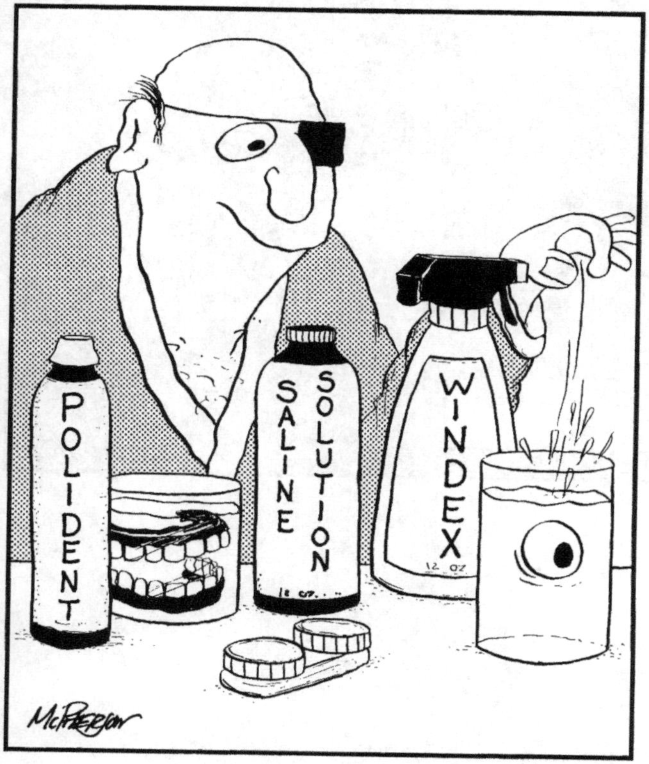
POLIDENT
SALINE SOLUTION
WINDEX
12 OZ
McPherson

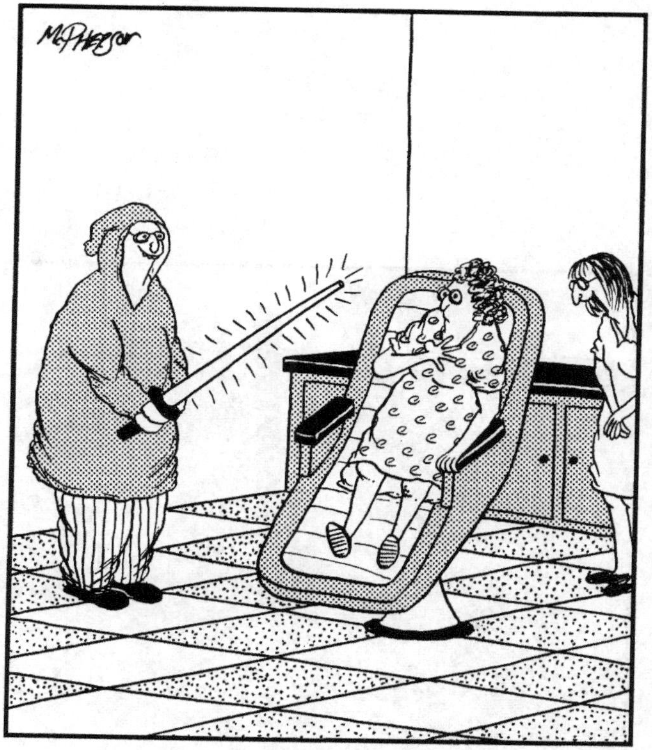
McPherson

"Just so you know, Dr. Wazley likes to be referred to as Obi-Wan Kenobi whenever he performs laser eye surgery."

THUNK!

NO. 7 PAR 4 420 YDS.

KURT'S EXPLODING GOLFBALL GAG GOES HORRIBLY AWRY.

McPHERSON

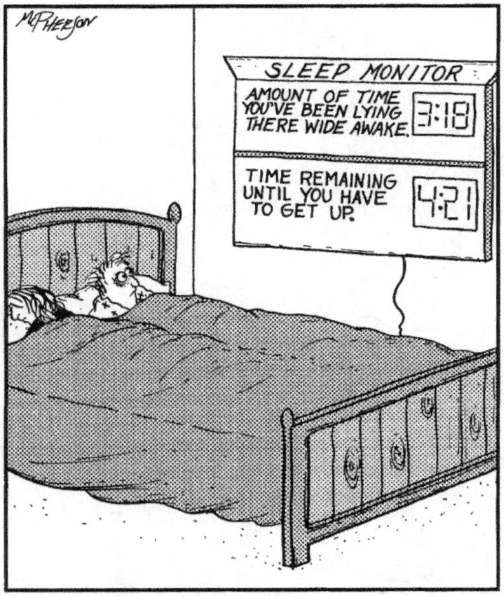
McPHERSON
SLEEP MONITOR
AMOUNT OF TIME YOU'VE BEEN LYING THERE WIDE AWAKE.
3:18
TIME REMAINING UNTIL YOU HAVE TO GET UP.
4:21

When technology is bad.

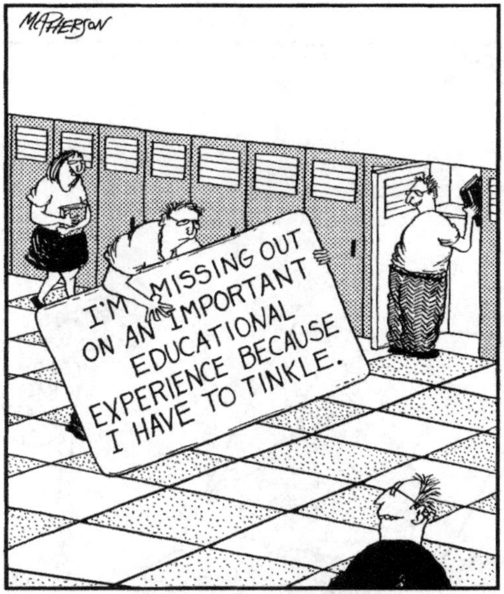
McPHERSON
I'M MISSING OUT ON AN IMPORTANT EDUCATIONAL EXPERIENCE BECAUSE I HAVE TO TINKLE.

The school's new hall passes proved to be extremely effective in discouraging frivolous trips to the restroom.

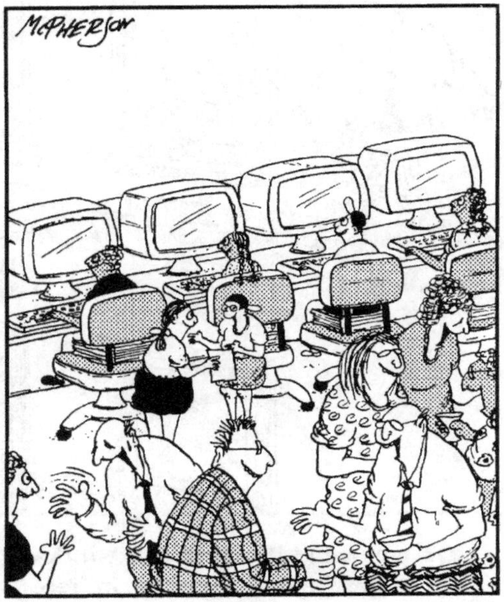
McPHERSON

When productivity soared 40 percent after the first Take Your Child to Work Day, the event was instituted on a weekly basis.

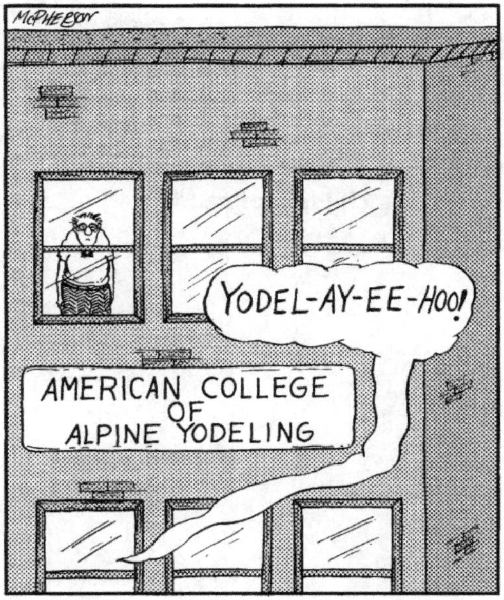
McPHERSON
YODEL-AY-EE-HOO!
AMERICAN COLLEGE OF ALPINE YODELING

Suddenly, Bruce understood why he'd been able to get his apartment for half the price of comparable apartments.

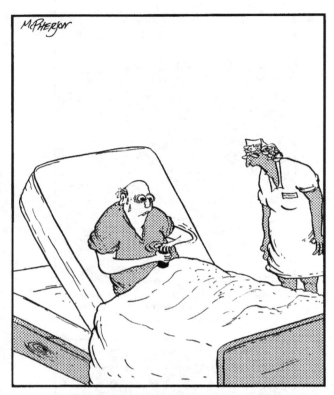

"Please keep trying, Mr. Fuller. We can't discharge you until you prove to us that you can open a childproof cap."

"Do you mind if I close this window? We're getting a nasty draft in here."

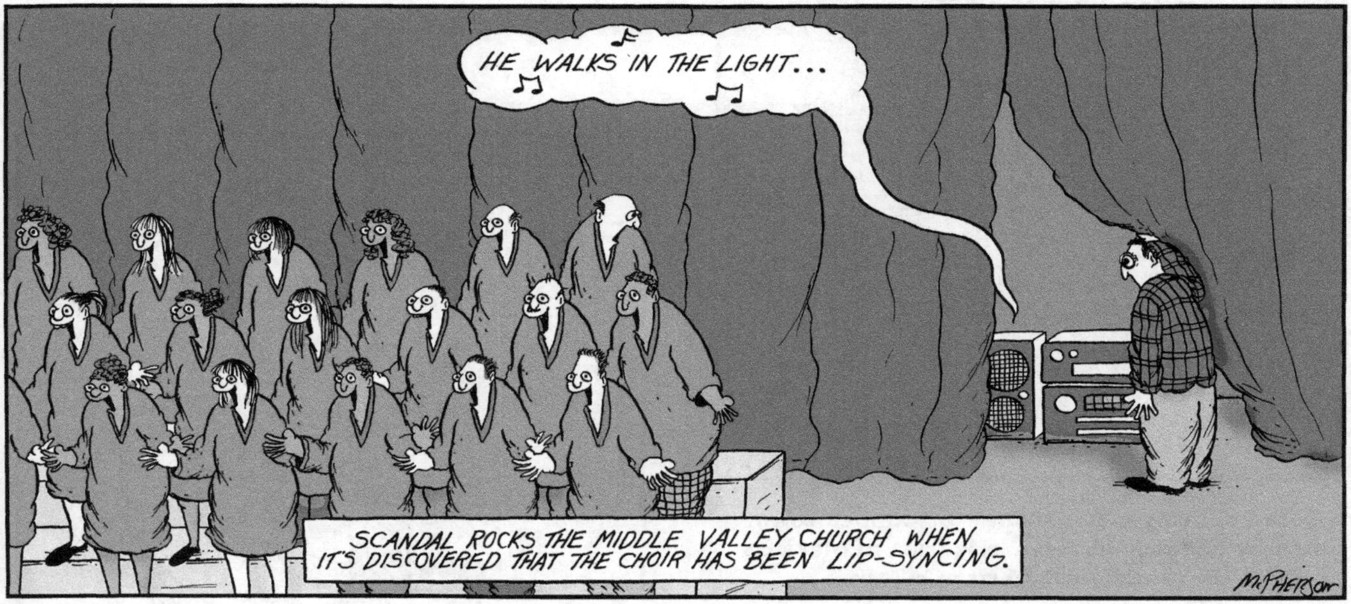
HE WALKS IN THE LIGHT...
SCANDAL ROCKS THE MIDDLE VALLEY CHURCH WHEN IT'S DISCOVERED THAT THE CHOIR HAS BEEN LIP-SYNCING.
McPherson

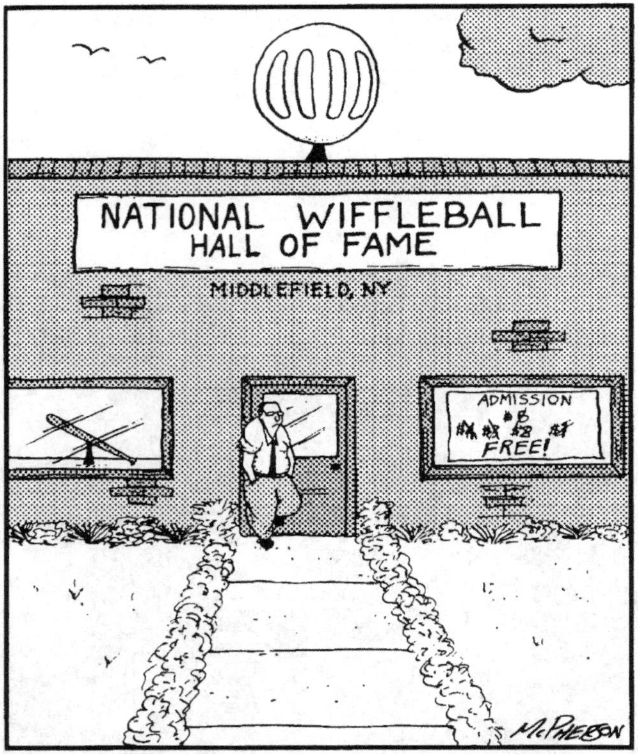
NATIONAL WIFFLEBALL
HALL OF FAME
MIDDLEFIELD, NY
ADMISSION
FREE!
McPHERSON

Tired of living in the shadow of Cooperstown, nearby Middlefield, New York, tries to make its own mark on American culture.

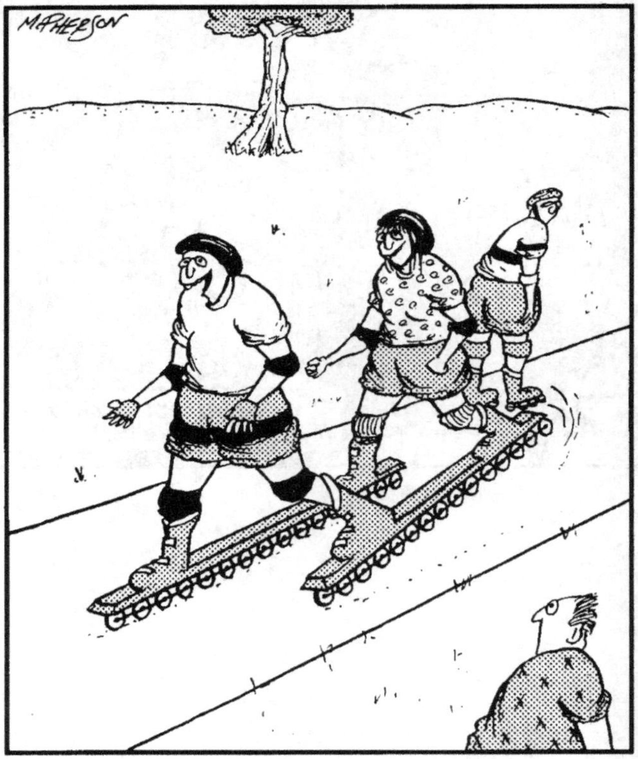
McPHERSON

This year's hot new sports fad: tandem in-line skates

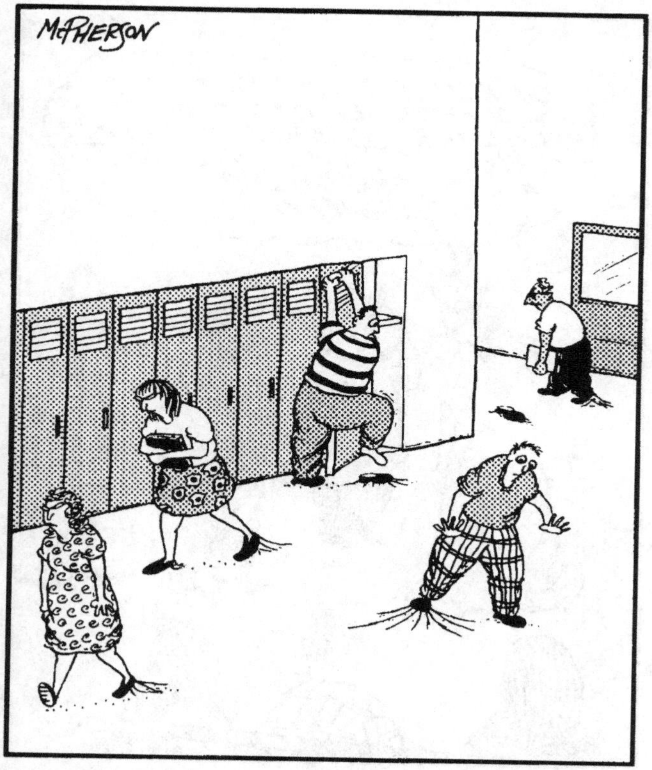
McPHERSON

Hoping to prevent students from running in the halls, the school's new flypaper flooring reduced accidents by 37 percent.

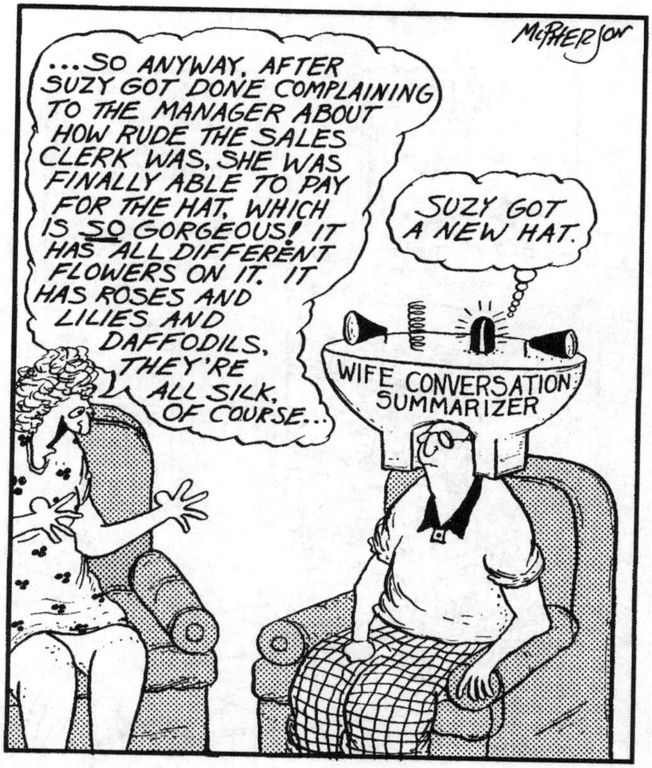
McPHERSON
...SO ANYWAY, AFTER SUZY GOT DONE COMPLAINING TO THE MANAGER ABOUT HOW RUDE THE SALES CLERK WAS, SHE WAS FINALLY ABLE TO PAY FOR THE HAT, WHICH IS SO GORGEOUS! IT HAS ALL DIFFERENT FLOWERS ON IT. IT HAS ROSES AND LILIES AND DAFFODILS. THEY'RE ALL SILK, OF COURSE...
SUZY GOT A NEW HAT.
WIFE CONVERSATION SUMMARIZER

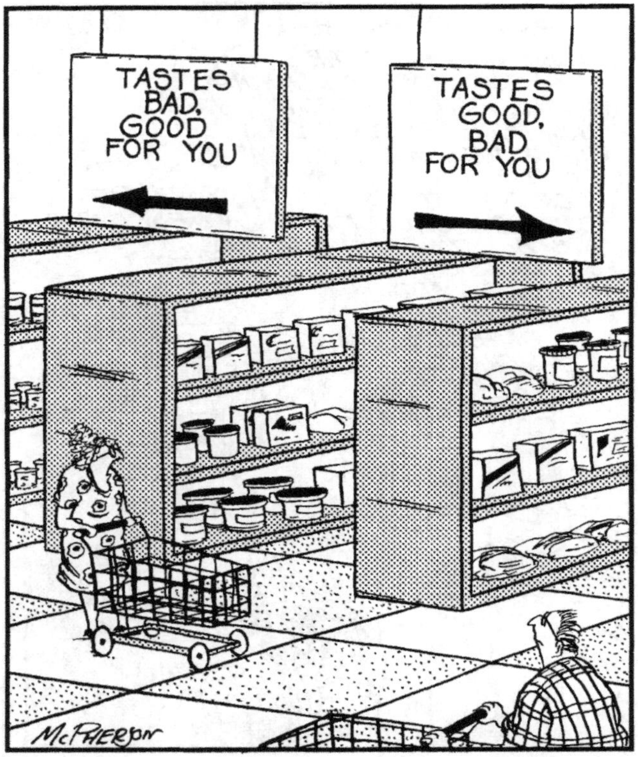
TASTES BAD, GOOD FOR YOU
TASTES GOOD, BAD FOR YOU
McPHERSON

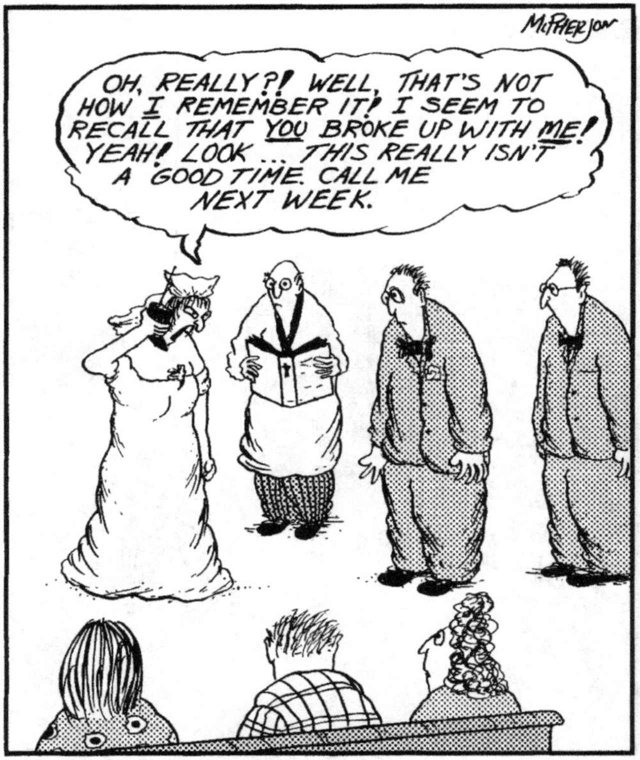
McPHERSON
OH, REALLY?! WELL, THAT'S NOT HOW I REMEMBER IT! I SEEM TO RECALL THAT YOU BROKE UP WITH ME! YEAH! LOOK ... THIS REALLY ISN'T A GOOD TIME. CALL ME NEXT WEEK.

Brad begins to have second thoughts.

CPSIA information can be obtained
at www.ICGtesting.com
Printed in the USA
LVHW061523030519
616573LV00001B/1/P

9 780740 761980